★ FRUITS BASKET STICKERS ★

Fruits Basket

Natsuki Takaya

We called it the "Cat" book so it could be like Kyo-kun: not quite part of the Chinese Zodiac, but loved by all the fans!

"Fruits Basket Fanbook (Neko – Cat)" cover

"Fruits Basket Fanbook (Neko – Cat)"
cover sleeve, front insert

"Fruits Basket Fanbook (Neko – Cat)"
back cover

"Fruits Basket Fanbook (Neko – Cat)"
cover sleeve, back insert

3

2004, issue 17, chapter intro page spread

2004, issue 19, magazine cover

2003 "Free to all who apply"
All Stars telephone card

2003 "Free to all who apply"
All Stars telephone card

2003, issue 18, magazine cover

2004, issue 22, chapter intro page spread

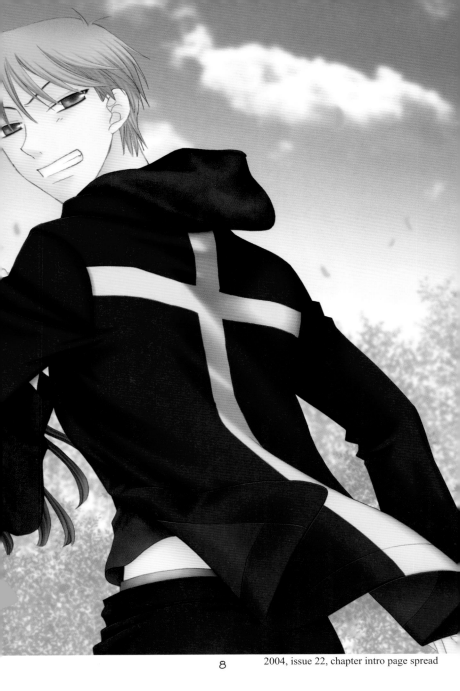

2003, issue 8, chapter intro page

2003, issue 4, chapter intro page spread

2005, issue 5, chapter intro page

The very first sketch is even rougher than this--I redraw it two or three times on the tracing table, and finally I wind up with this. I draw a clean copy of this rough sketch on the back of manuscript paper, using a 0.3 mechanical pencil with 2B graphite.

The Making of Color Illustrations

For the first time, Takaya-sensei offers a step-by-step explanation of how she creates a color illustration, using images of the work in progress!

After Cleanup

I change the color mode from gray to color, and make the lines dark brown. After that, I use the burn tool on a painted-over layer, and erase smudges and line mistakes. Maybe my scanner is too good-- there's always a lot of cleaning up to do.

Right After Scanning

I scan it in at 600dpi, then crop it to the specified size at 400dpi. The picture is dark right after scanning, so I adjust the brightness and contrast. When I'm done, I use the channel to select just the line drawing, leave that, and delete the layer.

Layer Division

The Layers Are...

•	Line drawing
•	Yun
•	Kyon
•	Lines
•	Collar/sleeves
•	Uniform/top
•	Uniform/bottom
•	Ribbon
•	Hair
•	Pupils
•	Eyes/mouth
•	Skin
•	Background

...the transparent sheets for creating pictures. By stacking several on top of each other, and changing the order, etc., you complete a single picture.

This is the hardest part of the process. The longer and more spread out the hair is, the more time and patience it takes (laugh). On this picture, there aren't a lot of characters or parts, so I made a lot of layers (I don't leave the channel there). I name each layer so that I won't get them confused, but I still mix them up sometimes. This is where I erase the checkered background that indicates blank space. By the time I'm done this part, I'm already wiped out (laugh).

This is the type of equipment and software I use!

My computer is a Macintosh G4, and the software is Photoshop 6. I have version 7 of Painter installed right now, but I don't use it (what a waste...). I haven't done much customizing, but I did fix up a color picture of all the characters I've drawn. I use it as wallpaper so I can check it to make sure I don't get the characters' coloring wrong (laugh).

Painting process

Basically, I use the airbrush tool. I change the pressure percentage depending on where I'm painting, and carefully shade things in. The square thing on the left is the school uniform shadow color. I leave it there so I don't mess up and lose track of what it was. The hair is the most difficult part in painting, too...

Painting complete

When I've finished painting, I check to make sure I haven't missed any spots, and that there are shadows in places that are touching (although sometimes I miss things...). At this point, sometimes I change the color of the clothes. The uniform has an established color, so it's easier in that respect.

How long does it take?

That depends on a lot of things, like how big the picture is, how many characters there are, how detailed their clothing is, and whether or not there's a background. From start to finish, I think it generally take three or four days. I don't know if that would be considered fast or slow, but that's how long it takes me when I'm working my hardest. At least, that's what I want to think (laugh). I think it would take longer if it were analog painting.

Layer merging

Characters
Background

If the picture has a background, I paint it at this point. This time I'm not in charge of the background, though, so I leave a blank background layer and merge the rest, preserving the character selection. That's a pretty broad explanation, but that's the gist of how I wrap things up. Thank you!

Finished!

Selected Fruits Basket Merchandise 2001-2004

A variety of cute and useful things to show how much you love Furuba! How many do you have?

Photograph:
Takeshi Yoshio

Chinese Zodiac Figures

(2003-2004, *HANA TO YUME*--FREE TO ALL WHO APPLIED)

FRUITS BASKET
NATSUKI TAKAYA
HANA TO YUME

The Riceball (onigiri), Tohru | The Tiger, Kisa | The Ram, Hiro | The Ox, Hatsuharu | The Horse, Isuzu

FRUITS BASKET
NATSUKI TAKAYA
HANA TO YUME

The Riceball (onigiri), Tohru | The Dog, Shigure | The Dragon, Hatori | The Snake, Ayame | The Rabbit, Momiji

FRUITS BASKET
NATSUKI TAKAYA
HANA TO YUME

The Rat, Yuki | The Cat, Kyo | The Monkey, Ritsu | The Bird, Kureno | The Boar, Kagura

Chinese Zodiac Figures

(2004 *HANA TO YUME* ISSUE 3 SPECIAL OFFER)

Exciting Yuki & Kyo bedroom items

(2003 *HANA TO YUME*, FREE TO ALL WHO APPLIED)

1) Comfy Kyo sheet (length, 90cm; width, 60cm)

2) Fuzzy Yuki slippers

Yuki & Kyo fuzzy plushes

(2002 *HANA TO YUME*, FREE TO ALL WHO APPLIED)

Yuki

Kyo

Natsuki Takaya Art Collection: Fruits Basket

(PUBLISHED 2004, HAKUSENSHA)

Illustrated by Natsuki Takaya
FruitsBasket
フルーツバスケット
高屋奈月

Fruits Basket Character Book

(PUBLISHED 2001, HAKUSENSHA)

フルーツバスケット
高屋奈月
キャラクターブック

Fruits Basket Animated TV Series DVD volumes 1 - 9

(RELEASED 2001 - 2002)

フルーツバスケット
BASKET

Sales agency:
King Records, Imagica

Selling agency:
King Records

Fruits Basket Animated TV Series DVDs Limited First Edition Figures (2 types)

FRUITS BASKET
FRUITS BASKET

Fruits Basket Animated TV Series Original Soundtrack CD: Memory for You

Memory for You
FRUITS BASKET

(RELEASED 2001)

Sales agency:
King Records

Fruits Basket

Fan Book
-Cat-

By
Natsuki Takaya

TOKYOPOP®

HAMBURG // LONDON // LOS ANGELES // TOKYO

Translation - Alethea & Athena Nibley
English Adaptation - Ysabet Reinhardt MacFarlane
Associate Editor - Stephanie Duchin
Retouch and Lettering - Jim Carruth & Michael Paolilli
Production Artist - Skooter
Graphic Designer - Christian Lownds

Editor - Paul Morrissey
Digital Imaging Manager - Chris Buford
Pre-Production Supervisor - Erika Terriquez
Art Director - Anne Marie Horne
Production Manager - Elisabeth Brizzi
Managing Editor - Vy Nguyen
VP of Production - Ron Klamert
Editor-in-Chief - Rob Tokar
Publisher - Mike Kiley
President and C.O.O. - John Parker
C.E.O. and Chief Creative Officer - Stuart Levy

A  Manga

TOKYOPOP Inc.
5900 Wilshire Blvd. Suite 2000
Los Angeles, CA 90036

E-mail: info@TOKYOPOP.com
Come visit us online at www.TOKYOPOP.com

FRUITS BASKET FAN BOOK [NEKO] by Natsuki Takaya
© Natsuki Takaya 1998 All rights reserved. First published
in Japan in 2005 by HAKUSENSHA, INC., Tokyo English lan-
guage translation rights in the United States of America and
Canada arranged with HAKUSENSHA, INC., Tokyo through
Tuttle-Mori Agency Inc., Tokyo
English text copyright © 2007 TOKYOPOP Inc.

ISBN: 978-1-4278-0293-4

First TOKYOPOP printing: September 2007
10 9 8 7 6 5 4 3 2 1
Printed in the USA

THE TALE OF THE ZODIAC

Oh yes, thank you.
We'll see you then, sir?

God said to the animals, "I'm inviting you all to my banquet tomorrow. Don't be late."

Hearing that, the mischievous Rat lied to his neighbor the Cat, and told him the banquet would be the day after tomorrow.

The next day, the Rat rode on the back of the Ox, and nimbly landed before the banquet hall. After him followed the Ox, the Tiger, and and all the rest, and together they feasted until morning.

Welcome to the banquet

All except for the Cat, who had been tricked.

THE HISTORY OF THE TWELVE CALENDAR SIGNS AND THE ZODIAC.

Chinese astrology was originally combined with the twelve calendar signs to express directions, times, and dates. Back then, there weren't any animals associated with astrology, and astrology wasn't used for fortune telling. No one knows how or why these particular twelve animals were chosen to make up the Zodiac, or why only one of those selected is mythical. At one time there was a movement in China to replace the mythical Dragon with the real-world Cat.

AKITO AND THE JUUNISHI EXIST IN A WORLD OF THEIR OWN...
...THAT OUTSIDERS LIKE US CAN NEVER FULLY UNDERSTAND.
A WORLD THAT IS THEIRS ALONE.
A CONNECTION FORMED FROM THE BLOOD THAT PULSES THROUGH THEIR BODIES.
A BOND OF BLOOD.

CONTENTS

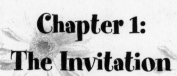

Chapter 1:
The Invitation

DIAGRAM
STORY
BACKGROUND
INTERVIEW 1

WE'VE ASSEMBLED LOTS OF INFORMATION TO GIVE YOU A MORE IN-DEPTH LOOK AT THE WORLD OF FRUITS BASKET, INCLUDING DIAGRAMS OF THE CHARACTERS' RELATIONSHIPS, A TIMELINE OF EVENTS, AN EXPLANATION OF THE WORLD'S BACKSTORIES, AND A WRITTEN INTERVIEW WITH TAKAYA-SENSEI!

Furuba Character Relationship Diagrams

We've created two charts showing the connections between the main characters in Furuba. The first one covers the relationships at Kaibara Public High School, and the second covers the Sohma family.

Kaibara Public High School Chart

Makoto Takei
A pain in the neck
Enemy
Enemy
Classmates
Hatsuharu Sohma
Deep affection
Deep affection
Sees his kindness
Respect
Momiji Sohma
Adores
Adores
Deep affection
Deep affection (looks to her for a mother's love)
True love(?)
Beloved
Regret
Tohru Honda
Love
Mother: Kyoko
Love and confusion
Love
Married
A Burden
Katsuya Honda
Awkwardness
Father
Parent and children (living together)
Tohru's aunt's family
Best friend
Best friend
Best friend
Best friend
Arisa Uotani
Reconciled
Father
Best friend
Best friend
Saki Hanajima
Love
Love
Father, Mother, Grandmother
Younger brother: Megumi
Crush
Kyo's classmate
Mayuko Shiraki
Key
Friendly
Hostile

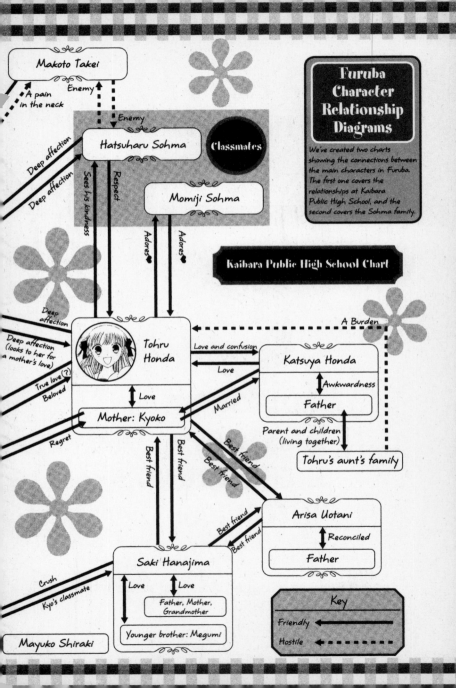

DIAGRAM
Student Council
Naohito Sakuragi
Reminded of how he used to be
Rivalry
Machi Kuragi
Half-siblings
Half-siblings
Budding romance?
Budding romance?
Kakeru Manabe
Commander of the Defense Force
Any friend of his brother's is a friend of his
Good Friend
Good Friend
Toxic friend
Toxic friend
Adores
Kimi Todo
Yuki Sohma
Troublesome brother
Darling brother
Awkwardness
Mother
Ayame Sohma
Torments
Enemy
Friendship
Budding romance
Ideal/Obstacle
Ideal/Obstacle
Motoko Minagawa
Adores
Adores
Adores
Friendship
Friendship
Rika Aida
Kyo Sohma
Hatred
Father
Minami Kinoshita
Love
Love
Prince Yuki
Mio Yamagishi
Kazuma Sohma

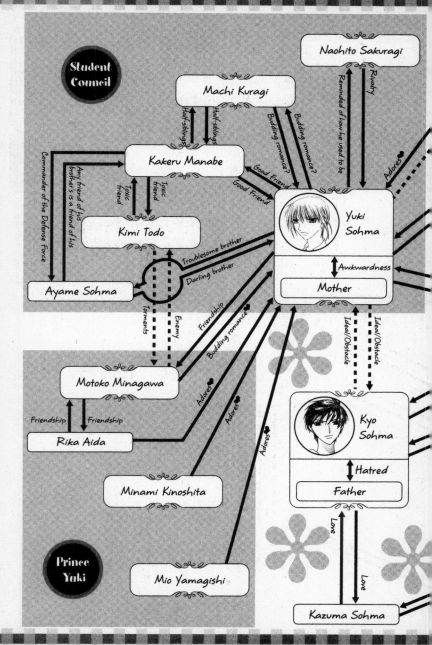

Sohma Family Chart

Key
Friendly
Hostile
The Monkey
Ritsu Sohma
Love
Mother: Okami-san
Unforgettable encounter
Arisa Uotani
Unforgettable encounter
The Horse
Isuzu Sohma
Fear
Father, Mother
Fear
Disgust
Unable to be herself
Friendship
Beloved
Beloved
Fear
The Ox
Hatsuharu Sohma
Unable to be herself
Worry
Tohru Honda
Love
Mother: Kyoko
Likes a lot❤
Thinks she's hopeless
The Ram
Hiro Sohma
Love
Mother: Satsuki
Adores❤
Adores❤
Adores❤
Adores❤
Budding romance?
Budding romance?
The Tiger
Kisa Sohma
Love
Mother
The Rabbit
Momiji Sohma
Erased
Mama
Adores❤
Little sister: Momo

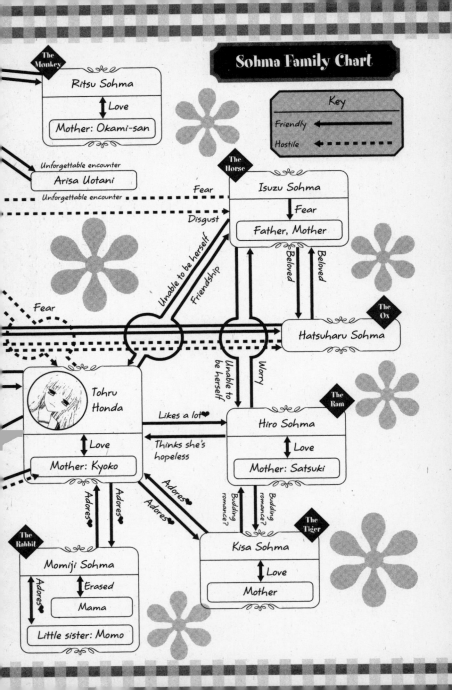

DIAGRAM

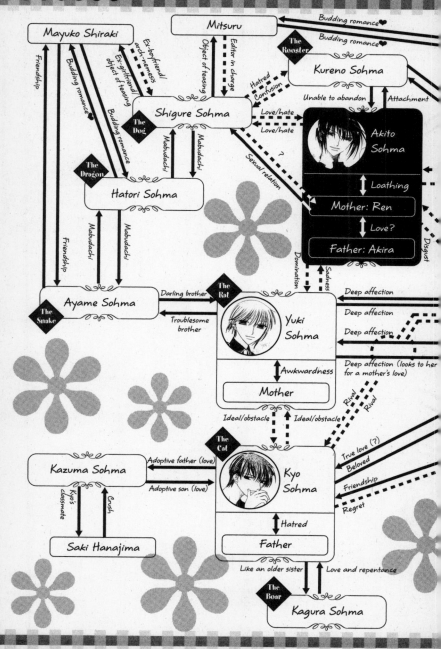

Mayuko Shiraki
Mitsuru
Budding romance
Budding romance
The Rooster
Kureno Sohma
Friendship
Budding romance
Budding romance
Ex-girlfriend/ object of teasing
Ex-boyfriend/ arch-nemesis
Object of teasing
Editor in charge
Hatred Confusion
Unable to abandon
Attachment
Shigure Sohma
The Dog
Love/hate
Love/hate
Akito Sohma
Mabudachi
Mabudachi
?
Sexual relation
The Dragon
Hatori Sohma
Loathing
Mother: Ren
Love?
Father: Akira
Disgust
Friendship
Mabudachi
Mabudachi
Domination
Sadness
The Snake
Ayame Sohma
Darling brother
Troublesome brother
The Rat
Yuki Sohma
Deep affection
Deep affection
Deep affection
Deep affection (looks to her for a mother's love)
Awkwardness
Mother
Rival
Rival
Ideal/obstacle
Ideal/obstacle
The Cat
Kyo Sohma
Kazuma Sohma
Adoptive father (love)
Adoptive son (love)
Kyo's classmate
Crush
Saki Hanajima
True love (?)
Beloved
Friendship
Regret
Hatred
Father
Like an older sister
Love and repentance
The Boar
Kagura Sohma

Furuba Timeline

Tohru's age	6-7 years old	Middle school age		First year in high school
Date (season)				May 1
Event	Tohru is chased around by boys from her elementary school and gets lost.	Tohru meets **Arisa Uotani** and they become best friends.	Tohru meets **Saki Hanajima** and they become best friends.	Tohru's mother, Kyoko, dies in a traffic accident.
Supplement	She is saved by a boy in a hat.	Arisa leaves her gang.	Saki learns to control her powers.	She is taken in by her grandfather on her father's side.

WHAT DO I DO?
SHE'S FOLLOWING ME!

When Tohru was lost, the boy who rescued her was like a prince on a white horse to her. Even now, she takes good care of the hat he gave her then.

The Events Of *Furuba*

We've put the events of Fruits Basket in chronological order following Tohru at the center.

The Story Begins

After her mother's tragic death, Tohru Honda winds up living in a tent. There, she runs into her classmate, Yuki Sohma--and learns that she's set up camp on Sohma property. Through Yuki's cleverness, Tohru is allowed to stay at Shigure Sohma's house, free of charge, and there she learns the Sohma family's deepest secret: that thirteen members are possessed by the animals of the Chinese Zodiac.

Chapter 1
Let's get this show on the road, shall we?
This is where the fun begins...
WOW...
IT LOOKS LIKE TODAY'S GOING TO BE ANOTHER HOT ONE.
OKAY, MOM. YOU'RE IN

Living in a tent after no longer being able to stay with her grandfather.

STORY

We lined up the events, not in the order they appear in the comics, but in the order in which they happened. Additional explanations are written in the "Supplement" row for events that so require.

● ●

December 31	Day after the Culture Festival		Culture Festival		Autumn	One week later	September
Yuki and Kyo decide to go back to the Sohma Estate, but, they got so worried about Tohru that they return to Shigure's house.	Under Hatori's orders, Tohru visits the Sohma Estate for the first time.	Momiji Sohma and **Hatori Sohma** come to the Culture Festival.	Yuki is forced to dress like a girl, wearing a costume made specially for him.	Class 1-D opens the food stand, "Onigiri Shop."	Her grand-father's new house is complete, and Tohru leaves the Sohma house. Tohru meets **Momiji Sohma** at the building where she works.	**Kagura Sohma** visits Shigure's house.	The next day, she meets **Kyo Sohma.**	Tohru comes to live free of charge at the home of **Shigure Sohma.**	Renovation begins on Tohru's grand-father's house, and Tohru begins living in a tent.
At the Sohma Estate, a Zodiac Banquet is held, with Akito at the center.	Saki opens a wave-fortune-telling booth.		That same day, Yuki and Kyo go to get her and bring her back.		Kyo lives at Shigure's house as well, and starts to attend Kaibara High School with Tohru and Yuki.	She learns the secret of the Chinese Zodiac.	For a week, she lives battling slugs and typhoons.

Tohru was about to greet the new year all alone. "There's no way anyone would be fine being alone." Realizing that, Yuki and Kyo rush home...?!

The Events of Furuba

	New Year's	Third term	February 14	Final exams	March 15	April 7		A few days later	May 1	May 2
Tohru's age						Second year in high school				
Date (season)	New Year's	Third term	February 14	Final exams	March 15	April 7		A few days later	May 1	May 2
Event	Tohru meets Hatori at the Sohma estate and sees his Juunishi form.	During the school endurance run, Tohru meets **Hatsuharu Sohma.**	Kagura arranges a double date: herself and Kyo, and Tohru and Yuki.	Tohru gets much better grades than usual on her exams.	Momiji unexpectedly invites everyone on a trip to a hot spring.	Momiji and Hatsuharu start attending Kaibara Public High School.	Akito shows up at orientation.	**Ayame Sohma** visits Shigure's house.	On the first anniversary of her mother Kyoko's death, Tohru visits her mother's grave.	Tohru visits a lakeside villa belonging to the Sohmas.
Supplement	Hatori learns that Kana, his ex-girlfriend, is engaged. Kana and Hatori had hoped to get married, but that desire brought Akito's wrath down on them. Hatori was blinded in one eye, and wound up ending their relationship by erasing Kana's memories.	Yuki's bronchitis acts up.			Their destination is a Sohma-run hot spring inn, where Ritsu's mother is the concierge.	Black Haru puts in an appearance.			Yuki, Kyo, Arisa, and Saki all join her.	Yuki, Kyo, Shigure, and Hatori all go with her.

THEY WON'T PLAY WITH ME AT ALL.
OUT.
DON'T I KEEP TELLING YOU TO LET IT BOUNCE?
SHUT UP!! WHY SHOULDN'T I HIT IT HARD?!
OUT.
BECAUSE THAT'S THE RULE.
AGAIN!?
THIS WAS DEFINITELY A BAD IDEA!
KYO-KUN-GOOD-LUCK!
Table tennis is a hot springs tradition! But **someone** in the group just can't play by the rules.

....
THESE...
THESE FOOT-PRINTS...
IT'S JASON!!
JASON ?!
THEY'RE BEAR TRACKS...
Discovering Jason's footprints by the lake sends them into a panic!

STORY

Summer vacation					July				June	Midterm exams	May	May 9	May 5
Yuki meets **Kakeru Manabe** and **Machi Kuragi** for the first time.	Tohru goes to a haunted house with Yuki, Kyo, Momiji, and Haru.	The next day, Ritsu meets Mitsuru.	**Ritsu Sohma** visits Shigure's house to see Tohru.	Haru goes Black at school and trashes his classroom.	Arisa, Saki, Yuki, and Kyo buy Tohru a swimsuit as a gift.	Tohru meets **Hiro Sohma.**	Yuki visits Ayame's shop.	**Kazuma Sohma (Shishou)** comes to see Kyo. Kyo's true form is exposed.	Kagura comes to see Kyo.	Tohru gets a red mark.	**Motoko Minagawa** and two other girls infiltrate Saki Hanajima's home.	Yuki agrees to become Student Council President.	Haru finds **Kisa Sohma** in her tiger form and takes her under his wing. She winds up staying at Shigure's house.
				He snapped and went out of control because Isuzu dumped him.	Arisa gets depressed when she sees Tohru in a school-issued bathing suit. When Shigure hears about it, it breaks his heart, too.	Hiro steals Tohru's notebook.	Tohru goes with him.	Tohru becomes Kyo's emotional support.		Tohru catches a cold and is bed-ridden.	Motoko and the others narrowly escape being cursed by Megumi.		

AN EMOTIONAL MEETING.
DON'T BREAK THINGS!!
WHAT THE HELL WERE YOU THINKING!? HOW THE HELL ARE WE GOING TO EXPLAIN THIS!?
YES, VERY TOUCHING.
WHAT A NICE STORY.
AND THEY LIVED HAPPILY EVER AFTER.

The plan was to go have fun at a haunted house. But when it gets too scary, they make up stories about the ghosts' lives--and wind up breaking the props!

?!
YOU HAVE TO GO BACK.
BACK HOME.
LET'S GO BACK.
YOU...

The revelation hits Tohru hard. But her feelings for Kyo are strong enough that she overcomes her fear.

The Events of Furuba

Tohru's age										
	Summer vacation (continued)							September 1		First Sunday in September
Event	Arisa meets **Kureno Sohma** while she's working a shift at a convenience store.	Tohru visits Shishou's house with Kyo.	Tohru goes on vacation to a seaside summer home owned by the Sohma family.	Shigure visits Mayuko Shiraki's house.	Hatori meets **Mayuko Shiraki** again.	Yuki kisses Tohru's forehead.	**Isuzu Sohma** meets Tohru near the summer house.	Yuki meets **Kimi Todo** and **Naohito Sakuragi**.	Tohru goes to ask Shishou if he knows how to break the curse.	Kyo goes on a date with Kagura.
Supplement		Kyo's father tells Shishou that Kyo will be confined when he finishes high school.	Yuki, Kyo, Momiji, and Haru go with her. Later, they are joined by Shigure, Kisa, Hiro, Hatori, Kureno, and Akito.		Afterwards, they stay in touch...					Kagura tells Kyo the truth about her one-sided feelings for him, and stops pursuing him.

IS THAT...
...SUPPOSED TO BE FUN?
OOOOH...
sizzle
BUT--! YOU HAVE TO TRY IT AT LEAST ONCE! IT'S REALLY WORTH SEEING!
I CAN'T SEE ANYTHING IN ALL THIS SMOKE.

When it gets dark, everyone gets together to light fireworks! The "snake firework" is the most exciting: "You have to try it at least once!! It's really worth seeing!!" (Is it really...?)

BUT IT LOOKS LIKE SHE'S NOT BREATHING.
EH?!!
GASP
GASP
GASP
GASP
GASP
GASP

When visiting a beach house, there's nothing like a swim in the ocean! And it seems like Tohru's a pretty good swimmer... or maybe not.

TOHRU KNOWS THAT THE CURSE CAN BE BROKEN! THE QUESTION IS, WHAT WILL SHE DO NOW..?

Third term	New Year's		End of the year	Cultural Festival	October				September

Tohru learns that Kureno's curse is broken, and that Akito is a woman.

At the Zodiac banquet, Akito flies into a rage at Yuki.

Tohru celebrates New Year's at Kazuma's (Shishou's) house with Kyo and Isuzu.

The student council has a celebration.

Kyo has a dream about Kyoko.

Class 2-D performs their play, "Sorta Cinderella".

Isuzu comes to Shigure's house and winds up baring her heart to Tohru.

School trip to Kyoto and Nara.

Tohru sneaks into the Sohma estate to talk to Kureno, and meets **Momo Sohma.**

Arisa starts a new job at a family restaurant.

Parent-teacher conferences (Yuki's is held on a different day).

Tohru's grandfather strains his back and is bedridden. Shigure ends up standing in for him at Tohru's parent-teacher conference.

During that conversation, Kureno frankly tells Tohru that he has no intention of ever seeing Arisa again.

The Zodiac Banquet is held at the Sohma estate, centering around Akito.

Isuzu is hospitalized.

Shigure attends as Tohru's guardian, and goes out of his way to torment Mayuko-sensei.

This year, Tohru and Kyo greet the new year at Shishou's house. Naturally, she throws herself into making a memorable New Year's Eve dinner.

At her parent-teacher conference, Tohru is frozen solid by the chilly atmosphere in the room.

The Mysteries of Furuba

The Mysteries And Laws Of Furuba

We've taken a closer look at the key points of some mysteries that have come up in Fruits Basket.

The Relationship Between Kyo And Kyoko

IN KYO'S DREAMS, KYOKO KEEPS BLAMING HIM.

I'LL NEVER FORGIVE YOU.
YOU HAVE TO GO INSIDE.
DO IT.
OR DO YOU WANT MORE TERROR?

A dream about Kyoko reminds Kyo of his mother, who committed suicide. Is it possible that he had something to do with the traffic accident that caused Kyoko's death?

Tohru doesn't know it, but Kyo and Kyoko once knew each other. Kyoko told Kyo about her past, and sympathized with him. A friendship began to develop between them, but...

The Conflict Between The Cat And The Rat

THE BET KYO MADE WITH AKITO

Kyo has always hated Yuki, believing the Rat's--Yuki's--existence was to blame for the suffering he's been through. But under the surface, their conflict has another source: a bet between Kyo and Akito.

THE BET YOU MADE WITH ME...
...ABOUT WHETHER OR NOT YOU COULD BEAT YUKI.
YOU CAN'T...
I TOLD YOU, DIDN'T I?
...CAN YOU?
IT'S IMPOSSIBLE, ISN'T IT?
YOU CAN'T WIN, CAN YOU?
YOU JUST CAN'T BEAT HIM, CAN YOU?
FROM THE BEGINNING, THE CAT WAS MADE SUCH THAT...
...IT CAN NEVER BEAT THE RAT.

God's sadistic offer: if Kyo can beat Yuki even once, Akito will reconsider his confinement.

The Relationship Between Tohru And Kakeru

Even before he met Yuki, Kakeru was interested in Tohru. He claims that he doesn't like or dislike her, but he seems to have met her before. And Saki feels like she once saw them together...

THE TWO SEEM TO HAVE SOME SORT OF CONNECTION, BUT WHAT IS IT?

MMM...
WHAT IF I WERE TO SAY THAT, ACTUALLY...
...I LIKE HER?
...IT'S JUST THAT...

Kakeru jokingly provokes Yuki with his interest in Tohru, but that's not how he really feels--he has a girlfriend he loves. How does she tie into the story?

I WONDER...
W-WITH ME...YOU SAY?!
EEEHH?!
REALLY?!
SPINNING MEMORIES
I'M SORRY... I DON'T KNOW... AT ALL.
NO, IT DOESN'T MATTER...

Even with Saki's prompting, Tohru can't remember a situation where she might have met Kakeru.

BACKGROUND

We've brought up some of the mysteries that are closely tied to the story, and analyzed the parts that have been explained and those that have yet to be brought to light.

Akito's Manipulations

Like Shigure, Akito has a secret hidden in her heart. Because of that desire, she allowed Tohru to live at Shigure's house. What does she really want?

AKITO'S TRUE DESIRE...

IF YOU HATE HER THAT MUCH...
IF YOU--!!
...THEN WHY DID YOU LET HER LIVE IN THAT HOUSE?!
THAT'S MESSED UP!! YOU COULD HAVE JUST SAID "NO"!!
WHAT ARE YOU THINKING?!
WHAT ARE YOU--
SCHEMING.

Kyo recognizes the contradiction in Akito's orders, and realizes that she is plotting something that involves Tohru.

Shigure's Manipulations

THAT PASSION...
PARALYZINGLY SWEET AND SAD.

Shigure has made it clear that he'll use any means necessary to reach his goals. He's even willing to use Tohru if that's what it takes.

I WANT TO HOLD IT IN MY HANDS!

Shigure is plotting something, out of a desire to take his childhood dream and make it real. Is it Akito's heart he wants to possess, or something else?

The Curse

TO BE TOGETHER ...
EVEN IF THEY WERE REBORN SEVERAL TIMES...
...FOR ETERNITY.
...THEY WOULD GO TO HIS SIDE, AND NEVER LEAVE.
THEY WOULD GO TO SEE HIM.
THEY WOULD ALWAYS ...

Isuzu explaining to Tohru what the curse is: a bond of blood that will tie them together forever.

...I DO NOT HAVE...
...ANY POSITIVE PROOF.
"BECAUSE THAT IS THE CURSE."
THE "BOND"...
...IS THE CURSE?

When Tohru goes to ask Kazuma how to break the curse, he explains its true nature, and tells her how it relates to Akito.

"THE BOND" AND "THE CURSE" ARE ONE AND THE SAME.

At its heart, the curse is a bond. A "bond" may be something precious, but it can also become a crushing burden if it shackles people together against their will, leaving them no way to escape. Akito's mother, Ren, mocks the bond Akito clings to and calls it a fake.

......
IT DOESN'T EXIST, AFTER ALL...
...DOES IT?
A WAY TO BREAK THE CURSE?

To those possessed by spirits, Akito--God--is both a source of terror that they can't defy, and someone precious that they love from the bottom of their hearts. Isuzu wants to release Hatsuharu from those feelings, and so she is struggling to break the curse...

The Laws and Customs of the Sohma Family

The Cat's Ultimate Destination

I ONLY MET MY GRANDFATHER ONCE.
"COME HERE, KAZUMA. HAVE SOME CANDY."
I DON'T WANT ANY!"
"IT'S CURSED!"

Young Kazuma was terrified of his grandfather, the Cat, and refused the candy he offered, saying it was cursed.

When the one possessed by the Cat, who transforms into a grotesque beast, reaches adulthood, he is closed in a dark storehouse and spends the rest of his life there. Kazuma's grandfather, too, died after such a life.

FROM NOW ON...
...BE A GOOD BOY...
...DURING THE SHORT TIME YOU HAVE LEFT...
...LIVING ON THE "OUTSIDE."

AKITO WHISPERS, "I'LL BE WITH YOU," TO KYO, WHO IS TO BE CONFINED.

Sohma Family Property

AH.
INSIDE?
OUTSIDE?
REMEMBER THAT TREE-LINED ROAD YOU TOOK TO THE MAIN HOUSE?
ALL THE PEOPLE WHO LIVE ALONG THAT ARE SOHMAS.
SHII-CHAN AND YUKI USED TO LIVE "INSIDE," TOO.
"OUTSIDE" THERE'S ABOUT EIN HUNDERT... ONE HUNDRED PEOPLE. "INSIDE" THERE SHOULD BE ABOUT FIFTY.

The property has a tree-lined road, with residential areas unfolding on either side of it. The entrance of outsiders is strictly limited.

The Sohma Family holds a very large amount of land, about as much as would fill a city. It is strictly divided into "inside" and "outside," and only those possessed by spirits and the very few who know the secret can live on the inside.

Ha'ri lives over here.
WOW...
EVEN THE GROUNDS ARE HUGE.
IT'S LIKE ITS OWN LITTLE TOWN.

As a general rule, minors possessed by spirits live on the Inside, and Momiji has been separated from his parents and lives by himself.

Memory Suppression

When suppressing memories, basically he overlaps them, preventing memories from coming back.

Memory suppression is not a special, psychic power, but a technique similar to hypnosis. It has been passed down for generations in Hatori's family of doctors, and they are in charge of the operation.

"HATORI IS LIKE SNOW."
...I ERASED HIS FRIENDS' MEMORIES.
THAT'S WHY...
"HE'S COLD LIKE SNOW."
FOR A LONG TIME, IF AKITO OR MY FATHER...
...ORDERED ME TO DO IT, I WOULD SUPPRESS ANYONE'S MEMORIES.
SO EVEN THOUGH I KNEW IT WOULD HURT YUKI...
...WHEN AKITO UTTERED THOSE WORDS...

Sohma Family Establishments

The Sohma family is an enterprising group, running various operations. The management ranks are filled with members of the Sohma family, and Momiji Sohma's father's company has its own building.

The hot springs inn at which Ritsu's mother serves as Okami is also a Sohma-run establishment. Additionally, it seems they own several summer homes.

THIS IS AMAZING!
MY FIRST OPEN-AIR BATH!
IT SEEMS LIKE SOMEONE MOMIJI-KUN'S SIZE COULD SWIM IN IT.
LET'S SEE...
NOW, NOW...
THAT'S RIGHT.

The Sohma family is full of mysteries. From among them, we have taken the parts whose truths have been revealed, and the parts that we have begun to learn about. Almost all of the Sohma mysteries have something to do with the curse.

The Ruler of Souls

Akito is not a member of the Zodiac, but the God who rules over them. Those possessed with spirits have feelings of reverence towards Akito, and it seems those feelings have also become the source of the curse, also known as their bond.

I WANTED TO SEE HIM.
I DIDN'T WANT TO SEE HIM.
THE OLDER ONES POSSESSED BY SPIRITS CRIED BEFORE HIM AS WELL.
WHAT ELSE COULD ONE CALL IT BUT A "BOND"?
LIKE AN UNBREAKABLE KARMIC LINK.
I WANT TO HOLD HIM CLOSE...
IT'S ALL RIGHT.
LOVED...
AND HATED.

Yuki's feelings are severely shaken by the God before him. He was so attracted that he wanted to embrace her, but so frightened he couldn't stop trembling......

WHAT?
WH-WHY ARE YOU CRYING, YUKI?
STOP THAT-- IT'S RUDE!
BUT...
...IT WASN'T UP TO ME.

When Yuki met Akito for the first time, he was so overcome with emotion that he wept. Yuki didn't understand himself why the tears were shed, but the maid taking care of Akito said that all those possessed with spirits cried as well.

DON'T MISUNDER-STAND.
THIS WORLD IS BLACK.
JUST LIKE YOUR LIFE, YUKI.
THERE ARE NO POS-SIBILITIES, NO HOPES....
YOU'LL LIVE ON A PITCH-BLACK PATH.

Yuki's mother sold him to Akito as a playmate. After Akito's mind was twisted, Yuki was confined in a dark room and continually forced to listen to the dreadful words Akito whispered.

The Relationship Between God And The Rat

The one possessed by the Rat is special, even among the Zodiac. The Rat, who arrived first at the banquet, is closest to God, and because of that it is said that the one possessed by the Rat is one step better at everything he is allowed to do. But the circumstances he has been left in...

WANTING TO HOLD TIGHT,
WANTING TO RUN AWAY
BELOVED, HATED
A CURSED "BOND OF BLOOD"...!!

...
TOHRU-SAN...
I HAVE...
...NEVER BEEN AFRAID OF AKITO.
HE IS JUST LIKE A SMALL CHILD.
HE ONLY KNOWS HOW TO SCREAM AND CRY AS IF HE'S ON FIRE.
A FRAGILE...
...CRANKY CHILD.
BUT TO THE MEMBERS OF THE ZODIAC, AKITO IS SPECIAL.
A GODLIKE BEING, A BEING TO BE FEARED AND RESPECTED.
WEAK OR STRONG, HE AFFECTS THEM ALL THE SAME.
WORDS THAT FROM ANY OTHER MOUTH WOULD MAKE THEM FLINCH...
...WHEN SAID BY AKITO, CAUSE SUCH PAIN IN THEIR HEARTS THAT IT'S AS IF THEIR BODIES ARE BEING TORN APART.

Kazuma tells Tohru that he has never been afraid of Akito. To outsiders, Akito is no more than a hysteric child. But those possessed by spirits cannot oppose Akito. The reasons for that are complex, and difficult to understand.

Facts About Those Possessed by the Zodiac

The Mystery Of The Transformation

The most obvious trait shared by all members of the Zodiac is their transformation. When they hug someone of the opposite sex, they transform into the shape of the animal that possesses them. But physical contact like holding hands or touching someone's forehead is safe.

The other Juunishi try not to transform, but Momiji doesn't care. He hugs Tohru hard enough to snap her neck!

I'M BACK! I'M BACK! I'M BACK!
TOHRU!!
MOMIJI! WHY, YOU LITTLE--!

IF THEY'RE BOTH MEMBERS OF THE ZODIAC, IT'S OKAY!

...OH. ♡
SHI~~ GU~~ RE~~

Because it's safe to embrace someone of the opposite sex if they're also part of the Zodiac, Kagura and Hatsuharu are each free to hold the person they love. In addition, Akito--as God--can safely embrace any member of the Zodiac, and has had sexual relationships with both Shigure and Kureno.

*THE BANQUET WITH GOD *

From New Year's Eve to New Year's Day, a banquet is held which only the members of the Zodiac can attend.

*ZODIAC DANCE *

THE BANQUET CAN ONLY BE ATTENDED BY THOSE POSSESSED BY THE SPIRITS OF THE CHINESE ZODIAC.
I WOULD LOVE TO HAVE SEEN THAT!
Wow!
THE ZODIAC MEMBERS REPRESENTING THE NEW YEAR AND THE OLD YEAR DANCE TOGETHER.
THIS YEAR IT WILL BE MOMIJI-KUN AND THE TIGER.
YUKI'S DANCE THREE YEARS AGO WAS BEAUTIFUL!
THE CAT CAN'T GO TO THE BANQUET.
YOU FINALLY MADE IT!
THE BANQUET IS STARTING!
HEY, MOMIJI!
I'M LOOKING FORWARD TO YOUR DANCE.

At the banquet, the Zodiac members who represent the passing year and the coming year perform a ceremonial dance together.

Treatment Of Those Possessed By The Zodiac

Households that bring up members of the Zodiac are given substantial amounts of money, and special treatment from the Sohma corporations. This extends to the household that raises the Cat. On top of that, the Juunishi themselves receive a set monthly allowance.

Those possessed by spirits have a variety of troublesome traits. Some of those traits turn into useful skills, but for the most part they just make the Juunishi's lives harder.

Special Characteristics Of Those Possessed By The Zodiac

Possessed individuals have distinct characteristics other than the physical transformation. They often share special traits with the animal spirit they're possessed by, and they also attract the attention of their animal counterparts and can communicate with them.

*WHEN THEIR BODIES ARE WEAK... *

WELL... MORE OR LESS. THAT NIGHT, EVERYONE WAS SICK WITH COLDS.
WHAT DID THEY EXPECT, PLAYING OLD MAID OUTSIDE IN SUCH COLD WEATHER...?
Of course they'd catch colds!
I ONLY TAKE FAMILY AS PATIENTS, AND I STILL GET WORKED TO DEATH...

They don't only transform when they hug or are hugged by members of the opposite sex. It can also happen if they are physically weakened. Isuzu and Kisa have both transformed from weakness.

THEY RESEMBLE THE ANIMAL THAT POSSESSES THEM

BUT WITH REGARD TO YOUR HAIR--CAN YOU PROVE THAT'S YOUR NATURAL COLOR?!
I CAN.
OHO?! AND HOW EXACTLY WOULD YOU PROVE IT?! I DEMAND LEGITIMATE EVIDENCE!!
grab

Hatsuharu's black and white hair, Kyo's beautiful orange hair, Kisa's pale eyes--Juunishi members sometimes share physical features with their animal spirit. Such features often mean that they're singled out for teasing.

THEIR FELLOW ANIMALS GATHER AROUND THEM

AAAA AHH!
CATS!
EEP!
What's wrong, meow?
meow
Why are you angry, meow?
A fight?
meow
meow
meow
meow
WHAT THE?!
WHAT?!
How...?

Cats appear out of nowhere to be with Kyo.

*THEY SHARE SPECIAL ABILITIES *

LEAVE ME ALONE!
EEEEK!!
STOP! THIS IS THE SECOND FLOOR!
......

IF SHE RUNS OFF IN DETERMINED MODE, I CAN'T CATCH HER.
SHE IS THE HORSE, AFTER ALL.
I DON'T KNOW HOW YOU DO IT, HARU. SO CAREFREE...

Kyo can land on his feet after jumping from the second floor; Momiji walks quickly; Isuzu runs like the wind; and Ritsu is extremely agile... Many possessed people also share desirable traits with their animals.

The Cat: The Irregular Zodiac Member

The Cat didn't make it into the Zodiac, but for some reason, there is a Cat in the Sohma family. Just like in the story, he is unceasingly persecuted.

*THE ROSARY THAT PREVENTS TRANSFORMATION *

HUMAN BONES.

The beads that keep the Cat from transforming into a hideous beast are made from the bones and blood of a virtuous priest. In other words, they exist because someone else's life was sacrificed.

The Secret Of *Furuba's* Origin

Natsuki Takaya Written Interview Part 1

We asked about the stages Furuba went through as it took shape. Questions marked with a star were received from readers.

Q1: What sparked the idea of *Fruits Basket's* story?

It's been a long time since I started drawing Fruits Basket, so I don't remember it clearly. But as a manga artist, one of my earliest goals was to be able to draw a domestic drama. I was obviously inexperienced when I was just starting out, so I couldn't draw very well; I gave up on the idea and worked on other projects, like Gen'ei Musou and Tsubasa o Motsu Mono. Eventually I thought, "Let's give it one more try!", and that's when I began to imagine Furuba.

Q2: Which part of the *Fruits Basket* story did you come up with first? Was it the plot or the theme that started everything, or the characters, or particular scenes?

There's a conversation that takes place somewhere in or near the final chapter. I expanded it from that.

Q3: Are there any scenes in *Fruits Basket* that you especially wanted to draw? Which scenes are they?

It's the things that each character clings to--pain, wishes, or love--that I want to draw. The moments when those emotions are rewarded are always what I love.

*Q4: Why did you adopt the theme of the Zodiac? (P.N. Totoran)

The dictionary I always use has a Zodiac chart in it, and whenever I would see it, I would think, "This is interesting--I wonder if I can use it for anything." Then when I drew Furuba, my editor said, "Let's add some kind of motif," so I said, "Oh, then, let's use the Zodiac." It was kind of a lighthearted choice. I didn't realize there would have to be so many characters (laugh).

Q5: When Fruits Basket began to be serialized, how many chapters were you planning?

I planned it for the length it is now, but I also prepared versions with six and twelve chapters. My self-confidence was a bit low, so I didn't think they'd let me keep drawing it for so long (laugh). I'm glad those shorter versions wound up being wasted effort.

Q6: What was your editor's reaction the very first time you explained *Fruits Basket's* concept?

It was a subtle reaction (laugh). I had another story prepared in addition to Furuba, but my editor said, "Why don't you do that one?" (laugh). But I asked them to let me do this one. It certainly wasn't from any solid confidence, but I was thinking, "Right now, this is what I want to draw."

*Q7: Before you decided on the title *Fruits Basket*, what did you call it? (P.N. Terasato, others)

What was it......? I forgot.... But I kind of get the feeling it was something really weird. I'm glad I went with *Fruits Basket*--I can't imagine it being called anything else.

The *Furuba* Characters

Q8: Which character was born first?

Let me see, who was it...? (fighting with fading memories). I think Tohru was first, and then Yuki and Kyo, but it's all pretty vague now. Oh, but the first character whose personality and looks really hit me...without any hesitation might have been Kyo. I seem to remember him being the one I was least hesitant about.

Never Seen Before: The Rough Draft for Chapter 107 *

*This is the name for Chapter 107. The character positioning, the way their facing, and other small details are different than what you see when it's published.

*Q9: Hana-chan, Kagura, and others add -kun to Tohru's name and call her Tohru-kun." Why is that? (P.N. Yuki)

Because I didn't think Tohru-"chan" suited her very well. I thought that a more dignified form of address, like Tohru"-kun," was a better choice for a spacey girl like Tohru.

Q10: I think Tohru has a very unique personality. How did you come up with her personality and background? Also, did you always plan for her to use such polite language?

I considered a lot of things. I thought that for a girl to accept other people's feelings so wholeheartedly, she'd have to have a slightly unusual way of looking at things so that she wouldn't be crushed by having so much empathy. But I still worried that I needed something else to flesh her out. And then the thought, "Oh, yeah--I'll make her use super-polite language, and use it incorrectly!" came to me all at once. After that, her character was completed in no time. (I think.)

Q11: Why did you choose to give Tohru's best friends such strong quirks, like making them a "yankee" and a "wave"?

I wanted Tohru, as the main character, to have best friends with such explosive personalities that they wouldn't be overshadowed by the Zodiac characters.

Q12: Are there any characters whose design/role/personality/etc. changed a lot from your original concept? What kind of changes did they undergo?

None of them have changed "a lot". I develop my supporting characters slowly, so that I have time to make them into what I need.

*Q13: When you started the series, did you think of Akito as a woman? (P.N. Eriko, others)

Yes, I did. For some reason, I've always loved drawing characters that are gender neutral, so you can't really tell what they are. Like, what's it called—moé? (laugh)

Q14: Did the previous head of the Sohma family and members of the Juunishi suffer under the curse the way Akito and the characters who are currently possessed do?

Good question. The past Juunishi and God weren't all together at once, and there were probably cases where they never met, so there might have been different feelings. But I think the suffering of the Cat is the one thing that hasn't changed.

Q15: Since we learned that Akito was a woman, the story seems to have gone in more mature directions. Did you plan this change in tone from the beginning?

Yes, I did. But the current mature, serious developments are not the part I wanted to draw most. Right now the characters are climbing a wall, and getting lost and making mistakes. And it's okay for them to be in terrible shape, but I want to draw what's on the other side of that wall, which is what this part of the story is building up to. That's always how it is for me.

Q16: I think that the traits of the animals each member of the Zodiac is possessed by are reflected in the characters and their designs, but did you refer to any Chinese Zodiac fortune-telling?

I didn't. I did pay attention to features (cattle are black and white, so there's White Haru and Black Haru; and Kagura is the Boar, so she charges, etc.) but ultimately I just created the characters I wanted to write.

Q17: There are many, many touching scenes in *Fruits Basket*, but are there any scenes that made you cry while you were drawing them?

I've never cried while reading it. But when I do the very first draft—a version so rough that no one else can decipher it, that sometimes I can't even decipher myself, because I've just scribbled whatever came into my head—there have been times when I've been moved to tears. But it's kind of embarrassing to say things like that.

Q18: There are plenty of humorous scenes as well. Have any of them ever made you burst out laughing?

When I'm writing, I'm thinking, "Maybe this would be funnier than that...", so I don't laugh at the time. Sometimes I do laugh when I reread the comic to check lines and flashbacks. But, no, really—it's embarrassing to answer this kind of question, so please stop asking (laugh).

Q19: What's the most important thing to you when you're making decisions about composition and layout?

I pay very close attention to things like the overall rhythm, the positioning, and which way the faces are turned. The result doesn't always look much like I imagined, though....

Q20: As you continue drawing *Fruits Basket*, what are the things that are most important to you?

What's at the very heart of the story.

To be continued on page 174

Chapter 2:
The Gathering

CHARACTER

IN THIS SECTION WE'LL BE INTRODUCING THE
MAIN CHARACTERS FROM FRUITS BASKET, FROM
TOHRU TO AKITO, AND DELVING DEEP INTO THEIR
INNER SELVES. WE ALSO HAVE CHARTS OF
EACH CHARACTER'S FAMILY TREE.

"I want
to protect
them.
I want to
protect it."

"The path
that everyone
is following,
with all
of my
power."

Tohru Honda

本田 透

A compassionate girl who always thinks of others before herself. She always uses slightly incorrect formal speech, a habit she picked up from her father. She's so soft-hearted that she can't get angry with anyone--it's so fundamental to her personality that she can't bring herself to say mean things, even in a school play. This profound kindness is what allows her to accept the Juunishi, curse and all.

After she starts living with Kyo and Yuki, she sees how much the members of the Zodiac suffer under the curse, and begins desperately wanting to free them.

Fashion Concept

She chooses clothes based on how sturdy and practical they are, rather than on their looks, so she dresses very plainly. To put it bluntly, she's unfashionable (laugh). But she's recently had a bit more money, so her newer clothes are somewhat cuter. When she wears particularly adorable outfits, like in chapter 25, they're usually things Shigure picked out. He gives her presents fairly often (I can understand how he feels...). Tohru did accept the maid's costume in chapter 18, but--no surprise here--Yuki and Kyo won't let her wear it. She keeps the costume safely in the dresser she uses for western clothes.

(From the 2001 Fruits Basket Character Book)

A second-year student at Kaibara Public High School. Nicknames: Tohru-kun, Tohru. She used to live with her mother, but went to live with her grandfather after her mother died in a traffic accident. Soon afterwards, her grandfather began renovating his house, and she decided to try living in a tent. She is currently living rent-free at Shigure's house.

BUT I...
ONIGIRI! THAT SOUNDS GOOD!
...I WAITED FOR SOMEONE TO CALL "ONIGIRI."
ALL RIGHT, HERE I GO! APPLE!
PEACH!
BUT NO ONE CALLED.
...AS THEY PLAYED THE GAME...

SHE CAN'T SAY IT.
TO TELL SOMEONE WHO CARES ABOUT YOU THAT YOU'RE BEING TEASED...
...IS REALLY IS HARD TO DO.
I... COULDN'T SAY IT EITHER.

Kisa thought she should be ashamed of herself for being teased. Tohru knew exactly how she felt.

Constantly Teased

Ever since she was small, the obedient, gentle Tohru has had to deal with bullying, such as being chased by boys and being left out of games by her classmates. It's partly a result of her strange, polite speech, but it's also possible that some of the boys teased her because they liked her. The day she met the boy with the hat, she had gotten lost while running away from bullies. Tohru still doesn't know that the boy who saved her and led her back to her mother was Yuki.

Anxious About Colds

IT'S NOT LIKE THAT. I THINK I'M GETTING A COLD.
OH...?!
TH-THAT'S TERRIBLE!
!
DO YOU HAVE A FEVER?!

Tohru is very quick to respond when people come down with colds--her father died of complications from a cold. But when she gets sick herself, she is slower to react.

Hearing that Yuki feels a cold coming on sends Tohru into a panic. Her father's death has left emotional scars as deep as the ones left from losing her mother.

Year of the Cat Fangirl!

When her mother told her the Chinese Zodiac fairytale as a bedtime story, Tohru felt so bad for the shunned Cat that she started to cry. Ever since, the Cat has had a special place in her heart.

...THE CAT WAS DREAMING OF A BANQUET THE NEXT DAY THAT WOULD NEVER HAPPEN.
POOR THING--SLEEPING SOUNDLY UNAWARE OF THE DECEIT.
WHAT SHOULD I DO NOW?
I LIKED HIM SO MUCH THAT IF THERE WAS A YEAR OF THE CAT CLUB I WOULD HAVE JOINED.
BUT HE HATES ME.

Tohru gets depressed when she meets her beloved Cat and thinks that he hates her.

A Part-Time Worker

UH...
THAT IS... UM...
I'VE GOT TO WORK HARD!

Tohru is flaky, but she's fiercely self-reliant. She pays for all of her own school expenses and clothes from her part-time salary. But even with her frugal lifestyle, buying Valentine's chocolate set her back far enough that she couldn't pay a deposit on her class trip. She currently works part-time as a cleaner in Momiji's father's company building.

Tohru's co-workers love her enthusiasm and talent for lightening the workload.

A Very Good Cook

Because her mother worked so hard, Tohru did all of their housework. Living at Shigure's, she's still in charge of the chores. She can cook just about any dish--Japanese, Western, or Chinese--and is also good at cleaning and laundry. She even got Shigure's disaster of a kitchen under control in the blink of an eye.

TODAY WE'RE HAVING HAMBURGER FOR LUNCH!
KYO-KUN'S IS IN THE SHAPE OF A CAT!

Tohru makes her own hamburger, of course; she also makes pies and sauces and everything else from scratch.

Tohru Quote Collection

"She worked so hard and I forgot to tell her to come home safe. I didn't even see her back as she left for work..." (->Shigure)

"It's true. I...... I wanted to be born in the year of the Cat......!" (->Kyo)

"You're always by my side, and that has been such a support to me. If I'm not grateful for that, I really will be punished. I love you...!" (->Arisa/Saki)

"......The reason people get jealous of each other is that they can see so clearly the umeboshi on other people's backs." (->Kyo)

"If you can really remember how you felt when you were a child, even when you're an adult or parent, then you can understand each other." (->Ayame)

"When Yuki-kun came here, something changed. And Kyo-kun, too. I don't know what it is, but I'm sure it's a very good thing. What about...me?"

YOU SEE...
...IT'S ALSO IMPORTANT TO THINK ABOUT WHAT YOU CAN DO NOW, WHAT YOU CAN DO TODAY.
AND IF YOU KEEP WASHING THINGS ONE AT A TIME...
...YOU'LL BE DONE BEFORE YOU KNOW IT.
BECAUSE FORTUNE IS LOOKING OUT FOR YOU.
SOMETIMES THE ANXIETY WILL START TO WELL UP, BUT WHEN IT DOES...
...TAKE A LITTLE BREAK.

(Shigure's advice to Tohru)

"I'M SO GLAD..."
"...THAT I HAD YOU, TOHRU..."
"I CAN GO ON SMILING EVERY DAY BECAUSE MY LITTLE GIRL IS HERE."
"MOMMY..."
"DOES THAT MEAN I WAS BORN..."
"...SO THAT I COULD MEET YOU?"

"I won't give up. I want to think that there's something... ...something I can do." (->Kazuma)

"...It's a mystery. Because of just a single sentence, I get shaken, or I get happy. Kyo-kun is mysterious indeed."

Other People's Words To Tohru

"It would be okay to complain... be selfish...say what you want...once in a while. It's okay to let yourself be sad." (Kyo)

"...Honda-san isn't the type to see her life as a glass half empty..." (Yuki)

"...Why didn't I realize? How could I miss that? So at peace all by herself... No one's like that." (Yuki/Kyo)

"If there is anything you can do, it may just be... to smile for them. Because when you smile, the world... seems just a little kinder." (Kazuma)

"...You won't break, being like that...?" (Isuzu)

"She won't show it to anyone. On the other side of the door, I feel like she's quietly breaking. I get that feeling somehow." (Isuzu)

Tohru Honda's Family Tree

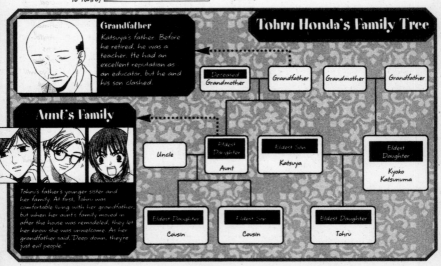

Grandfather

Katsuya's father. Before he retired, he was a teacher. He had an excellent reputation as an educator, but he and his son clashed.

Aunt's Family

Tohru's father's younger sister and her family. At first, Tohru was comfortable living with her grandfather, but when her aunt's family moved in after the house was remodeled, they let her know she was unwelcome. As her grandfather said, "Deep down, they're just evil people."

Deceased
Grandmother
Grandfather
Grandmother
Grandfather
Uncle
Eldest Daughter
Aunt
Eldest Son
Katsuya
Eldest Daughter
Kyoko Katsunuma
Eldest Daughter
Cousin
Eldest Son
Cousin
Eldest Daughter
Tohru

By saving Tohru, Yuki also saved himself. Kindness rewards itself.

I DON'T KNOW WHO OR WHERE HE IS...
...AND I DON'T EVEN REMEMBER WHAT HE LOOKED LIKE.
WHY DID YOU KEEP IT? IT'S SO... WORN OUT.
BECAUSE IT'S A PRECIOUS MEMORY.
BECAUSE I REALLY WAS...
...VERY HAPPY...
...THAT HE HELPED ME.

Tohru says that, looking back on it, the boy with the hat might have been her first love. A wonderful, reliable Prince Charming, who appeared out of nowhere in her time of need.

BUT EACH TIME...
HE WOULD WAIT FOR ME.
HE WAS A MYSTERIOUS BOY.
......
THEN I REALIZED...
...THAT HE HAD LED ME HOME.
I WENT TO THANK HIM, BUT I COULDN'T FIND HIM ANYWHERE.
THE ONLY PROOF THAT HE WAS EVER THERE AT ALL WAS THE HAT HE GAVE ME.

I already told you!
SHE'S AN ADORABLE GIRL WITH AN ADORABLE VOICE AND FACE, WEARING ADORABLE CLOTHES AND WITH ADORABLE POM-POMS IN HER HAIR!
GOT IT?!
I'M AFRAID NOT.

Kyoko's overly-threatening attitude frightened Yuki so much that he almost cried.

A Hat Full of Memories

Tohru has an old boys' hat. It is a cherished keepsake from the boy who helped her when she was little and got lost. Tohru still doesn't know that that boy was Yuki, or that the hat originally belonged to Kyo.

"In a way... that boy was my first love."

A SELFISH WISH

...I THINK THAT...
...I WANT TO BREAK THE CURSE.

Tohru visits Kazuma, looking for information about the curse. When he hears her intentions, Kazuma tells her about its true nature.

IF THERE IS...
?
...IT MAY JUST BE...
...ANYTHING YOU CAN DO...
...TO SMILE FOR THEM.
BECAUSE WHEN YOU SMILE...
...THE WORLD...
...SEEMS JUST A LITTLE KINDER.

I'M SORRY, BUT NO! I WON'T STAY OUT OF IT!!
STOP...
STOP SCREWING AROUND!
JUST AS YOU HAVE THINGS YOU CAN'T GIVE UP, ISUZU-SAN...
...SO DO I.
THAT'S WHY.
SHUT UP, SHUT UP!
NO...!
SHUT UP...!
THERE ARE THINGS... I CAN'T GIVE UP.
SHUT UP! THERE ISN'T ONE!!

"If the day will come that all of them, freed from everything, can cry from their hearts, can smile from their hearts, even if I really am punished, I want to break the curse."

The vengeful spirits' curse was originally a promise made long, long ago to always be with God. That's why they are bound to the Sohma family—and to Akito. When Tohru learns the true nature of the curse, and that Kyo will be confined after he graduates from high school, she resolves to find a way to break the curse.

Even when threatened and told not to interfere, Tohru refuses to back down. Even she has something she can't give up.

THE PAIN OF A HEART ABOUT TO BE TORN APART

Rough kindness. Loneliness. Sadness. Solitude. Love... Everything Kyo says or does either hurts Tohru's heart or makes it skip a beat. Without realizing it herself, she's beginning to fall in love with him--which fuels her desire to break the curse. Yuki and Shigure seem to be aware of her feelings.

...AH...
YES.
THANK Y--
......
WHA...
I--
I DON'T KNOW... FOR SOME REASON, T-TEARS SUDDENLY...
WHY ARE YOU CRYING?!
WH-WHY DOES...
...MY HEART...

When Tohru hears Kyo say, "When there's a guy you like, I'll help you out," she starts to cry. But she doesn't quite understand why.

WHAT HAPPENS TO ME IS MY OWN--
WAIT!
BUT THAT WOULD MAKE ME...
...VERY...
...UM...

Tohru is hit hard by the line, "Locked up in the castle until you die," in the "Sorta Cinderella" play.

...NN?
WHAT'S WRONG...?
AH
BLUSH
AH! NO... UM--!
Y-Y-YOU SUDDENLY WALKED AWAY AND I WAS WONDERING WHERE YOU WERE GOING, SO...
IT'S JUST, THAT...
AH, I SEE.

"...I wonder if he'll push me away like that someday, too."

IT SEEMS LIKE YOU'VE BEEN GUESSING EVERYTHING RIGHT ABOUT ME RECENTLY, KYO-KUN.
YOU DON'T THINK YOU'RE TOO EASY TO READ?
TH-THAT'S NOT TRUE...
YOUR VOICE IS GETTING QUIETER, YOU KNOW?

When he hears this exchange between Kyo and Tohru, Yuki is convinced that the two of them are falling in love with each other.

Will she also be pushed away one day? Suddenly anxious, Tohru involuntarily grabs Kyo as he starts to leave--and he looks back and takes her hand with a surprisingly gentle smile.

COME ON.
......!

Unable to shake off her fear that Kyo might someday reject her, Tohru almost cries when he's curt with her. On the other hand, every smile or kind word makes her happy.

I WANT TO GO SEE HIM.

......
...WAS THE LAST PROMISE I WAS ABLE TO MAKE...
I WANT TO WORK...
...ONCE I'VE SAFELY GRADUATED HIGH SCHOOL...
AFTER ALL...
...TO MOM.
THAT...

"Don't go. Come back. Don't, don't take Mom away."

Tohru gets scared when her grandfather says, "I want to go see Katsuya." She remembers her mother saying the same thing long ago.

"I WANT TO GO SEE HIM."

Her mother's wish—for Tohru to graduate from high school in her place, since she herself hadn't been able to attend high school--is now a source of comfort for Tohru.

......
THAT... IS...

When Hiro asks her why she has such a mother complex, Tohru withdraws into herself.

I'M OFF...
NO!
YOU CAN'T GO!
YOU'LL BE...
...TOHRU.
DON'T GO!
COME BACK!
DON'T GO!

The day her mother died, Tohru slept in after staying up late to study for a test, and didn't have a chance to tell her to come home safely. She still regrets not saying goodbye. And the memory of her mother's breakdown after her father's death still haunts her.

The night she meets Isuzu, Tohru dreams about her missed chance to say goodbye to her mother.

"No. It's not as simple as that. The truth lies much deeper."

EH...?
THE THING THAT'S MOST IMPORTANT TO YOU...
WHAT IS IT?
......
WHY...
THE THING YOU CAN'T GIVE UP...WHAT IS IT?
...DO YOU WANT TO BREAK THE CURSE?
IT'S...

"What is it that's most important to you?" Tohru is struck speechless at the question. It used to be a question she could easily answer, but now it paralyzes her.

BEING BY YOURSELF...
...IS SCARY.
BEING ALONE...
...IS A FRIGHTENING WAY TO LIVE.

A HEART THAT IS QUIETLY BREAKING

Unknown to anyone, a dark fear is gradually eating away at Tohru's heart. She has lost so many people already that she lives in fear of losing anyone else, and of being left alone. Only one person--Rin--has even the vaguest idea of how fragile Tohru is.

本田今日子

Kyoko Honda

"I'm always an idiot. I always have to lose my way once or I can't reach my own answer."

BUT SHE SAID THAT KINDNESS IS SOMETHING THAT GROWS INSIDE OF EACH PERSON'S BODY...
...BUT IT'S UP TO US TO NURTURE THAT KINDNESS IN OUR HEARTS.
THAT'S WHY KINDNESS IS DIFFERENT FOR EVERY PERSON.

Kyoko Quote Collection

"There are feelings that you don't understand unless you get hurt and cause problems. And there are feelings you understand for the first time after falling to the bottom of life. You resist beautiful things, but after being beat up, you start to love beauty for the first time. Pain needs kindness, and for darkness to stand out, it needs the sun. You can't make light of either of them. You can't say either of them is worthless." (->Arisa)

"How could I have said that? Back then, I don't know what my mother felt when she heard that, but if my child had said that to me, I would want to die. I said a terrible thing. I didn't have any problem saying something to someone that would hurt me if I had been told it."

"I needed him. I loved him. I was finally able to meet him, but no matter where I go back to, there is no one to welcome me."

I...WOULD NEVER TELL ANYONE!
MY MOM ALWAYS TOLD ME THAT GOSSIPING IS WRONG!
NO, IT'S NOT THAT.
I PROMISE! I'LL SIGN MY NAME IN BLOOD OR BURN MYSELF WITH A CIGARETTE OR ANYTHING YOU WANT!
I'm pretty sure my mom did stuff like that.
No, I told you that's not it.
WHAT KIND OF PERSON WAS HER MOTHER ...?

Katsuya Honda

A mild-mannered, unusually polite young man. But he has a cynical side, and a rebellious streak. When he was younger, he was even more difficult. He died while on a business trip, after contracting a severe cold. Tohru's awkwardly formal speech is an imitation of his.

IT SAVES ME FROM CRITICISM WHEN I TRY TO PUSH BOUNDARIES.
MY FATHER'S INFLUENCE IS WORTH USING.
IF YOU KNOW HOW, THAT IS.

Katsuya points out that he can just use his father's influence to get out of trouble. He's quite audacious.

WHY?
YOU'RE ASKING ME?
WHY...
THAT'S WHAT... THAT'S WHAT I WANNA KNOW.
...DID I...?!
WHERE DID SHE GO WRONG?
WHAT WAS HER MISTAKE?
I'M MISERABLE.

If she was honest about it, she hated how wretched she was. But she felt she couldn't change.

WANTING TO BE LOVED BY OTHERS

Kyoko was raised in a cold household, and became a girl who rejected others and couldn't open up to them. But she desperately wanted to be loved. Katsuya, who'd come to Kyoko's middle school as a student teacher, was the first person to recognize her heart's desire.

LISTEN.
TOGETHER.
LET'S MAKE SURE TO APOLOGIZE.
THEN WE'LL HOLD IT AGAIN.
...HOW ABOUT THAT?
WE'LL RAISE IT LIKE THAT.
NOT...
...BY MYSELF.

!
AT THE TIME...
YOU WERE STILL IN MIDDLE SCHOOL, AND I WAS SENSITIVE TO THAT.
SO?
CHOOSE ME.
BUT I NEVER INTENDED TO LET YOU GET AWAY.
IF YOU STILL CAN'T BELIEVE ME,
...I'LL SAY WHATEVER YOU NEED TO HEAR.
I'LL SAY IT AS OFTEN AS YOU LIKE.
THAT I DON'T LIKE WASTING WORDS.
JUST REMEMBER...

When Kyoko got pregnant, she cried because she felt incapable of raising a human being.

"WHY...DID I...TURN OUT... LIKE THIS...? WHY...? WHY DID I...? I'M SAD... I'M LONELY..."

I'M SORRY.
I'M HOME.
THANK YOU.

"He's not here.
He's not here anymore.
He's not anywhere.
He's not here. Katsuya."

When her parents abandoned her, Katsuya alone understood and loved Kyoko. After his death, Kyoko's entire world crumbled, and she eventually tried to take her own life. But at the last minute, her love for her daughter held her back.

!!
I...
I'M HO...
...I'M SORRY!
I'M HOME!
WHAT'S WRONG WITH ME?
I'M HOME...!
I'M SO SORRY!
I'M SORRY!

When Kyoko finally comes to her senses, Tohru welcomes her home.

IT CAN BE HARD TO FIND YOUR OWN ANSWERS.
IT MAKES ME WONDER.
...HOW LONG YOU'LL TAKE.
HOW LOST YOU'LL ALL GET...

Kyoko describes her painful history to a young Kyo.

DON'T LEAVE ME!
PLEASE!
HE'S NOT HERE!
KATSUYA!
D-
DO...
DON'T...
...LEAVE ME...!

"Even I want someone who lives on my level. I want to need someone, and be needed in return. I don't want to just sleep. I don't want to just receive. I want to give something only I can give."

草摩由希
Yuki Sohma

Zodiac: The Rat

Everything Yuki touches seems to turn to gold, so he acquired the nickname "Prince Charming". But he thinks of himself as insignificant, and has a complex about his feminine looks.

When he was small, he was brought to Akito as a playmate, and the two of them lived together. After Akito's mind was twisted, Yuki was locked in an isolated room and suffered severe psychological abuse. Even after he was let out, he had no idea how to behave around people--the wall he'd built around himself seemed too high.

A second-year student at Kaibara Public High School, and current president of the Student Council. Nicknames: Yun-Yun, Prince Charming. He lives at Shigure Sohma's house. When he was very young, he lived at the main house as Akito's playmate. Name origin: The sound "Yuki" just popped into my head.

Fashion Concept

There's no particular reason why he likes and wears Chinese-style clothes--I just like Chinese clothing. But I think they suit the androgynous Yuki very well. (What do you think?) He especially likes shirts with a thin, light feel, and he hates accessories. When I was designing Yuki and Kyo's clothes, I deliberately chose very different styles so they could both think, "I wouldn't be caught dead in the clothes you wear--and besides, they'd look awful on me."

(From the 2001 Fruits Basket Character Book)

Awkward

Despite his refined appearance, Yuki's lazy around the house. He's terrible at cleaning, and when he cooks, he does odd things like adding takuwan to curry. On top of that, his hands are so clumsy that he can't even fold paper cranes.

THAT'S TERRIFYING. LET'S NOT DO THAT!
PLEASE-- ALL I'M LACKING IN IS DRIVE.
I think.
YOU MEAN TALENT!

When Tohru is gone overnight, Yuki decides to try cooking for the first time in a while. Shigure panics and tries to stop him, but Yuki refuses to listen. The resulting culinary achievement is... indescribable. Self improvement is a noble idea, but maybe some things are better left alone.

...THERE.
I DID IT.
THANK YOU VERY MUCH.
!
flappity flop
ガタガタ。

He took his best shot at first aid when Tohru injured her hand, but mostly just kept wrapping the bandage around and around. At least he tried.

Secret Base

SOHMA-KUN, IS SOMETHING WRONG?
AH.
A FARM?
A VEGETABLE GARDEN, ACTUALLY.
?!
SOHMA-KUN, YOU DID THIS?!

Yuki has a private vegetable garden on the (Sohma-owned) mountain behind Shigure's house. He calls it his "secret base", and doesn't tell anyone about it.

Yuki's reasons for growing vegetables are similar to Ayame's reasons for making clothes.

Not A Morning Person

HMMM...
WHAT SHOULD WE DO...?
HIS EYES ARE OPEN, BUT HE'S TOTALLY UNAWAKE!
YUKI...?
IT'S ALMOST TIME FOR BREAKFAST...
KYON, WAKE HIM UP!
WHAT? WHY ME?
LEAVE HIM.

Yuki and mornings don't get along. When he first gets up, he's basically sleepwalking--and he's a better fighter in that state. But if something pushes his buttons, he'll snap awake.

Released From The Darkness

DO YOU KNOW WHY...
...AT GURE-NII'S HOUSE?
...YOU'RE ABLE TO LIVE...
HARU BEGGED HIM...
...TO GET YOU OUT OF THERE.
HE WANTED TO HELP YOU.

Akito kept Yuki locked up in an isolated room for a long time Eventually, Shigure arranged for him to leave, after Hatsuharu pleaded for his release.

Yuki didn't know why he had been released until Isuzu told him.

An Exclusive Private School

Since he was the Rat, Yuki was forced to attend a famous private school where he didn't know anyone. He wanted to go to school with Kyo and the other Zodiac members instead.

IT'S A SHAME, CONSIDERING I ENROLLED HIM IN A BETTER SCHOOL THAN THE OTHER ZODIAC CHILDREN.
OH--AND PLEASE DROP ME OFF BEFORE YOU TAKE HIM TO SCHOOL.
I'LL BE COMING HOME LATE.
YES, MA'AM.

He was chauffeured to elementary school in an expensive foreign car, but he wished he could walk to school with everyone else. His mother's vanity kept him from going to school with his friends, adding to his suffering.

[Tohru's words of friendship]

Yuki Quote Collection

"Thank you for always listening to me. Thank you for always accepting my weakness." (->Tohru)

"He needs to realize. That he (Kyo)... and I are both made that way. That in the end... that's all we are." (->Shigure)

"Back then, when she abandoned me, when she threw me away everything lost its color. I thought that everything was over."

"Never talk to him again'... The part of me that panicked and said something so senseless... That part of me... I might not hate it so much."

"...again and again, she accepted me... like a 'mother'..."

"I don't like making it anyone's fault anymore. If I blame someone else, no matter how much time passes, I won't be able to change." (->Akito)

...MIGHT BE SOMETHING THAT YOU DON'T LIKE.

...SOMETHING THAT I CAN BE PROUD OF.

...BUT I WANT IT TO BE.

Yuki Sohma's Family Tree

Mother	Father
Second Son Yuki	Eldest Son Ayame

Other People's Words To Yuki

"It's all right. You are not a 'tool.' If someone like me can have someone who is there for me, then surely a good kid like you isn't as alone as you think you are." (Ayame)

"I see... You know, you're a pretty interesting guy." (Kakeru)

"...Yuki, you're weak. But Yuki... you're also kind." (Hatsuharu)

"You are my toy. Your mother gave you to me." (Akito)

"You easily jump over people who are trying so desperately. Someone like you would never understand how I feel. A 'Prince Charming' who lived without any worries would never understand the feelings of someone who couldn't get anything." (Kyo)

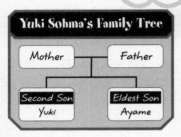

Young Yuki's silent pleas don't reach his mother, who sees the world through her own distorted values. If she ever looked at him, maybe she'd understand...?

I'M DECIDING FOR YOU.

The Mother Who Sold Her Own Son

Yuki's Mother

A vain woman who thinks only of herself. Because she gave birth to the Rat of the Zodiac, she has many privileges from the Sohma family, and lives a life of idle luxury. Even though Ayame is her son, she can't handle him and his regal attitude; since she couldn't control him, she tried to make Yuki into her ideal son. She's ruthless, and has never asked Yuki's opinion. She thought being Akito's favorite would be good for him.

THEN, I'LL BE GOING HOME, TOO.

DON'T —

YUKI.

DON'T... USE IT WASTE-FULLY.

Yuki has to get his mother to sign a cell phone contract. After signing it, she says something motherly for the very first time.

"SO WHAT ARE YOU SAYING? WHAT IF YOU ARE A 'TOOL'?"

50

BECAUSE SOMEONE WILL NEED YOU...

His very first friends... The first time in his life he felt wanted.

BE...
FRIENDS?
SURE!
NOW C'MON!
WE WANNA PLAY, YUKI!
FRIENDS.
FRIENDS.

"Was I able to help a little? If so, I'm happy. I'm happy. I'm very happy."

BUT RIGHT NOW...
...SHE'S COUNTING ON ME.
SHE WANTS TO FIND HER WAY AGAIN.
SHE'S DESPERATE— THAT'S WHY SHE'S TRAILING AFTER ME.
SHE'S...
SHE'S ENTRUSTING ME WITH EVERYTHING.
...COUNT-ING ON ME.
ME.

A series of events leads to Yuki being the one to take Tohru home when she is lost. Realizing that he truly helped her gives him a sense of fulfillment.

BUT IT WAS ONLY ONCE, WHEN WE WERE VERY SMALL. I NEVER LEARNED HER NAME.
WHEN I MET HER AGAIN, I DIDN'T RECOGNIZE HER.
...I WANTED TO TRY MY BEST.
I KNEW THERE WAS MORE THAN DARKNESS IN THE WORLD.
I WANTED TO TRY TO LIVE THE BEST LIFE I COULD.

Yuki loses his will to live when he loses his only friends. After helping Tohru he felt able to try again, but being confined by Akito fills him with resignation and despair. He becomes incapable of reaching out to people.

A PERSON REJECTED BY EVERYTHING

YOU NEED ME.
IF I DIDN'T CARE ABOUT YOU...
...THERE'D BE NO REASON FOR YOU TO BE ALIVE!
AFTER THAT...

His innocent heart was exposed to Akito's malice.

"HOPE TURNED TO DESPAIR, ASPIRATION TURNED TO JEALOUSY. I WANTED TO BE LIKED... I WANTED HIM TO BE MY FRIEND, THAT'S ALL. AND YET..."

THAT WAS ALL I WANTED.
THAT, AND NOTHING ELSE.

He yearned for warm people around him, a family that welcomed him, and friends to play with.

He was sold by his mother, ignored by his brother, and hated by Kyo. Yuki hadn't even had real contact with the other Juunishi, and because he didn't know how to interact with people, he also didn't have any friends at school. But he craved companionship.

OH.
UM, YES.
I'LL NEVER...
...FORGIVE YOU.
DO YOU HEAR ME?
I'LL NEVER FORGIVE YOU!
SOME-ONE AS ROTTEN AS YOU...
IT'S ALL YOUR FAULT, RAT!
EVERY-THING'S YOUR FAULT!
...OUGHTA DO US ALL A FAVOR AND JUST DISAPPEAR!
IT'S ALL BECAUSE YOU EXIST!

When Yuki and Kyo first meet, Yuki doesn't understand the rage Kyo directs at him.

A REBORN BOND BETWEEN BROTHERS

Because they were raised apart, a rift grew between Yuki and Ayame. Ayame regrets the distance between them, and tries to bridge it with his unique style of love. Yuki is also trying to understand Ayame, and the rift is slowly closing.

put it on forthWITH!!
WHAT HAVE YOU DONE?

But his brotherly love often runs wildly out of control. "I live for my older brother"? What is he thinking???

...ISN'T AS ALONE...
...AS YOU THINK YOU ARE.
THERE...
FINISHED.

Yuki grew up being treated as an object by his parents and brother. Ayame is trying to heal those wounds in Yuki's heart with his brotherly love.

THAT'S NOT TRUE. NII-SAN...
...IS RELIABLE.
I MEAN...HE'S OUTLANDISH IN LOTS OF WAYS, BUT...
...HE'S NOT...
..."GOOD-FOR-NOTHING."

Ayame attends Yuki's parent-teacher conference. Yuki's mother dismisses Ayame as a good-for-nothing, but Yuki defends him.

FACING HIS INFERIORITY COMPLEX

"I guess I could never truly hate someone who is capable of saying he's in love."

Kakeru somehow reminds Yuki of his brother and Kyo. He lives at his own unflappable pace, no matter what, and this triggers Yuki's inferiority complex. But Yuki refuses to run away, and their constant clashes grow into a friendship where they can talk about anything.

DON'T CRY, YUN-YUN!
OW.
THAT HURT!
I DON'T APPRECIATE THE SUDDEN THREAT OF A NOSEBLEED!
GAH!
HEY, I'M JUST TRYING TO CHEER YOU UP!
AND IF YOU EVER GOT A NOSEBLEED, I'D USE MY CELL PHONE TO SHOW EVERYONE!
You stink!
YOUR CELL PHONE DOESN'T EVEN HAVE A CAMERA!
You stink!

Hitting each other with a volleyball cemented their friendship.

"NEVER...
...SPEAK TO ME?"
NE--?!!
"NEVER SPEAK TO YOU"? WHAT AM I SAYING?!
NO, UH, THAT WAS...!
I SOUND LIKE A LITTLE KID! "NEVER SPEAK TO YOU AGAIN"...?! "NEVER SPEAK TO YOU AGAIN"...?!!
WHAT AM I SAYING?! WHERE DID THAT COME FROM?!
STEP...
WHA...
SAYING THAT WON'T HAVE ANY EFFECT WHATSOEVER!! I'LL BE LAUGHED AT!!

"I'll never speak to you again." Yuki said it without thinking, and is embarrassed by how childish he sounded.

"YOU'RE A PRETTY INTERESTING GUY."
I WAS...
THAT REALLY WAS THE FIRST TIME...
...I'D BEEN TOLD ANYTHING LIKE THAT.
SO IT MADE ME A LITTLE...
......
...A LITTLE TAKEN ABACK.
...HAPPY.

Kakeru said, "You're a pretty interesting guy." Yuki realized he'd always wanted someone to say that to him.

WHAT HE WANTED WAS UNCONDITIONAL LOVE

FOR NOW, ALL I CAN TELL YOU...
...IS THAT I'M DOING WELL.
SO, DON'T WORRY ABOUT ME.

Yuki comforts Tohru when she senses his doubts.

BECAUSE...

Yuki realizes that his feelings for Tohru aren't romantic.

LIKE THE SKY...
...BOTH NEAR AND FAR.
AND AGAIN...
LIKE A REAL MOTHER WOULD.
...SHE'S ACCEPTED ME.
THAT BELOVED HUMAN BEING.

"I WAS LOOKING... FOR A 'MOTHER,' FOR A 'MOTHER'S LOVE.'"

"I KNOW."
"I UNDERSTAND...
...WHAT YOU WANT, WHAT YOU'RE SEARCHING FOR...
...IN TOHRU HONDA."
"I KNOW ...
...WHAT YOU'RE LOOKING FOR...
...IN HER..."

Akito sees into his heart and points out what he didn't want to admit to himself.

From the beginning, Yuki knew he loved Tohru. But he also knew those feelings weren't romantic. What he craved was unconditional love from someone who would never reject him, something his mother had never given him. Flustered by his childish longing, he tries to persuade himself that he's in love with Tohru. But in the process of opening up to Kakeru, he confronts and comes to terms with his real feelings. He's now able to watch over Tohru and encourage her happiness.

FEELINGS THAT SPREAD LIKE WAVES

"TO SAY HELLO... SHE WAS CHASING ME JUST FOR THAT? SHE DIDN'T... GO TO ANYONE ELSE."

There is just one girl who says that Yuki is "not like a prince," and sees how lonely he is, even when he's surrounded by people. Yuki is beginning to have feelings for Machi, a fellow student council member who sees him for who he is. Seeing how hard it is for her to express herself reminds him of himself.

THANK YOU.

Machi wore herself out chasing him all over the school, just so she could say hello to him. Realizing what the gesture means, Yuki is filled with a quiet happiness.

WHAT DOES THE WORLD LOOK LIKE THROUGH YOUR EYES?
YOU MAKE ME WONDER.

Yuki was curious about the kinds of things Machi normally thinks about.

"I knew. Really, I knew. Just like there's rejection in the world, there are people who will hold out their hand to you."

草摩夾
Kyo Sohma

I JUST WASN'T REALLY...
I JUST...
...FEELING VERY WELL.

Zodiac: The Cat

おまえが謝ることは
な

The person possessed by the Cat, despised by the Sohma family. Kyo's mother brought him up without letting him see anyone; she loved him, but was still afraid of him. After her suicide, Kyo was taken in by Kazuma, who gave him his first taste of untainted love. But he continued to be a fierce, unmanageable boy during elementary and middle school. He was supposed to attend a local boys' high school, but instead trained in the mountains with Kazuma for three months. After he got back, he began living at Shigure's house and attending Kaibara Public High School.

A second-year student at Kaibara Public High School. Nicknames: Kyon-Kyon, Kyonkichi. Possessed by the Cat. Kazuma Sohma's adopted son. His fate is to be confined deep within the Sohma estate after he finishes high school. But if he can ever defeat Yuki, he won't be imprisoned.

Fashion Concept

Of all the male characters I've drawn, he's the one that looks best in V-neck shirts (I think). He likes rough clothes that are easy to move in and don't need looking after. He absolutely hates clothes that are tight around the neck. And he doesn't wear accessories except for his beads, which he only wears because he has to. Anyway, he doesn't like wearing things that feel oppressive--he even hates wearing socks. He really liked the pants he was wearing when he first appeared, but they're all torn up, so he can't wear them anymore. (Sorry, Kyo.)

(From the 2001 *Fruits Basket Character Book*)

Least Favorite Food

EAT IT!

He's not very picky about food, but he hates leeks, green onions, and miso. He hates the smell of leeks and the taste of onions, and while he can tolerate miso soup, he can't stand miso dengaku. Tohru has still been known to obliviously cook leek and liver.

Against Kyo, leeks become a dangerous weapon. Once, when he was arguing with Yuki in front of the supermarket, Yuki stuffed a bunch of raw leeks into his mouth and nearly made him vomit.

He Hates Water

Kyo hates water. It's bad enough that rain exhausts him, but it also means he doesn't like swimming. Apparently this is because his true form hates water.

IT'S--
IN THE MORNING...
--BETTER THAN YOU DAMMIT! YOU CAN'T EVEN...
...WAKE UP...

Even the rain makes Kyo lethargic. He gets so listless that Tohru asks (with some embarrassment) if he would rather turn into a cat and have her carry him.

What He Really Can't Handle

BECAUSE WE'RE GOING TO BE MARRIED!
WHEN DID YOU DECIDE THAT?!

Kyo seems like a troublemaker, but he's surprisingly sensible--and can't cope with people like Momiji and Hatsuharu, who march to their own drum. Kagura is the most trouble for him, though: he's likely to get hurt regardless of whether she's showing the dreamy or aggressive side of her personality.

"Because we're going to be married!" Kyo has never understood why Kagura is so attached to him.

YOU'RE ENGAGED?!
THAT'S SO GREAT THAT YOU FOUND SOMEONE TO BE YOUR WIFE.
CON-GRATU-LATIONS.
CUT-IT-OUT!!

He Likes High Places

Whenever something upsets him, Kyo goes to the roof of the school, the roof of the house, or some other high place to calm down. When Kagura first visited and spent the night, he immediately evacuated to the roof.

I FOUND YOU!
I KNEW YOU'D BE HERE!
WAH!
YOU ALWAYS SNEAK UP ON ME...
KYO-KUN, YOU REALLY LIKE HIGH PLACES, DON'T YOU?
AH! HELLO, MR. KITTY.

His attraction to high places is only natural for the Cat.

Ignorant

BUT IT'S BEING BROADCAST NATIONWIDE.
YOU'RE KIDDING!
I'M KIDDING.
......
KYO'S PRETTY DUMB WITH MODERN TECHNOLOGY.
HE SURE IS!

Because he was locked up in his house when he was small, and became so absorbed in his training when he was older, he's very ignorant about the world. He'd never heard of Jason, and didn't even know what DVDs were.

He was completely shocked to see his performance in the Cultural Festival play on the TV. Even Tohru made fun of his surprise.

A Surprisingly Good Cook

IS THIS FOR TOHRU-KUN?
WHAT?!
You got a problem?!
YOU CAN'T EXPECT A SICK PERSON TO COOK FOR HERSELF.
......
BUT I DIDN'T SAY ANYTHING.
BY THE WAY, WHAT ARE WE GOING TO EAT?

Because his Shishou, Kazuma, is so appallingly bad at cooking, Kyo became good at it to survive. He also has a knack for forming onigiri.

When Tohru was sick in bed, he voluntarily made some medley soup for her.

I CAN'T HELP IT.
I'M...
...NOT MADE FOR INTERACTING WITH PEOPLE.

YOU...
...DESTRUCTIVE IDIOT!!
HANG IN THERE, DESTRUCTIVE IDIOT.
SHUT UP!!
LEAVE ME ALONE!!

[Encouraging words from Yuki]

Kyo Quote Collection

"I wish I could be like that, too...!" [->Yuki]

"I hate this! Losing her, being pitied, being miserable... having this fate forced on me."

"Anyway, why do people have to ask stupid questions like, 'What are you going to do when you graduate?' They just don't get it. Being possessed by the Cat, it's not that easy. I don't even know if I'd be able to live with normal people. Just thinking about it, I freeze up." [->Tohru]

"She won't ever come back. I couldn't fulfill it, but even so, it blossomed in front of me. It kept blossoming. A small, small flower. A tiny, precious flower." [->Tohru]

"I want to be near you until the time when I must go away. I want to be with you 'til the end." [->Tohru]

Other People's Words To Kyo

"Together. I want us to live... Eat meals, study ...share our troubles, like we did before... together. I want to stay together......!!" [Tohru]

"From now on you will have to breathe the air of higher places." [Kazuma]

"You should have been the one to die. However you look at it, everyone would have been a lot happier if you had never been born." [Akito]

Kyo Sohma's Family Tree

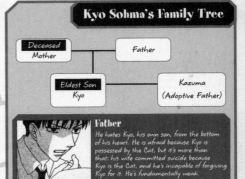

Deceased Mother — Father

Eldest Son Kyo — Kazuma (Adoptive Father)

Father

He hates Kyo, his own son, from the bottom of his heart. He is afraid because Kyo is possessed by the Cat, but it's more than that: his wife committed suicide because Kyo is the Cat, and he's incapable of forgiving Kyo for it. He's fundamentally weak.

The Person Who First Showed Kyo Love

Kazuma Sohma

He manages a karate dojo on the Sohma "outside". Because his grandfather was possessed by the Cat, Kazuma grew up "inside". He came to regret his coldness toward his grandfather, and originally took Kyo in to atone for it. But now he loves Kyo like a true father.

"...I will take your means of escape. Will you lose her, or will you not? I will help you find the answer."

SHISHOU! WHAT ARE YOU BURNING THIS TIME?!
EH?

He is educated, but his day-to-day skills are weak. He is especially horrible at cooking. But somehow, he keeps getting the idea that he can do it.

...WE KEPT MISSING EACH OTHER
ALL THIS TIME...

Kazuma felt that they had finally became a real father and son, and finally understood each other.

Kunimitsu Tomoda

Kazuma's number one student, and his assistant. When he was young, he caused a lot of mischief, but now he's reformed completely and Kazuma has complete trust in him. He has the same attitude with everyone, even when dealing with people with strong personalities, like Kyo and Isuzu.

A GROTESQUE MONSTER

I NEVER THOUGHT...
...TOHRU.
TOHRU...!
...TO HEAR THOSE WORDS.

He didn't need her to love everything about him. He just wanted her to be at his side.

"IT'S OKAY IF YOU'RE SCARED. IT'S OKAY IF YOU DON'T LOVE MY HIDEOUS SELF. BUT, EVEN SO, 'LET'S GO ON LIVING TOGETHER.'"

...TRUE FORM?

The true form of the one possessed by the Cat. It is truly a monster: brutal and ugly, with a smell like something rotting. Faced with it, Tohru feels sick to her stomach, and leaves the area, but...

The human possessed by the Cat has a "true form": a grotesque form that gives off a putrid smell from its whole body, and has inhuman speed and jumping ability. It is usually sealed away with beads made of human bone and blood, but he transforms if they are removed. No one knows why only the Cat has this deformed other shape.

STOP.
I'M GOING TO MAKE YOU MISERABLE.
GET LOST!

I DON'T KNOW HOW MUCH OF THAT'S TRUE, THOUGH.
APPARENTLY, BECAUSE IT WAS MADE
...BY SACRIFICING THE LIVES OF OTHERS. IT'S SUPPOSED TO BE A POWERFUL PROTECTIVE CHARM.

Beads made from the bones of others. A mother who took her own life because of him. Kyo doesn't understand why his mother killed herself and not him.

THE AIR "OUTSIDE"

Kyo desperately protected himself from the people who blamed him for his mother's death. The one person who understood and accepted him was Kazuma Sohma, who took Kyo in and raised him in the outside world. Under his care, Kyo gradually began to blossom.

"I'll be the kind of guy who's worthy of calling you my dad, Shishou."

...HE WAS THE FIRST ONE TO SHOW ME THE "OUTSIDE" WORLD.
HE TOOK MY HAND...
...AND STAYED BY MY SIDE.
HEY, YOU'RE A SHISHOU, RIGHT?
EH?
Ah ha ha!
THAT MAY BE RIGHT.
BUT...
ON TV THEY WERE CALLING A KARATE INSTRUCTOR "SHISHOU." SO YOU'RE A SHISHOU, RIGHT?
...NONE OF MY STUDENTS WILL CALL ME THAT.

Kazuma tries to shield Kyo from the malicious gossip.

KYO.
......
...MY TROUBLE-SOME...
TH...
...SON.

"My troublesome son." Kyo accepts those words with an uncharacteristic meekness, and from then on, they begin sharing their burdens.

THE CAT AND THE RAT, DESTINED BY BLOOD

THE FATE SET BY YOUR BLOOD.
YOU WILL NEVER IN YOUR LIFE BE ABLE TO BEAT YUKI.
THAT'S HOW YOU WERE MADE FROM THE BEGINNING.
I'VE TOLD YOU...
IT'S THE COURSE OF DESTINY CARVED OUT BY THOSE POSSESSED BY VENGEFUL SPIRITS...

The one possessed by the Cat can never win against the Rat. Akito says that's naturally how it is: it's the destiny carved out for those possessed by spirits.

"SOMEONE LIKE YOU WOULD NEVER UNDERSTAND HOW I FEEL. THE STUPID WISH OF A STUPID GUY WHO WANTS WHAT HE DOESN'T HAVE. YOU'D NEVER..."

WANT TO COMPETE WITH US?
IF YOU JOIN, KYO WILL GET INTO IT.
splash
splash
LIKE HELL I WILL! I'M NOT THAT SIMPLE!
...
MAYBE I WILL JOIN...
THERE'S NO WAY I'M GONNA LOSE!!
I'M GONNA KICK YOUR ASSES!
SEE, YUKI? WHAT'D I TELL YA?

Kyo always gives in to his feelings of rivalry toward Yuki. He'll even get into water, which he hates, to compete with him.

"...YOU WOULDN'T KNOW WHAT TO DO WITH YOURSELF, WOULD YOU?"

Those possessed by the Rat and the Cat are seen as rivals by the Sohma family, and Kyo and Yuki have a natural enmity toward each other. When Akito tells him that he won't be confined if he beats Yuki before graduating from high school, his feelings of rivalry intensify. Kyo sees Yuki, who is incredibly talented in many areas, as undeservedly blessed.

But the truth is, he knew what he was doing--that he needed someone to hate in order to hide from his own emotions.

YOU HAVEN'T CHANGED...
"IF I DIE TOO, YOU'LL BE SATISFIED, RIGHT?!"
"IT'S HIS FAULT! IT'S ALL HIS FAULT!"
"I'LL KILL HIM AND THEN I'LL KILL MYSELF!"
"THEN YOU'LL BE SATISFIED, RIGHT?"

Kyo believes that the Rat is to blame for all of his problems. At his mother's funeral, he shouted at his father, saying he would kill Yuki and then kill himself.

A RELATIONSHIP BURIED AT THE BACK OF HIS MIND.

"Even you smiled at me, but now you hate me."

...I'M SORRY...
...OKAY...?

As Tohru naps after visiting Kyoko's grave, Kyo apologizes to her for something.

Kyo has another secret that he can't tell Tohru: he met Kyoko more than once when he was young, and talked with her many times. He even saw Tohru when they were both children. And he might know something about Kyoko's death...

MAYBE IT'S BECAUSE MOM IS SO HAPPY...
...THAT EVERYONE IS COMING TO VISIT HER GRAVE.
...

In front of Kyoko's grave, Kyo's face shows something like regret. Saki easily picks up on his conflicted waves.

A TINY, PRECIOUS FLOWER

"WHEN DID I START THINKING MY NAME HAD A SPECIAL RING TO IT WHENEVER SHE WOULD SAY IT?"

Y-
YOUR...
...HAND...

When Kyo returns to the classroom after having an argument with Yuki, he is calmed by a smile from Tohru, who had been waiting for him.

BUT THAT WOULD MAKE...
...ME...
...VERY...?
...ABOUT THAT STORY.

When Tohru blurts out, "That would make me..." during the play, "sorta Cinderella," the words give Kyo a faint hope.

There is a girl who said she likes the Cat that is hated by the Sohmas. A girl who helped him think that he might have value on his own, rather than living in Yuki's shadow. A girl who saw his deformity and embraced it without giving in to her fear. It was probably inevitable that she would become someone dear to Kyo.

YOU DON'T KNOW HOW SCARED SHE WAS THEN!
HER HANDS...
SO HOW CAN YOU SAY THOSE THINGS?!

When Akito insults Tohru, Kyo forgets Yuki's warning, and unintentionally talks back. But Akito refuses to listen.

I...
I WON'T LOSE!
WHY HIDE IT? I'M THE MEAN STEPSISTER!
UH, YOU'RE NOT THE ONE BEING MEAN.
PAT
AND HOW OLD ARE WE TURNING THIS YEAR?
!
YUKI-KUN.
NOT TO INTERRUPT, BUT MIGHT I HAVE THE PLEASURE OF ENTERING MY HOME?
SO WHICH IS IT?
IT'S NOT!
......!
OUH

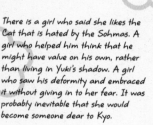

He takes Tohru's script and teases her about it, and thinks she's cute when she blushes with embarrassment.

I LOVE YOU...
...THE WAY YOU ARE.
I LOVE YOU.
I LOVE YOU SO MUCH!

"I am not worth any special mention. I have no power, and little merit. I'm worthless, the worst kind of man."

草摩紫呉
Shigure Sohma

Zodiac: The Dog

Shigure hides his true self under a pretense of constant silliness. He's kind to Tohru, and generally friendly, but sometimes his eyes are cold. He seems to know something about the Zodiac curse, but he dodges questions about it. It's not entirely clear whether he has Tohru, Yuki, Kyo, or anyone else's best interests at heart, but he's obviously plotting something that involves Tohru. A couple of years ago he dated Mayuko Shiraki, Tohru's homeroom teacher, who called him a "ripple in the water."

Fashion Concept

He latched onto the idea that novelists should wear kimonos, so he started wearing them--sloppily--to get into the spirit of things. Before he became a writer (when he still lived at the main house), he wore rougher clothes like t-shirts and jeans because it suited his idea of that life. "Sort of getting into the spirit of things" is really just another of his games, as if he's proving that he's not committed to anything.

Author (pen names: Shigure Sohma, Noa Kiritani, others). Nickname: Gure-san. Akito has ordered him to live on the Sohma "outside". He is raising Yuki and Kyo. Name origin: from a name for the Tenth month: Shigurezuki *Autumn showers month

(From the 2001 Fruits Basket Character Book)

Shigure Quote Collection

"Mingling with people, hurting them, getting hurt by them... that's how you learn about others, and about yourself. If you don't, you'll never be able to care about anyone but yourself." (->Kyo)

"You remember the morning we had that dream? You and me and Aaya all cried, remember? That morning..." (->Hatori)

"...I may be the most cursed of us all..." (->Hatori)

"The most important thing to me has always been me." (->Mitsuru)

"Whatever we choose to do, Akito will be the one to pay for it in the end." (->Hatori)

"Please, do your best. Keep struggling. That's your job as young people, isn't it?" (->Hatsuharu)

"I have no power, and little merit. I'm worthless, the worst kind of man." (->Isuzu)

"I love Akito. Then and now. I love him. I love him so much, I want to spoil him rotten. I want to trample him to a pulp."

"I will be here. I'll always be here. You just don't realize it. Just like that day, I'm waiting."

Other People's Words To Shigure

"I'm not going to be on your side. But I won't be your enemy, either." (Hatori)

"It's almost impossible to find words to describe a man like Shigure... He's like a ripple in the water." (Mayuko)

"That's low, even coming from you. You don't even treat the people you like as human beings." (Mayuko)

Shigure's Weakness

Since he grew up with Hatori and Ayame, the other Zodiac members his age, Shigure is close enough to them to sometimes show his true self. When he does, Hatori usually lectures him for being annoying--so he gets nervous on the rare occasions when Hatori doesn't rebuke him.

WHAT'S GOING ON?!
AT A TIME LIKE THIS, HATORI IS SUPPOSED TO GIVE ME A STERN LECTURE!!
I WON'T.
SHAKE SHAKE
OUCH! THAT'S DIRTY!
YOU KNOW THAT IT HURTS THE MOST WHEN YOU TAKE THAT ATTITUDE!

Shigure assumed he'd be scolded for inviting Akito to the summer home, but...

Author Of... Belles Lettres?

Tohru didn't realize it at first, but Shigure is an author of belles lettres. What's more, he has several pen names, and writes a whole variety of things. His bestselling books are the shojo novels written under the name "Noa Kiritani."

WHAT WAS IT? BELLES LETTRES?
I had no idea.
YUP. THAT'S RIGHT.
I WRITE THESE.
OH, I'M SORRY. WRONG ONE.
THIS. THIS IS THE REAL ONE!
THIS IS A BOOK I PUT OUT ON A LARK.
夏色の吐息
1
DOESN'T THAT STILL MEAN YOU WROTE IT?!
THAT'S AMAZING!
WHAT'S SO AMAZING ABOUT BEING A PERV?
FOR ONCE, I AGREE WITH YOU.
きりたに のあ

Adult Advice

Shigure always seems to be messing around, but sometimes he gives serious advice as the adult of the house. He compares spending time with people to martial arts practice, and advises Kyo, who's awkward around people, to "not run away. Keep training".

THE MORE YOU'D THINK ABOUT IT, THE MORE ANXIOUS YOU'D GET.
SO WHAT DO YOU DO, TOHRU-KUN?
BUT TIME KEEPS PASSING, AND THE LAUNDRY DOESN'T WASH ITSELF.
IT MIGHT BE A GOOD IDEA...
...TO START WASHING THE LAUNDRY RIGHT AT YOUR FEET.
OF COURSE IT'S IMPORTANT TO THINK ABOUT WHAT LIES AHEAD, TOO...
...BUT IF YOU ONLY LOOK AT WHAT'S DOWN THE ROAD...
...YOU'LL GET TANGLED IN THE LAUNDRY AT YOUR FEET AND YOU'LL FALL, WON'T YOU?

Shigure usually offers advice in metaphors, which isn't surprising coming from a novelist.

A Man Like A Jellyfish

Shigure hides himself so well under his frivolous comments that he's impossible to grasp. Hatori says he's a "jellyfish", and Mayuko calls him a "ripple", meaning "he's a man who can't be caught".

!
HMM... THE TRUTH IS...
...Rin and I are going out.
Eh ...?!
AH! R-R-REALLY?! I-I'M SORRY, I SHOULDN'T HAVE PRIED!
NAH, I'M JUST PULLING YOUR LEG. SORRY, SORRY.
PAY ATTENTION TO THE CIRCUMSTANCES BEFORE YOU MAKE SUCH FLIPPANT COMMENTS.

Does he ever say anything that's not a lie or a joke? Tohru's seriousness makes her the constant victim of his nonsense. At times like those, it's still Hatori's job to play the straight man.

"I WILL GET IT. AND I'LL DO WHATEVER IT TAKES TO GET THERE. EVEN LIE OR USE PEOPLE. I WILL MAKE THAT DREAM LAST FOREVER."

Shigure and the other Zodiac members his age all had a dream the moment Akito was conceived. They went to Ren and cried for joy, because she was pregnant with their God.

A COOL-HEADED SCHEMER

Behind Shigure's sociable facade lies a shrewd strategist. He'll use anyone to get what he wants: Tohru, Yuki, Kyo... even Akito. He doesn't cooperate with or rely on anyone, and nothing seems to stir his heart--not even Isuzu's struggle to break the curse.

Shigure is aloof from the world and doesn't get too attached to things, but there is one person who means more to him than anything else: Akito.

Akito is annoyed when she hears that Tohru and the others have gone to a summer home. Shigure tempts her into following them.

His relatives believe Shigure is the one Akito trusts most among the Juunishi. They don't know how deep his plotting goes...

His relationship with his parents isn't very good, but unlike Momiji, he doesn't seem to have been rejected by his mother.

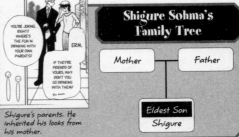

Shigure's parents. He inherited his looks from his mother.

Shigure Sohma's Family Tree

Mother		Father
	Eldest Son Shigure	

THE MOST CURSED OF THE ZODIAC

BESIDES, THAT'S NOT EVEN MY JOB, IS IT?
THAT'S LOW, EVEN COMING FROM YOU.
YOU DON'T EVEN TREAT THE PEOPLE YOU CLAIM TO LIKE AS HUMAN BEINGS.

Mayuko's casual comment hits home. Shigure's expression says that he knows he's twisted.

...
IT WOULD BE NICE IF YOU COULD REALIZE IT, TOO.
AKITO ...
...

Akito can't endure the idea of any of the Juunishi being drawn to anyone but her. Shigure knows that her irrational hatred isn't helping anyone, least of all her.

"I WANT TO TRAMPLE HER TO A PULP."

"I LOVE AKITO. THEN AND NOW. I LOVE HIM. I LOVE HIM SO MUCH, I WANT TO SPOIL HIM ROTTEN. I WANT TO TRAMPLE HIM TO A PULP."

Shigure knows his love for Akito is a dark, distorted thing--and that knowledge is why he mocks himself and claims to be the most cursed of the Zodiac.

AREN'T I BEING NICE TO YOU!?
......
BE NICER!!
HER...
YOU DO!
NICER, NICER, NICER!
YOU USED TO BE MUCH NICER.
YOU LOOKED ONLY AT ME.
AS IT SHOULD BE!
AT ME...
THAT WOMAN... YOU REALLY—

Shigure's history with Ren torments Akito. But Akito betrayed him once, as well, and doesn't realize how much that betrayal has twisted him.

WHY?!
WHY DO YOU TEST ME LIKE THAT?!
I'M NOT TESTING YOU.
DON'T YOU GET IT?
THE REASON I SLEPT WITH THAT WOMAN...
...IS BECAUSE YOU SLEPT WITH KURENO.

In a sense, the one most bound to Akito—to God—is Shigure. The strength of his warped love sometimes hurts her. Shigure knows it sometimes makes her suffer, and is deliberately driving her into a corner, as if he wants to see her break.

PLEASE TAKE YOUR JOB A LITTLE MORE SERIOUSLY.
ISN'T YOUR JOB IMPORTANT TO YOU?
HUH? THE MOST IMPORTANT THING TO ME...
...HAS ALWAYS BEEN ME.

"What are you talking about?" You know! That thing from that horror movie!

SHIGURE-SAN...!
UM...
HEY, WELCOME BACK.
SE...
ZENZEI!!!
THIS IS MY EDITOR.
UAAAAAH

She tries to hang herself, or slit her wrists...

Did you know?!
THERE'S A DEVIL WHO PRETENDS TO BE HUMAN ADRIFT AT SEA AND GETS ON THE BOAT!
EXCUSE ME?

"THIS TIME I ABSOLUTELY, POSITIVELY, DEFINITELY, WILL NOT LET YOU GET AWAY."

The Editor Who Wrestles With The Devil

Mitsuru

Her nickname is Mitchan. She's the editor in charge of Shigure's novels, and has raised worrying to an art form. Shigure baits her by disappearing before his deadlines, and takes a perverse glee in the resulting meltdowns. Mitchan becomes good friends with Ritsu, who's also prone to coming apart at the seams.

Zodiac: The Bear

草摩楽羅

Kagura Sohma

"Caring for someone isn't based on logic. You can't really rationalize emotions. Once I think 'I like him,' it's all over."

A demure young girl who is prone to dreaming. She is shy and quiet, but when she gets excited, she becomes a destructive force of nature. Her behavior is especially uncontrollable when she's with her beloved Kyo. She's been trained at Kazuma's dojo, so her capacity to wreak havoc is unparalleled.

When she was young, she happened to meet Kyo, and they started playing together. Since Kyo's mother had forbidden him to speak to anyone, Kagura is his only childhood friend. She's loved him wholeheartedly ever since, but her feelings are rooted in a secret sadness.

Fashion Concept

She wears cuter clothes than most twenty year olds because she's baby-faced, and because she thinks she'll look too old for Kyo if she dresses like a grown-up. She made her cat backpack by hand, and has several more in reserve. Her bedroom is overflowing with plush orange cats—enough orange in one place to hurt the eyes.

(From the 2001 Fruits Basket Character Book)

A second-year student at a private girls' junior college. She lives on the "inside" of the Sohma estate. When she gets excited, she goes berserk, and has caused a lot of property damage at her home and Shigure's house. Her dream is to be a daycare worker. She is good friends with Ritsu. Name origin: from a name for the Eleventh month: Kagurazuki *Month of Shinto song and dance

Kagura Quote Collection

"Please, just a little longer... Just humor me a little longer." [->Kyo]

"I... I was sad that I was born possessed by a vengeful spirit. After all... When I was young... my parents often fought because of me. Whenever I saw Mama crying by herself afterwards, it made me really sad." [->Kyo]

"I was...relieved. I realized that, compared to the Cat, I had it easy." [->Kyo]

"That's why I was with you. ...I was always looking down on you, Kyo-kun..." [->Kyo]

"I thought that, if I could shorten the distance between us, and if you would like me back, then the me that ran away—the dirty me—would be washed away." [->Kyo]

"...There's nothing to feel sorry for on my behalf. I've just been a very selfish girl. For the first time, I was finally able to see that. Thank you for worrying about me, Mama." [->Kagura's mother]

"But I'm fine. I'm fine. Caring for someone isn't based on logic. You can't really rationalize emotions. Once I think 'I like him,' it's all over." [->Yuki]

Other People's Words To Kagura

"I want to be someone like Kagura-san, who can find the wonderful things about the person she likes." [Tohru]

"Why don't you stop forcing yourself on him and calling it love? It's painful to watch." [Isuzu]

"Kagura, you know that's the second time you've destroyed that door in as many months." [Kagura's mother]

"Kagura. ...Regardless of what your reason was, when you played with me... I was happy. Thanks." [Kagura]

Valentine's Day Starts With An Ambush!

...AH!
AH...!
KYO...
...KUUUN!

When it comes to romance, Kagura is proactive. The day before Valentine's, she lies in wait by the gate to Tohru and the others' school and captures Kyo, who had realized she would come but failed to make his escape. Not surprisingly, she can predict his behavior and thoughts after knowing him for so long. She later visits Shigure's house and makes arrangements for them to go on a double date with Tohru and Yuki the next day.

SHE DID COME!
LOOOOOOOOOVE!

Where did the cuteness from the previous page go? The moment she sees Kyo, she loses it!

Knowing A Secret...

"HEY, JUST FOR A LITTLE!
JUST FOR A LITTLE BIT...
...LET ME WEAR THOSE BEADS."
YOU...
...DIDN'T WANT TO, KYO-KUN.
BUT I...
...FORCED YOU.

Scared by Kyo's grotesque form, young Kagura ran away. Her behavior still haunts her.

Kagura knows Kyo's secret. When they were young, she playfully stole his beads; after that, Kyo's mother let him outside even less, and Kyo began distancing himself from Kagura.

Relationship With Rin

Kagura's parents took Isuzu in when her own parents treated her badly, and she now lives with them. Isuzu doesn't get along particularly well with Kagura, but her own difficult love may give her some insight.

PROBABLY YUN-CHAN, PROBABLY SHII-CHAN, AND HARU-CHAN...
AND I BET KYO-KUN IS THERE!! ♡
AND, ISUZU, YOU HAVEN'T MET TOHRU-KUN YET, AND—
KAGURA.
WHY DON'T YOU STOP FORCING YOURSELF ON HIM AND CALLING IT LOVE?
IT'S PAINFUL TO WATCH.

Isuzu sees right through Kagura, and knows her secret. She says things that cut right to the truth.

Shyness doesn't keep her from attacking with remarkable strength.

ONE OF THE REASONS FOR KYO-KUN'S DISLIKE.

"KYO-KUN...! YOU'RE MEAN... YOU'RE SO MEAN. WHEN I (FIVE SECONDS BEFORE LAUNCH) ...WHEN I LOVE YOU SO MUCH!!"

Her outrageous behavior toward the man she loves isn't malicious--she just loses control of herself as her emotions well up. Even Kyo can't really get mad at her.

Once she gets going, Kagura can't be stopped, and Kyo bears the brunt of her energy. Hatori says Kagura's behavior is like "bullying the one you love," and it's overwhelming to the person on the receiving end. When she met Tohru, for example, her rampaging sent her crashing into a man, and she transformed.

YELLING AT A GIRL IN PUBLIC IS THE WORST THING YOU CAN DO!!

Even for a Zodiac member, Kagura has an intense personality. When she does this to Kyo, he can usually endure it, but...

An Ordinary Mother Who Loves And Worries About Her Daughter

•Kagura's Mother•

Kagura's parents are average people who love their daughter dearly. But for parents of a Zodiac member, they're exceptional--although they often fought about Kagura when she was young. They've taken Isuzu in, but they're at a bit of a loss because she won't open up to them.

"THIS DOESN'T LEAVE THE ROOM, BUT... IF YOU WERE TO GET BADLY HURT, TOO... MAMA WOULD JUST BREAK DOWN."

Kagura Sohma's Family Tree

Mother		Father
Living with Them		Eldest Daughter
Isuzu		Kagura

66

A FORCED LOVE

Kagura bears the curse of being possessed by an animal of the Zodiac. But Kyo, possessed by the Cat, was more "pitiable". It made her feel better to know there was someone more miserable than her--and that's why she started playing with Kyo. Not wanting to acknowledge her selfish motives, she tried to ignore them by falling in love with him. She thought that if she really loved him, that "dirty" side of her would disappear.

"THE WHOLE TIME, I WAS ONLY CHASING AFTER YOU FOR MYSELF. I'M SORRY... I'M SORRY, KYO-KUN."

IT'S YOU...
...WHO DOES THAT. KYO-KUN.

Kagura's memories of long ago are very bitter—and very sweet.

I REALIZED THAT...
...COMPARED TO THE CAT...
...I HAD IT EASY.

Young Kagura looked down on Kyo because he was more pitiful than she was. Now, she confesses the truth to him.

WANT ME TO PLAY WITH YOU?
REALLY?!
......
YEAH!
OF COURSE. REALLY. STARTING TODAY...
...I'LL BE WITH YOU!!
I'LL ALWAYS BE BY YOUR SIDE!
KYO-KUN...
KYO-KUN I'M...

BUT AN HONEST LOVE

"YOU STAYED BY ME UNTIL I STOPPED CRYING. THIS KYO-KUN IS MINE ALONE."

KYO-CHAN!
THERE WAS A PART OF ME...
KYO-CHAN...!
...THAT CHASED AFTER HIM BECAUSE...
KYO-CHAN...
I WANTED TO...
KYO-CHAN...
KYO-CHAN...
I DO LOVE YOU...

I LOVE YOU!
BELIEVE ME.
BELIEVE ME!
BELIEVE... ME.

Her love started out as something she forced, but her feelings were sincere. Kagura's cry after she revealed everything was heartbreaking.

There was one more thing that Kagura wanted to erase: the part of herself that saw Kyo's true form and ran away. She idealized the memory of Tohru accepting him, and at the same time she understood that she could never truly bridge the distance between herself and Kyo. Her love had been born out of selfishness, but she had truly come to love him for himself.

草摩紅葉
Momiji Sohma

"If I keep them, and keep trying, without running away... If I keep trying, then someday... Someday I'll be strong enough that those memories can't defeat me. I believe that"

Zodiac: The Rabbit

Because he's half-German and half-Japanese, he can speak both languages. Confused by his childish appearance and behavior, Tohru believed for a long time that he was an elementary school student, but he's actually only a year younger than her. She learned his age six months after they met, when he told her he'd be going to her school.

Momiji looks extremely young, but he has surprising maturity. He still loves his mother deeply, even though she rejected him and had her memories of him erased. He also has the courage to stand up to Akito, who everyone is afraid of, when he thinks she's wrong.

*A first-year student at Kaibara Public High School. Nickname: Momitchi. He is half-German, with a German mother and a Japanese father. He lives by himself on the Sohma "inside". Name origin: from a name for the Ninth month: Momijitsuki *Autumn leaves month*

Fashion Concept

I let him wear whatever clothes he wants, as long as they're Loli-Loli. He has a lot of clothes, probably more than he could ever wear (he probably doesn't even know what it all looks like anymore). He occasionally has clothing made at Ayame's shop, and loves pumpkin-shaped pants. I like the way he looks in the boys' uniform, too (can I say that, since I'm the one drawing him?).

(From the 2001 Fruits Basket Character Book)

Momiji Quote Collection

"I closed my eyes and thought about the traveler. I thought about the traveler who was tricked into being nothing more than a crying head saying, 'Thank you.' And I thought, 'How lucky he was......" (->Yuki & Kyo)

"I wonder if I really helped Mama..."

"I want to... believe that. Because I want to think that there's no such thing as a memory that's okay to forget. That's why... that's why I really didn't want Mama to forget. I wanted her to keep trying. ...But that was my selfishness, so it's a secret." (->Tohru)

"...My goal might be impossible for me. Even so... I think it would be great if it came true. So I keep believing." (->Tohru)

"Even though I left her, I still want to make memories with Tohru. I'm so selfish. I like Tohru so much." (->Kyo)

"What should I do...? What should I do!? I'm so happy..."

Other People's Words To Momiji

"Right now you're traveling full speed down the road to failure!!" (Makoto Takei)

"Ask Momiji if he'll be Momo's brother. Momo... wants a big brother to talk to and play with. Momo started learning to play the violin, so we could play together. I bet it would be fun. You can see him every day. So ask him. Ask him, okay?" (Momo)

Momiji and Kyo

YOU KNOW...
...YOUR HYPER ENERGY REALLY PISSES ME OFF!
WAAAH!
KYO IS A MEANIE!
MOMIJI-KUN, ARE YOU HUNGRY?
I am! ♡

Momiji's friendly innocence and Kyo's antisocial tendencies are completely incompatible, and Kyo is often sharp with Momiji. It's not uncommon for Kyo to get irritated enough to hit him. But Momiji says Kyo's been nicer lately, since meeting Tohru.

Kyo gets irritated by Momiji's intense cheerfulness, and always attacks him.

Helping at Tohru's Workplace

Tohru first met Momiji at the building where she works part-time as an evening cleaner. The building belongs to a company owned by the Sohma family, and Momiji's father is the company president. Momiji had been there to secretly look at his mother and sister when they came to see his father.

IT'S GREAT THAT YOUR TESTS ARE OVER.
YOU CAN FINALLY TAKE A BREAK FROM STUDYING!
YES! IT'S ALMOST TIME FOR SPRING BREAK AND THEN THE NEW TERM...
TIME REALLY DOES FLY.
IT SURE DOES.

Ever since they met, Momiji has sometimes helped out at Tohru's work.

The Face of Real Kindness

YUKI?
KYO?
DO YOU REALLY THINK THAT'S STUPID?
......
WHEN YOU CLOSE YOUR EYES...
...WHAT DO YOU THINK?

"The Most Foolish Traveler in the World": The story of a soft-hearted person who is constantly deceived but never doubts people, who gives freely without expecting anything in return. As he told the story, Momiji thought of Tohru.

Momiji feels that the story of the traveler, who doesn't worry about his own well-being, is very tragic. He wants to do something for people like that.

If The Uniform Fits, Wear It!

Tohruu-- ♡
MOMIJI...
...KU-
!!
KYO-
KYO-KUN, CALM DOWN...!
ARE YOU RETARDED ?!

When Momiji starts attending Kaibara High, he shows up wearing the girls' uniform! He wears shorts underneath, of course, but it causes trouble at the school. Momiji takes the criticism in stride, and just says "this one looks better on me."

CUTE!

AND SHE LOOKS JUST LIKE MAMA!

SHE'S SOOOO SPOILED!

SHE FOLLOWS MAMA AROUND LIKE A BABY CHICK.

SHE'S SOOO—

BUT SHE DOESN'T SPEAK MUCH JAPANESE.

SHE HAS A LOT OF TROUBLE WITH IT.

His mother rejected him and had her memories erased. His little sister doesn't know who he is. But Momiji loves them dearly, and watches over them. He says that he wants to hold on to even his most painful memories, even if they only hurt him. He believes that he can someday be someone who won't be crushed by them.

"IF I KEEP THEM, AND KEEP TRYING, WITHOUT RUNNING AWAY... IF I KEEP TRYING, THEN SOMEDAY... SOMEDAY I'LL BE STRONG ENOUGH THAT THOSE MEMORIES CAN'T DEFEAT ME. I BELIEVE THAT."

IT'S A SECRET.

He shares his true feelings with Tohru: he'd wanted his mama to keep trying.

From the shadows, he quietly watches his mama and sister, who have come to his father's company.

SOMEDAY...

AND WE'LL HAVE PRECIOUS MEMORIES.

...WE... OVERCOME THE PAIN...

If his mother and family are happy, that's enough for him. Momiji wants to accept even the painful memories and move on with his life.

If he can overcome the painful things that happen in his life rather than rejecting them, maybe something will change someday.

I WANT TO...

...BELIEVE THAT.

BECAUSE I WANT TO THINK...

...AS A MEMORY THAT'S OKAY TO FORGET.

...THAT THERE'S NO SUCH THING...

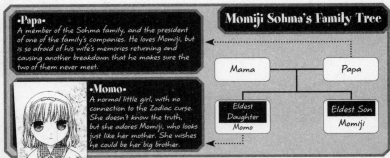

Momiji Sohma's Family Tree

•Papa•
A member of the Sohma family, and the president of one of the family's companies. He loves Momiji, but is so afraid of his wife's memories returning and causing another breakdown that he makes sure the two of them never meet.

•Momo•
A normal little girl, with no connection to the Zodiac curse. She doesn't know the truth, but she adores Momiji, who looks just like her mother. She wishes he could be her big brother.

Mama		Papa
Eldest Daughter Momo		Eldest Son Momiji

THOUGHTS AND WISHES THAT CAN'T BE ERASED

SHE'S BEEN WATCHING YOU ALL THIS TIME, MOMIJI-KUN.
JUST LIKE YOU'VE ALWAYS...
...WATCHED OVER HER!
MOMO-SAN HAS BEEN LISTENING TO YOUR VIOLIN!
SHE SAYS... SHE WANTS TO TALK...
...TO YOU.
SHE WANTS TO PLAY WITH YOU.
SHE... SHE WANTS...
...TO KNOW IF YOU'LL BE HER B-- HER BROTHER...!

Tohru's eyes fill with tears while she tells Momiji about Momo.

MY DREAM, YOU KNOW?
I WANT TO BE A VIOLINIST...
......
IT'S TO BE A VIOLINIST.
WHY?
...AND HAVE A SMALL CONCERT...
AND...
WHY CAN'T THEY SEE EACH OTHER?
WHY CAN'T THEY LET THEIR FEELINGS GROW?
...PAPA AND MAMA AND MOMO WILL LISTEN TO ME PLAY!
TOHRU.

Momiji tells Tohru his small, unattainable dream. He can't stop wishing, even knowing it will never happen.

ASK MOMIJI IF HE'LL BE MOMO'S BIG BROTHER!

Momo had been secretly coming to listen to Momiji play the violin. She'd only met Momiji once, in her father's company building, but she never forgot him.

Momo, who's been kept in the dark, adores Momiji and wants to see him. When Tohru tells him that, she starts to cry. It breaks her heart to think that two people can be kept apart no matter how close they are, or how badly they want to see each other. But Momiji was happy, knowing there was someone who would cry in his place.

"YOU'VE MADE ME SO HAPPY. I'M SO HAPPY BECAUSE...THERE'S SOMEONE WHO WILL CRY FOR ME..."

IS THAT YOU, MOMIJI-CHAN?
WHAT ARE YOU DOING...
...IN A PLACE LIKE THIS SO LATE AT NIGHT?

A Mother Who Rejected Her Son With Her Whole Body

•Momiji's Mama•

She fell in love with Momiji's father when they were in college, and they got married. However, their child was born under the Zodiac curse, and changed into a strange baby animal when she first held him. Unable to accept it, she rejected Momiji; she became hysterical and irritable, and then mentally unstable. In order to save her, Momiji's father decided to have her memories suppressed, and she chose to forget her son.

"THE GREATEST REGRET I HAVE IN THIS LIFE IS THAT THAT 'CREATURE' CAME OUT OF MY BODY."

草摩はとり
Hatori Sohma

Zodiac: The Dragon

"All that I can do now is watch over them, so that they don't make the same mistakes. So that they don't lose the will to smile."

He comes from a long line of Sohma family physicians, and is carrying on the family tradition. He mostly attends to Akito, but he also makes house calls when a member of the Sohma family is injured or gets sick, and treated Tohru when Shigure asked him to. As well as being a doctor, he knows the technique of manipulating memories, and is responsible for suppressing them when strangers learn the Sohma family secret. When Yuki transformed in front of his friends, Hatori was the one who suppressed their memories. He gives the impression of being quiet and calm, but that's largely due to his resignation over the way his life has turned out.

He is the family doctor for the Sohmas (mainly Akito) Nicknames: Tori-san, Haa-san, Ha'ri. He lives on the Sohma "inside". He is almost completely blind in his left eye. Name origin: from a name for the Fourth month Konohatorizuki *Month of taking leaves (to silk worms)

Fashion Concept

He's not actually attached to wearing suits, but he thinks they're the easiest thing to wear without needing to spend a lot of time deciding on an outfit. He lets his housekeepers pick them out (Kana did it when they were together), but sooner or later someone's going to get on his case about it.

(From the 2001 Fruits Basket Character Book)

Hatori Quote Collection

"I started crying. It was the first time in my life that I felt forgiven. Like I was saved. Like the frozen snow that's melted by the breath of spring, the tears wouldn't stop."

"He's just... he's still a child. There are still a lot of things he can't give up. There's no rush." (->Ayame)

"It's over between Kana and me. We're not going to get back together. Even if we were together, I would only miss her......" (->Shigure & Ayame)

Other People's Words To Hatori

"I understand. You must have been scared. You didn't want anyone to know your secret. Naturally, you would distance yourself from others. Especially if it was someone you loved. But there's no need to be scared anymore. Don't push me away. I'm...happy I met you, Hatori. I'm happy that I fell in love with you. I want to be near you." (Kana)

"I think it would have been better if we'd never met... It would have been better if we'd never met." (Kana)

"It becomes spring! No matter how cold it is now, spring will come again! Without fail... It's strange, isn't it...?" (Tohru)

"Next time, when you meet a new woman, I hope that she is someone you wouldn't have to stay distant from, even when you're with her. A woman who you can be truly happy with." (Shigure)

"So it can't be true, Hatori-kun. That you can't be happy... It can't be true!! If it is, I won't believe! I won't believe in anything!!" (Mayuko)"

I'm sorry. ...I was so childish. And you... were hurting yourself, Hatori." (Yuki)

An Avid Reader

After Shigure, he is the most avid reader among the Zodiac. When they went to the lake house, Shigure brought a huge stack of Western books for him. Shigure has even used Mayuko's family's secondhand bookstore as part of a scheme to mend her relationship with the book-loving Hatori.

YOU CAN'T BE BORED, HAA-SAN!
I BROUGHT AN ASSORTMENT OF RECOMMENDED BOOKS.
HM?
WHAT BETTER WAY TO TAKE ADVANTAGE OF THIS CAREFREE LEISURE TIME THAN BY CATCHING UP WITH YOUR READING?!
Because next to me, what Haa-san loves most is a good book.
......
No... well, I do like reading...
They're mostly Western books.
!
I SEE...

A Secret Complex

He threatens Shigure when Shigure tries to reveal his animal shape. You wouldn't expect threats from someone who seems so composed.

I WILL TELL EVERYONE IN THE PUBLISHING INDUSTRY EVERYTHING I KNOW ABOUT YOU, STARTING FROM WHEN YOU WERE FOUR YEARS OLD...
SORRY, TOHRU-KUN. MY LIPS ARE SEALED!

When he transforms, Hatori becomes a seahorse, also called "the dragon's bastard offspring." Even the other Juunishi think it's funny, so he's developed a secret complex about it. Tohru doesn't learn what he becomes until he winds up transforming in front of her. Kana was the first person not to laugh when she saw his Juunishi form.

Hatori Sleeps?

AH!
HATORI-SAN, WE'RE ABOUT TO TAKE OFF...
...OKAY...?

Dozing on the sofa. Ayame's about to wake him up, though.

Kyo is surprised to see Hatori taking a nap at the lake house. Hatori doesn't often let himself indulge basic human needs in front of others, so apparently he felt very comfortable at the lake house.

Serious

Huh?
NOW THAT I NOTICE, YOU'RE NOT WEARING A SUIT TODAY?
YEAH, WELL...
I DIDN'T WANT YOU TO GET HOT LOOKING AT ME, AGAIN.
fwip
......
TEE HEE...

Hatori is basically a serious person. When Mayuko jokingly tells him she gets hot seeing him in a suit, he takes it seriously and makes sure to wear something different when he returns the next day. But he sometimes does mischievous things, like deliberately giving Shigure needles in places that will hurt.

IS SHE MAKING FUN OF ME?

IT BECOMES WATER OF COURSE.

WRONG!

IT BECOMES SPRING!

SPRING IS MY FAVORITE SEASON!

Hatori can't see out of his left eye. He lost its vision when Akito went into a frenzy and attacked him over Kana. Kana, who saw him hurt so badly in front of her, tortured herself over it until she broke down. In order to save her, Hatori suppressed her memories of him. Kana is now happily married to another man.

"I PRAY. EVEN IF I DIE SURROUNDED BY SNOW THAT NEVER MELTS, I DON'T CARE. PLEASE, PLEASE..."

Kana Sohma was assigned to be Hatori's assistant. Hatori is gradually attracted to her cheerful innocence.

I WANT TO BE NEAR YOU!

I'M HAPPY THAT...

...I FELL IN LOVE WITH YOU.

I STARTED CRYING.

Kana accepted Hatori, even when he transformed. To Hatori, she was spring incarnate.

KANA...

WHAT SHOULD I DO?

WHAT CAN I DO? IT...

...PROTECT HIM!

IT...

IT CAN'T BE FIXED, IT'S ALL MY FAULT.

I WAS RIGHT THERE, BUT HE GOT HURT SO BADLY!

PROTECT HIM.

I COULDN'T -

Hatori quietly accepts Kana's marriage, and is happy for her. He knows they can never go back to the way they were.

ISN'T IT YOUR FINAL DUTY TO FREE HER FROM THAT PAIN?

I THINK SHE TRULY WANTS TO BE RELEASED.

WHAT'S HURTING HER RIGHT NOW IS HER MEMORIES OF YOU.

SHE WANTS...

HER LOVE FOR YOU.

EVEN IF WE MISS TIME TOGETHER

I WOULD ONLY MISS HER.

WE CAN'T GO BACK TO THE WAY IT ONCE WAS.

THE FEELINGS OF GUILT AND SHAME WON'T DISAPPEAR.

THEY'LL MELT AND TURN INTO A CURSE.

EATING AWAY AT HER AND ME.

Their happiness ended in an instant. Kana blames herself so much for what happened to Hatori that she makes herself sick, and Akito persuades Hatori to suppress her memories.

Father

When Hatori was in high school, his father died of an illness (he also lost his mother to illness, when he was in elementary school). As the Sohma family doctor, his main responsibility is to look after Akito, and when Yuki was a child Hatori treated his bronchitis. Both of his parents were very strict, and his home life wasn't very warm; this may explain some of Hatori's overly-serious nature. Hatori inherited the memory suppression technique directly from his father. It isn't a special power, but a technique that has been handed down in his family for generations. It works something like hypnosis.

Hatori Sohma's Family Tree

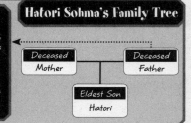

Deceased Mother		Deceased Father
	Eldest Son Hatori	

THE FIRST BREATH OF SPRING COMES AGAIN

I SUPPOSE THIS MAKES ME LOOK...
...PRETTY IMMATURE, HUH?
NO, NOT AT ALL.
YOU CRIED IN PLACE OF ME.
...THANK YOU.

Mayuko cries in frustration over Hatori's lack of happiness.

Shigure manipulated Hatori and Mayuko into running into each other by arranging for Hatori to pick up a book at the secondhand bookstore run by Mayuko's family. When Mayuko realizes her ex-boyfriend is meddling with her love life, and that she was taken in by his lies, she is outraged.

AFTER ALL...
...IT'S SUCH A NICE DAY.
ALL RIGHT!
I WILL!
I'LL HAVE BEER. DRAFT BEER.
YOU WOULD DRINK IN FRONT OF SOMEONE WHO'S GOING TO DRIVE?

Hatori's heart lightens a little when Mayuko cries in his place.

"IS THIS MY PUNISHMENT? I NEVER THOUGHT I'D HAVE TO ERASE WITH MY OWN HANDS THE MEMORIES OF THE ONE PERSON MOST IMPORTANT TO ME. THE MEMORIES MOST IMPORTANT TO ME."

PLEASE...
PLEASE!
D-DON'T ERASE THEM!
THEY'RE MY FRIENDS!
THEY'RE THE FIRST...
...FRIENDS...
...I EVER MADE.

Yuki pleads with Hatori not to erase the memories of the first friends he'd ever made, but to no avail.

If his father or Akito ordered it, Hatori would unhesitatingly erase someone's memories. Even when it hurt Yuki and Momiji, he did his job with such indifference that Akito said he was as cold as snow. But eventually, Hatori has to seal away the memories of his own love.

MEMORIES ERASED BY HIS OWN HANDS

I COULDN'T...
PRO...
...TECT... YOU...
......
...RY...
I'M SORRY
I'M SO SORRY.
I'M SO SORRY!
HATORI...
...I'M...

Unable to watch Kana deteriorate, Hatori erased her memories. He thought it was his punishment for erasing other people's memories.

IMPRESSED YOU NOTICED.
I WONDER IF IT'S THE POWER OF PERSISTENT LOVE!
GRRRRAAH! HE'S REALLY PISSING ME OFF!
THERE'S REALLY NO NEED FOR YOU TO HATE ME SO.
IF YOU AND HAA-SAN GOT MARRIED...
...I'D BE RELATED TO YOU, AFTER ALL.

The biggest mistake of her life: dating Shigure to try getting over her feelings for Hatori!

MAYU...?

She and Kana are still friends, despite everything. She is heartbroken that Kana forgot Hatori.

The Woman Who Cried, And Wished for Hatori's Happiness

•Mayuko Shiraki•

Mayuko was Kana's best friend from college. When she was introduced to Hatori, she immediately developed a crush on him, but she ignored it. She doesn't know about the curse, but she wholeheartedly wants him to find happiness.

"WHAT I WANTED TO FORGET AND HAVE DISAPPEAR WAS NOT THE TWO FROM THOSE DAYS."

"Don't judge me based on some story and laugh."

草摩溌春

Zodiac: The Ox

When he was growing up, the adults teased him mercilessly for being possessed by the foolish Ox, which would have been first in the Zodiac if not for the Rat. He responded by becoming a passive but easily enraged person. His parents couldn't handle him, so they enrolled him in martial arts to help him control his temper. But it wasn't very effective--when he snaps and "goes Black", he still goes wildly out of control.

Normally, he is quiet and easygoing. He doesn't always seem to be paying attention, but very little escapes his notice. Sometimes he speaks very bluntly, even with Yuki or Hatori. Yuki, who helped him overcome his issues when they were young, is very special to him. Haru and Isuzu (another member of the Zodiac) are lovers.

Fashion Concept

He used to dress more like Kyo, but Isuzu's influence made him adopt a flashier look. Now he dresses that way because he likes it, too. Like Momiji, Haru has a lot of clothes--he spends money on his wardrobe shamelessly. He's especially fond of leather, so he enjoys winter.

(From the 2001 Fruits Basket Character Book)

A first-year student at Kaibara Public High School. Nicknames: Haru, Haa-kun. He lives on the Sohma "inside". He has two aspects to his personality, nicknamed Black and White. But he doesn't have a split personality. Name origin: from a name for the First month: Hatsuharu *Early spring

Hatsuharu Quote Collection

"As long as I have to hug someone, she might as well be cute." (->Tohru)

"He was my first love, you know... Yuki" (->Tohru)

"Let me ask you this. If I wear a three-piece suit, does it mean I won't resort to blackmail? If I won't pierce my ears, does it mean I won't break someone's heart? If my hair is black and shiny, does it mean I won't kill you?" (->President Takei)

"Why do I still want to see her so badly...?" (->Yuki)

"...I'm not going to give up on her yet. I don't think Rin realizes just how much I like her." (->Yuki)

"And I'd like it... if you wouldn't laugh like that." (->Akito)

"Rin thinks that she's been 'bad,' but don't you think that you've done anything 'bad'!!? Having people take their anger out on us, being laughed at, being made light of--we kids get hurt just like you do. Why can't you understand something so simple!!? Apologize! Apologize...!! Apologize to Rin!!" (->Isuzu's mother)

Other People's Words To Hatsuharu

"Ahaha! Oh, Hatsuharu... Hatsuharu, you always say funny things. Heheh...Ha......" (Akito)

"Ha ha ha! Really, Haru... I don't know if you're saying that because you understand, or not..." (Yuki)

"Haru-nii, you...! Really are nice... To everyone. Uselessly so...! But that kindness might have been what made Rin so sad..." (Hiro)

No Sense of Direction

He has absolutely no sense of direction, so when he went to Shigure's house to challenge Kyo, he spent three whole days wandering the streets. And once, when he was very young, he managed to get lost on the way to the bathroom and needed Kyo's help to find it.

I SET OUT ON SUNDAY...
...AND FOUND MYSELF IN AN UNFAMILIAR TOWN. NEXT THING I KNEW, THREE DAYS HAD PASSED.
A mystery...
JUST SAY IT. YOU GOT LOST.

It took him three days to get from the Sohma estate to Shigure's house. What on earth did he do at night? More importantly, how did he bathe???

Kyo vs. Hatsuharu

Haru studied martial arts at Kazuma's dojo, and his relationship with Kyo centers around that. He has a one-sided rivalry with Kyo, and challenges him to fights whenever he can, but he never quite wins. He just might annoy Kyo as much as Momiji does.

Sometimes he visits from the Sohma estate just so he can challenge Kyo.

SPLISH
I CHALLENGE YOU TO A CONTEST.
SPLISH
STOP IT, YOU IDIOT! LET GO!
SPLASH
YOU TRYING TO KILL ME?!

Empathy For Others

IT'S MY PERSONALITY, I GUESS.
I WANT YOU TO ENJOY LIFE.
STILL...
...I HATE WATCHING YOU SUFFER.

He sympathizes very keenly with others, since he knows from experience just how badly words can hurt.

His Black side can't be discounted, but he's fundamentally kind, and worries more about others than himself. He is extremely sensitive to the moods and heartaches of the people he cares about, like Kisa, Yuki, and Kyo.

Off-The-Wall, But Easygoing

When he's not Black, he often misses the point, and he says and does unexpected things. Yuki notes that "Normally, Haru's a bit of a pushover." Haru's very deadpan when he jokes around, so sometimes it's hard to tell if he's serious or not.

A MAN'S BACK IS HIS LIFE.
EH ?!
R-R-REALLY?!
HONDA-SAN... YOU SHOULDN'T TAKE HARU TOO SERIOUSLY.

When things get tense, he clears the air with a well-timed, ridiculous joke.

...HE SEEMS DOWN.
A MAN'S "BLUE DAY"...?
HAARUUU!

In addition to being violent, Black Haru is an aggressive flirt. But thanks to Yuki, he now loses control much less often.

"YUKI LET ME SAY WHAT WAS IN MY HEART. HE FREED ME."

The Ox that appears in the Zodiac fairy tale is made fun of in the Sohma family. The adults may have been half-joking, but the teasing wounded young Hatsuharu deeply. After talking to Yuki, he became less irritable and slower to lose his temper.

"Are you really stupid?" Because of Yuki's understanding, Haru was able to let go of the hurt that had been building in his heart.

Being an object of mockery is more painful to Haru than anything else. He asserts himself quietly but firmly, even with Akito.

SOMEONE WHO UNDERSTANDS YUKI

From listening to the Zodiac fairy tale, Haru had assumed that the "Rat" was a dirty coward. But once he got to know Yuki, he realized that he, too, had been perpetuating that idea. He began visiting Yuki in the isolated room, and their friendship secretly grew.

"IT'S BECAUSE YOU'RE LIKE THAT, YUKI, THAT I KNOW THAT THERE'S SOMEONE OUT THERE WHO WILL UNDERSTAND YOU. AND SOMEDAY, YOU'LL FIND EACH OTHER."

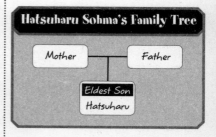

Hatsuharu Sohma's Family Tree

Mother		Father
	Eldest Son Hatsuharu	

THE DEPTHS OF LOVE

I GOT DUMPED.
I...
IT DIDN'T SINK IN AT FIRST...
...BUT AS THE DAYS WENT ON, I GOT MORE AND MORE IRRITATED.
AND TODAY, I WAS THINKING ABOUT IT, AND GETTING WORKED UP...
...AND I JUST SNAPPED.
YOU MEAN, AKITO...
IT WAS KIND OF A SECRET THAT WE WERE GOING OUT.
THIS IS THE FIRST TIME I'VE TOLD ANYONE.
SINCE...
...WE'RE BOTH IN THE ZODIAC, I THOUGHT...

Isuzu unexpectedly broke up with Haru after she was injured. He doesn't understand why.

IN COMMEMORATION OF YOUR COMING TO THE MAIN HOUSE AFTER SO LONG...
AND FOR ME.
FUNNY... YOU DON'T LOOK SICK.
OH, I'M NOT.
I HAD TO KNOW WHAT HAPPENED NEXT IN THIS GAME, SO I TOOK THE DAY OFF.
I SEE
THEN...
ARE YOU ALL RIGHT?
ABOUT RIN?
HNN...?
YEAH.
I'M NOT GOING TO GIVE UP ON HER YET.
...JUST HOW MUCH I LIKE HER.
I DON'T THINK RIN REALIZES...

...I DON'T HAVE ANY CONFIDENCE AFTER ALL...
IT SEEMS...
I THINK THAT MIGHT HAVE BEEN HOW SHE REALLY FEELS.
I GUESS I'M JUST SCARED.
MAYBE...
...HER WORDS HURT ME...
...MORE THAN I REALIZED.
...HM...
AH...
HUH?

Even after she breaks up with him, Haru's feelings for Isuzu don't waver.

"RIN... DID I NOT UNDERSTAND SOMETHING? DID I FAIL TO HEAR YOU CALLING OUT TO ME WHEN YOU NEEDED ME MOST?"

...OF NEEDING HER.
...WANT TO SEE HER SO BADLY?
WHAT ARE YOU...
...THE FEELINGS...
...GOING TO DO NOW?

To Haru, Isuzu's presence is irreplaceable and absolutely vital. The thought of losing her is unbearable.

Haru was the one who found Isuzu after she collapsed from being abused, and a connection formed between them that grew into love. But after she was horribly injured, she began to avoid him rather than telling him what had happened. He tries to win her back, but...

A sudden kiss: the surest way to uncover Isuzu's feelings.

IN THAT CASE, HARU-KUN, PLEASE KEEP STRUGGLING.
SHE IS YOUR EX-GIRLFRIEND, AFTER ALL.
IF THERE'S SOMETHING BOTHERING YOU, YOU SHOULD ASK HER DIRECTLY.
THAT SOUNDS NICE.
DID SHE SWEAR YOU TO SECRECY?
YOU COULD SAY THAT.
I HAVE TO KEEP MY PROMISE.
WOULD YOU TELL ME IF I CALLED YOU "HONEY"?
AH HA HA!
Sorry. I would really hate that.
YOU MUSTN'T...
...CUT CORNERS, HARU-KUN.

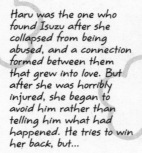

Hatsuharu agrees to call Shigure "Sensei" if he will arrange for Yuki to live "outside".

I bid you. Please take good care of my little Yuki.
WH-WHAT'S THIS ALL OF A SUDDEN...?
I PROMISE I WILL MAKE YOUR DAUGHTER HAPPY!!
HEY... YOU TWO, WHAT ARE YOU SAYING?
NOW, YUKI... YOU HAVE A MEETING TO RUN, DON'T YOU?
YOU MUST BE GOING.
EH? AH, BUT...
GOOD LUCK.
TO BOTH OF US.
"DON'T STAY LOST."

When he meets the new vice president, Kakeru, Hatsuharu senses that he is someone who will change Yuki.

IS ALL THE SUN GETTING TO YOU?
YOU DON'T LOOK SO GOOD.
YUKI-KUUUN!
OR HAVE YOUR FEELINGS MADE YOU DIZZY?
AH... OKAY!
COME JOIN US, YUKI, HARU!

草摩綾女

Ayame Sohma

"Maybe I wanted to know if there could be 'something that wouldn't exist without me."

Zodiac: The Snake

He is always intense, noisy, and self-centered, and he acts like royalty. He is incredibly charismatic, and served as student body president in high school.

These days, he's such a doting older brother that he drives Yuki insane, but when he was younger, he ignored Yuki completely. There is a ten year age difference between them, and Yuki grew up in isolation, so although they both lived "inside", they never spoke. By the time he realized that he'd sacrificed Yuki for his own freedom, a rift had grown up between them. Since then, Ayame has been aggressively trying to build a brotherly bond with Yuki.

He manages "Ayame", a custom clothing and handicraft shop.
Nickname: Aaya
He lives on the Sohma "outside". Yuki Sohma's older brother. Name origin: from a name for the Fifth month: Ayamezuki *Month of irises

Fashion Concept

Since the younger brother wears Chinese-style clothing, I simply decided to make the older brother wear it, too. (Lately I'm not sure it makes sense.) Ayame designs what he wants to wear, and Mine makes it for him--he'd never let anyone else do it! He loves gorgeous clothes, and his favorite colors are red and gold.

(From the 2001 Fruits Basket Character Book)

Ayame Quote Collection

"Rather than regret, it may be closer to repentance. So it may be that I do want to repent and erase the ignorant self from my childhood. Maybe that's what they mean when they say adults are selfish." (->Tohru)

"Rin thinks that she's been 'bad,' but don't you think that you've done anything 'bad'?!! Having people take their anger out on us, being laughed at, being made light of--we kids get hurt just like you do. Why can't you understand something so simple!!? Apologize! Apologize...!! Apologize to Rin!!" (->Isuzu's mother)

"...Tohru-kun resembles you a little. She spends all her energy helping other people. I'm really bad... at that sort of thing... I really can't compete with you, Tori-san..." (->Hatori)

"Listen to this, Gure-san!! Yuki--yes, that Yuki--came to me with tears in his eyes, saying that by all means he would like to visit me at my shop!!" (->Shigure)

"I was cruel... insensitive to your pain. The first and only time you came to me for help, you reached out to me with those trembling hands. And I just brushed you off. It's not as if I've forgotten." (->Yuki)

"Maybe I wanted to know if I could create something tangible with my own hands. If there could be 'something' that wouldn't exist without me." (->Yuki)

Other People's Words To Ayame

"Anyway, Nii-san... does and says too many things that are uncalled for." (Yuki)

"...You really have a gift. Being able to change the interpretation of things to suit your own purposes." (Yuki)

"Do you want him to turn into a good-for-nothing ingrate like you?!" (Yuki's mother)

"Thanks...for coming...today" (Yuki)

Mother/Son Relationship

For a selfish mother who thinks of her children as possessions, Ayame's imperious behavior and disregard for her plans are more than she can handle. By now their relationship is poor enough that they could be called archenemies.

...
EE... EYAHH!!!
WHA?!
WH-WH-WHAT ARE YOU DOING HERE?!
THESE ROSES ARE FOR YOU, MADAME.
THEY ARE FILLED WITH RESPECT FOR THE WONDERFUL BEING THAT IS THE FEMALE TEACHER WHO GUIDES MY DEAR YOUNGER BROTHER AND WHOSE FAIR VISAGE INSPIRES ROMANTIC FANTASY...
Now then!
LET US BEGIN THE CONFERENCE FORTHWITH!
ANSWER MY QUESTION, AYAME!!

"Ayame": The Shop That Sells Romance

"Ayame": a shop with an extremely questionable sign that says, "Trust comes first; Ayame; value from the heart." It's the shop Ayame manages, and it sells handicrafts and custom-made costumes. The costumes include things like wedding dresses for men.

MEN'S ROMANCE!
MAIDS AND NURSES, WAITRESSES AND STEWARDESSES AND SECRETARIES!
SAILOR SUITS AND CAT EARS, RABBIT EARS... THERE'S TOO MANY TO LIST!
IN THESE SIMPLE FASHIONS, MEN CHASE THEIR DREAMS AND BRING THEIR ROMANTIC FANTASIES TO LIFE! THERE'S NO CRIME IN PURSUING YOUR DREAMS TO ESCAPE THE HARSH REALITY OF LIFE.
IT'S NO DIFFERENT THAN THE ROMANTIC URGE TO PEEK INTO A WOMAN'S BATH!!

The more serious he gets, the more idiotic he sounds.

Regal Airs

For some reason, his raging ego was indulged at school. Some things can only be explained as "because he's Aaya".

Ayame carries himself proudly, and always marches to the beat of his own drum. He defied his high school's rules and wore his hair long, and dealt with his vulnerability to heat and cold by being chauffeured to the school's gate in summer and wearing fur in winter.

BECAUSE THE CAR THAT TOOK ME TO SCHOOL WOULD DRIVE RIGHT UP TO THE SCHOOL'S GATE!
......
Oohh, it's Ayame-san!
He's acting like a king today, too.
Ayame-san arrives...
Is that a new parasol?

Mabudachi Trio

He is good friends with Shigure and Hatori, who are his age. Shigure plays along with Ayame's boundless energy, while Hatori handles damage control. Hatori is the only person Ayame listens to.

YOU DIDN'T CHEAT ON ME WHILE WE WERE APART, DID YOU...
...GURE-SAN?
WHY WOULD I DO SOMETHING LIKE THAT...
...AAYA?
ALL RIGHT!!
WHAT'S ALL RIGHT?!

A friendship-affirming ritual--and not exactly the kind you'd expect from men their age.

...ON WHAT'S IMPORTANT.

NOT REALIZING HOW MUCH YOU HAVE TRAMPLED...

Their mother still hasn't realized what a good kid Yuki is.

Talking to Tohru, Ayame accuses himself of being selfish in his desire to make things right with Yuki after so long. Tohru suggests trying to meet Yuki halfway.

His exuberant love erupts into unnecessary behavior and emotional outbursts, and annoys everyone around him.

YOU MUSTN'T DIE, YUKI!

THE SETTING SUN WE WATCHED THE DAY WE PLEDGED BY THE SEINE TO DIE TOGETHER SPARKLES LIKE GOLD IN MY HEART, EVEN NOW!

WE NEVER SAW THAT WE NEVER PLEDGED!

When Ayame was young, he felt nothing at all about Yuki; he didn't love or hate him. But now, imagining how it would feel to have Yuki be that indifferent to him, Ayame fears the loneliness of being unnecessary. He regrets having brushed off Yuki's first and only plea for help. He's also very happy that Yuki is now trying to understand him despite that rejection.

"I HURT MANY PEOPLE... ABANDONED THEM. I WAS SO FOOLISH."

Crab and peaches were two of Yuki's favorite childhood foods. Bringing them is a gesture of love from someone inept at expressing it.

The two brothers just can't relate. But Ayame sees the value in Yuki's vulnerability and kindness.

Ayame Sohma's Family Tree

•Mother•

Their mother only thinks of Yuki as a tool for getting money. Ayame is disgusted by her overwhelming desire for social status and power. For her part, their mother thinks of him as a devil--she screamed and recoiled when he showed up at Yuki's parent-teacher conference.

Mother		Father
Second Son Yuki		Eldest Son Ayame

AN ENTERTAINER

?!!
NOW, NOW, EVERY-ONE...
THIS BUSINESS WE CALL RAIN IS TRULY A PROFOUNDLY MYSTERIOUS THING!
AFTER HINDERING MY AWAKENING, IT DID NOT EVEN GRANT ME THE FAVOR OF ALLOWING ME TO FIX MY HAIR!
BUT THERE IS NO LONGER NEED FOR WORRY, YUKI!
I APOLOGIZE FOR MAKING YOU WAIT!
I, WHO AM NUMBER ONE IN AFFECTION FOR MY YOUNGER BROTHER, HAVE NOW HUMBLY ARRIVED!!
pat

He shows up at the parent-teacher conference with a bouquet of roses. He's impossible to miss.

"IF IT COMES DOWN TO 'ATTACK' OR 'ACCEPT' I CHOOSE TO 'ACCEPT'!!"

FROM NOW ON...
...DIRECT YOUR PASSIONS AT ME!!

Ayame offers a lengthy, deadpan explanation of Kandora-sama. No wonder the principal slowly backs away.

IT WAS FROM KANDORA-SAMA, WHO ILLUMINES THE FOUR DIRECTIONS WITH GOLD AND RED LIGHT. WHEN KANDORA-SAMA CHANTED "MA RUDU MAN," HIS FOREHEAD SHONE WITH A BLUE LIGHT AND, LIKE A PONY STRUCK BY A WHIP, RURUBARA-SAMA'S HONORABLE PERSON WAS LIBERATED. WITH A WAVE OF WARM COMPASSION, LIKE TREES THAT BEND IN A LIGHT BREEZE, HIS SUPPLE TRESSES GREW...
...NOW, MEANWHILE, KASHIPARUU-SAMA WAS IN HIS CHAMBERS SLEEPING PEACEFULLY, LIKE A FLOWER WAITING TO BUD, AND HE GAVE VOICE TO THE PAIN THAT WAS IN HIS HEART, "KAMPANIRU...!"

Ayame sometimes says outrageous things and gets treated like an idiot, but his flamboyant appearance and unique behavior made him popular at school. He even served as president of his high school's student body, and says that he made many changes to the school's rules to make things more fun.

THE PERSON HE WANTS TO BE LIKE.

HELLO, TORI-SAN!! YOU'RE NOT GOING TO BELIEVE WHAT YUKI JUST TOLD ME!
DON'T REPORT EVERY LITTLE THING TO HATORI!!
IT'S SUCH A WASTE.

He calls to report every detail of his life. Recently, he's also started using email.

SHE SPENDS ALL HER ENERGY HELPING OTHER PEOPLE.
HOW IS IT THAT HE...
...ALWAYS SAYS WHAT I WANT HIM TO SAY?
HOW...
I'M REALLY...
...BAD...
...AT THAT SORT OF THING.
I REALLY CAN'T COMPETE WITH YOU...
...TORI-SAN...

Hatori says what Ayame truly needs to hear.

Ayame, whose arrogance makes it hard for him to empathize with others, wishes he could be like people who place others above themselves. That's why he listens to Hatori, and why he likes Tohru. But since Hatori can keep him in line, he's always getting dragged out to deal with Ayame's situations.

"HOW? HOW IS IT THAT HE ALWAYS SAYS WHAT I WANT HIM TO SAY?"

The Woman Who Understands "Boss"

•Mine Kuramae•

Ayame's employee. The maid outfit she wears isn't the store uniform--she just enjoys it. She wants to dress up every cute girl she sees. She also understands Ayame's fears and regrets, and hopes he and Yuki can grow at least a little closer.

"BECAUSE WHAT BOSS IS MOST AFRAID OF IS 'NOTHINGNESS'."

ARE YOU SAD?
I'M NOT SAD. I'M DOWNRIGHT PATHETIC.

DRESS-ING UP...
DO YOU ENJOY DRESSING UP?
Eek!
MINE-SAN, PLEASE BE SENSIBLE!

When Mine visits Kaibara High and is surrounded by cute high school girls, she nearly has a breakdown.

草摩杞紗
Kisa Sohma

"I have to... try my best. Or I'll... become worse and... worse. Even if I can't make up with them, even... if they all ignore me... I still have to try my best."

Zodiac: The Tiger

A shy, quiet girl. When she first met Tohru, she had lost her voice after being horribly teased when she started middle school. The bullying began over her hair and eye color, but escalated to shunning and mockery when she protested. It was severe enough that she stopped going to school entirely. But Tohru, Hatsuharu, and Yuki help her, and she regains her voice and finds the courage to face the bullying.

Not long ago, Akito struck Kisa hard enough to hospitalize her. To Kisa, the unprovoked attack came out of nowhere. She's been afraid of Akito ever since.

A first-year student at a private middle school. Nickname: Satchan She lives on the Sohma "inside". She was teased because of the color of her hair and eyes, and withdrew from others. She has been hospitalized by Akito's violence. Name origin: from a name for the Second month: Kisaragi changing clothes month

Fashion Concept

She's starting to like dresses. Personally, I want to have her wear more feminine, frilly dresses (laugh), but I don't think Kisa herself wants to wear clothes like that. (So I make her wear them in color pictures and whatnot.) She doesn't like flashy colors.

(From the 2001 Fruits Basket Character Book)

Kisa Quote Collection

"Mom, and all of you... You're all here... for me. That's why I can do my best..."

"What's wrong? Why would you...? When you... do sad things like that... I don't like it." (->Hiro)

"When I'm...with Onee-chan, I feel warm inside..."

".... I always thought that Hiro-chan hated me... When I was still in elementary school, he would always... play with me, but recently he started acting distant...And even when he did talk to me, he was so cold... I didn't... know why. So I was really surprised...I was so happy..." (->Tohru)

"I shouldn't always tag along with Hiro-chan... I have to make the invitation sometimes..." (->Tohru)

"...Yesterday, maybe... I shouldn't have... talked the way I did, either. So... I'm sorry..." (->Hiro)

"I get the feeling you'll be a caring older brother, Hiro-chan..." (->Hiro)

Other People's Words To Kisa

"Even though they were ignoring her, whenever Kisa said anything, they'd laugh. They'd just start giggling. You know... I've... never had that happen to me in class. All I can do is imagine, so that's what I did. Wondering how I'd feel if everyone started giggling at me every time I said something. It ...it was a very... very sad feeling..." (Momiji)

"I think when you hear someone say they like you, for the first time... then you can begin to like yourself.... I think when someone accepts you for the first time you feel like you can forgive yourself a little, you can like yourself......" (Yuki)

"And if you get sad again, or if things get too rough, come here. Here is where she is." (Yuki)

"I couldn't be any help back then... You were having a hard time, Kisa, but I couldn't do anything. But now... now you're always saying 'Onee-chan, Oneechan!' But I... but I... I was really... worried about you, too, Kisa...!" (Hiro)

She Always Greets People With "Kyuu"

KISA-SAN!
SHEESH... AND WE ONLY JUST GOT HERE!

When they meet up at the beach house after a long time apart, Kisa and Tohru greet each other with "kyuu".

Kisa says that when she's around Tohru she always "has a warm feeling inside." Since Tohru reached out to her when she was being teased, Kisa has become very attached to her. When they see each other, they always run to exchange hugs.

Even Older Boys Like Her

ANYWAY, BE CAREFUL AROUND HERE.
HUH?
THAT'S NOT WHAT I'M WORRIED ABOUT.
STUPID SCUM. GET LOST!
DON'T WORRY, HIRO-CHAN.
THIS PLACE MAY BE CROWDED, BUT I WON'T BUMP INTO ANYONE!

Kisa is oblivious to her situation.

Kisa got through the teasing and began to brighten up. Her lovely smile is irresistible to others--when she went to the Kaibara High Cultural Festival, all the male students' eyes were on her. Maybe that appeal is part of why she was teased?

Her Favorite Food is "Nira-Tama"

Ta-dah!
HUH?
IT'S AMIDA KUJI!

OKAY, IT'S DECIDED!
TONIGHT WE'RE HAVING...
...Nira-tama!*

When Kisa can't even summon her voice to say what she wants to eat, Tohru draws an Amida-kuji. The verdict is "nira-tama".

Kisa's mother was emotionally exhausted while Kisa was being teased, but she still worried and made sure to call Tohru to tell her Kisa's favorite food. She unquestionably loves her daughter. (Incidentally, Kisa hates eating dry, crumbly foods.)

...WITH COURAGE.

...YEAH.

YEAH.

I WAS SO HAP...

...PY...

YEAH...

You can't just decide to like yourself, with no one to help you. Having someone else say they like you makes it possible to see yourself as likable. That's why Tohru's affection helped Kisa so much.

" ...SHE DIDN'T WANT YOU TO HATE HER. IT'S BECAUSE SHE LOVES YOU THAT SHE COULDN'T TELL YOU..."

A Mother Who Loves Her Daughter So Much That She Becomes Overprotective.

Kisa's Mother

Her daughter stopped going to school and then stopped talking. What is she thinking? Why is she upset? Kisa's mother gets frustrated with her daughter's silence, and that stress only adds to the stress of having a Zodiac-possessed child.

" DO YOU ENJOY WORRYING YOUR MOTHER? WHY WON'T YOU SAY ANYTHING?"

Kisa's mother criticizes her, wearing a blank expression. But the next time we see her, she's back to being a kind mother.

TELL ME...

...EVERYTHING'S OKAY.

She is afraid that her mother might hate her for being teased.

Immediately after entering middle school, Kisa started being teased. Her entire class ignored her, and laughed whenever she spoke, so she stopped going to school. Ashamed of being teased and of being unable to cope, Kisa was afraid to say anything to anyone. What helped bring her back out of her shell was...

I'LL TRY, TOO.

...COME HERE.

...HERE.

AND IF YOU GET SAD AGAIN...

...OR IF THINGS GET TOO ROUGH...

IS WHERE SHE IS.

With Yuki's encouragement, Kisa decides to keep trying; she knows she can visit Tohru again if it gets too hard.

Kisa Sohma's Family Tree

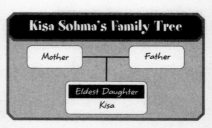

Mother		Father
	Eldest Daughter Kisa	

HIRO AND KISA SHARE FEELINGS THEY CAN'T TALK ABOUT.

When Hiro's careless comment hurts Tohru deeply, Kisa is genuinely angry. There are so many words that can cause pain...

YOU SHOULDN'T ...
...ASSUME THINGS LIKE THAT...
!
WH-WHY DO I HAVE TO...
I DON'T CARE ABOUT HER FEELINGS!
WHY SHOULD I HAVE TO WORRY ABOUT THAT?!
WHY DID YOU COME HERE, HIRO-CHAN...?
DID YOU COME HERE TO CAUSE TROUBLE FOR ONEE-CHAN...?
Turn...

"HOW DO YOU KNOW... SHE WAS FINE...? YOU DON'T KNOW... WHAT SHE'S HOLDING ONTO IN THE BOTTOM OF HER HEART... YOU SHOULDN'T... SAY 'IT'S NOT A BIG DEAL'..."

WHEN I WAS STILL IN ELEMENTARY SCHOOL, HE WOULD ALWAYS...PLAY WITH ME...
...BUT RECENTLY HE STARTED ACTING DISTANT... AND EVEN WHEN HE DID TALK TO ME, HE WAS SO COLD...
I DIDN'T... KNOW WHY...
SO I WAS REALLY SURPRISED...
'I WAS REALLY WORRIED ABOUT YOU, TOO, KISA!'
I WAS SO HAPPY...

Kisa thought that Hiro hated her. She didn't understand why Hiro, who had been her friend, would suddenly start giving her the cold shoulder.

Kisa says that she and Hiro were friends when she was in elementary school, and often played together. But after she was hospitalized with serious injuries, Hiro started to avoid her. They began talking again after she was bullied, but things are still awkward sometimes.

WHAT? DO I HAVE TO SPELL IT OUT FOR YOU?!
FIGURE IT OUT!!
HIRO'S TALKING CRAZY!
SHUT UP, RABBIT!
BUT I...
I WAS REALLY...
...WORRIED ABOUT YOU, TOO, KISA!

Kisa learns how Hiro really feels when he finally talks to her. The truth is that he had liked her all along, and had been extremely worried about her.

...YESTERDAY...
...I SHOULDN'T HAVE...
MAYBE...
...TALKED THE WAY I DID... EITHER.
SO...
I'M SORRY...

After getting mad at Hiro, Kisa reconsiders her reaction and wonders if she should have handled things differently.

AKITO'S IRRATIONAL ANGER

Akito's attack on Kisa was completely out of the blue. Kisa had absolutely no idea what she had done to make Akito hurt her so badly. Later, she finds out it was because of Hiro's feelings for her.

I'M VERY...
...WORRIED ABOUT THAT...
HE WON'T DO ANYTHING MEAN...
...TO ONEE-CHAN, WILL HE...?
LIKE HITTING HER...?
I'M SORRY. PLEASE DON'T BE OFFENDED...
Eh?!
NO, OF COURSE NOT! I'M ALL RIGHT, SO... YES...
Phew...

Having been assaulted by Akito herself, Kisa is afraid that the same thing might happen to Tohru. It's the first thing that crosses her mind when Akito appears at the beach house. Tohru and Akito don't wind up crossing paths at that point, but later on Kisa's fears turn out to be justified.

草摩燈路

> "How shameful.
> I want to be
> the only one
> who can help
> the one I
> care about."

Zodiac: The Ram

He's only a sixth-year elementary school student, but he enjoys quibbling and can talk circles around most adults. He uses pretentiously large words, and can just keep arguing without even pausing for breath, until people like Tohru can't keep up. Worse, he often sounds accusing, and often makes the people listening to him dislike him unnecessarily. He realizes that he should stop talking so harshly, and hates himself for picking trivial fights, but he has such trouble expressing his feelings honestly that sometimes argumentative things are all that come out.

He is worried about Kisa and Isuzu's situations, but he isn't free to talk about them.

Fashion Concept

He hates slovenliness, so he dresses carefully and always wears neatly tailored clothing. He doesn't like wearing accessories, unless it's something small to accent Western clothes. So I think he prefers winter clothes, like Haru.

(From the 2001 Fruits Basket Character Book)

A sixth-year student at a private elementary school.
Nicknames: Hiro, Hii-kun. He lives on the Sohma "inside". He happened to be passing by when Akito pushed Isuzu, and saw it all. He will have a little sister soon.
Name origin: from a name for the Seventh month: Fumihirogetsuki *Month of Publication

Hiro Quote Collection

"You're so gullible! Don't you have any standards? So if I told you to spin around, you'd do it? If they told you to jump off a cliff, would you do that, too? I can't stand people who have no individuality!!" (->Tohru)

"So, what are you saying? You mean if your wife wasn't controlling you, you wouldn't be a villain? You mean you've never thought that it's just because you're incompetent? And what's that line supposed to mean, anyway?" (->"Mogeta")

"Since when did the Cat set the rules for this house? You mean to tell me that you contribute more to this house than anyone else? Do you pay all the bills? I can't stand people who do absolutely nothing but complain all the time!" (->Kyo)

"I'm just a kid...! I'm pathetic. I hate myself so much I could die. Not like this... I don't want to be like this... I want to be a much, much better grown-up."

"Watch. I'll become one. I won't fail. ...But even when I die, I'll never thank her." (->Tohru)

"That's right. I'm sure...she is, too. Hiding feelings she hasn't shared with anyone... in the bottom of her heart."

"Endure it, Hiro...! If you get angry here, you'll never be a man! Composure! Show some composure...!!"

"I'm so stupid...! I did it again!! Again!! I got annoyed and took it out on him. I thought I'd never do it again......!!"

"It doesn't exist, does it? After all. A way to break the curse." (->Isuzu)

A Born Worrier

IT'S NOT LIKE YOU DON'T KNOW THAT MY MOM'S REALLY CLUMSY, RIGHT KISA?
JUST RE-CENTLY, SHE CAME RE-ALLY CLOSE TO FALLING HEADFIRST...
Huh?
Eek!
HIRO CHIAAAN!
Oh!
YOU, TOO, SATCHAN! WELCOME BACK!
What'd I tell ya?
DON'T RUN!!!
'specially not on stairs!!

His clumsy mother isn't any better about watching her step now that she's pregnant. Hiro is constantly on edge with worry.

When his mother calls to tell him she's pregnant, he ends the conversation with "Try not to fall down." He acts aloof, but he actually worries a lot.

Other People's Words To Hiro

"You smart-mouthed brat...! You act so mature, but you're not out of grade school yet, damn punk...!" (Kyo)

"I wanna punch him......! I wanna wring his little neck...!!" (a passing Kaibara High student)

"My mom said that there are a lot of people who are afraid to admit that they're still 'children.' They do everything they can to avoid it.... So...so people who can admit that... have a lot of courage, she says." (Tohru)

"Why? Are you going to worry about me forever...? If you're worried because you happened to see that, forget it. Keep on living peacefully loved by your kind mama and papa." (Isuzu)

The Straight Man

Being surrounded by the rest of the Furuba cast, with its many easygoing and flaky characters, poor Hiro is an eternal straight man, much like Kyo. He contrasts nicely against Tohru and Kisa's combined natural airheadedness, although it must be tiring for him to react to absolutely everything.

CONGRATULATIONS, HIRO-CHAN... THAT'S WONDERFUL!
YOU'LL HAVE TO THINK OF A NAME...!
I'M SURE THE BABY WILL BE JUST AS CUTE AS YOU ARE, HIRO-SAN!
Wait a minute!
WILL YOU STOP TALKING LIKE IT'S MY CHILD BEING BORN?!
CONGRATULATIONS!

SATSUKI-SAN... SO YOUNG...
THAT'S MY MOM YOU'RE TALKING ABOUT! COULD YOU CUT THAT OUT?! YOU'RE FREAKING ME OUT!

Whether he's dealing with Tohru, Kisa, or Shigure, he finds himself playing the straight man.

Surprisingly Bashful

I'M SURE IT WILL BE A KIND CHILD LIKE HIRO-CHAN! ♡
YES YOU ARE! ♡
I'M NOT THAT KIND.
HEY, SATCHAN, HE MAKES YOU WANT TO MARRY HIM, DOESN'T HE? ♡
EH...?
Hey!
WOULD YOU STOP ASKING KISA THINGS LIKE THAT?!

He freaks out when his mother plays matchmaker with him and Kisa.

Hiro gets awkward when he tries to talk about his feelings, and isn't good at accepting compliments. He reacts with embarrassment when his mother talks about him to the girl he likes. He may pretend to be an adult, but he's still an elementary student, and some subjects still make him blush.

IT'S NOTHING...

I HAVEN'T GROWN UP AT ALL. WHENEVER I'M FACED WITH SOMETHING I DON'T LIKE...

"...I TAKE IT OUT ON OTHER PEOPLE.

"BUT THEN I GO AND MAKE HER CRY. I'M SO STUPID. I REALLY AM LOSING POINTS. I'M A NO-GOOD, HOPELESS LITTLE BRAT, BRAT, BRAT."

LOOK WHO'S TALKING!!

IF ALL YOU HAVE TO CONTRIBUTE IS COMPLAINTS, EVEN A SNOT-NOSED KID CAN DO THAT.

YOU MEAN TO TELL ME THAT YOU CONTRIBUTE MORE TO THIS HOUSE THAN ANYONE ELSE? DO YOU PAY ALL THE BILLS?

SINCE WHEN DID THE CAT SET THE RULES FOR THIS HOUSE?

STOP, STOP, KYO-CHAN!

HAH?!

HII-KUN IS AT A REBELLIOUS AGE.

I CAN'T STAND PEOPLE WHO DO ABSOLUTELY NOTHING BUT COMPLAIN ALL THE TIME!

He wants to improve, for himself and for Kisa, but even small changes don't come quickly...

At any rate, he has a way with words, and if someone argues with him he'll return it tenfold. He feels bad about upsetting Tohru and Kisa with his careless harshness, but can't quite apologize. But he doesn't like the childish part of him that lashes out that way, and he wants to quickly mature into a composed adult.

An Airheaded Mother Who Said, "I Love Sheep!"

Hiro's Mother, Satsuki

Common wisdom says that mothers of the Zodiac either overprotect or reject their children, but Hiro's mother breaks the mold. When Hiro was born, she was completely unfazed, and cheerfully said that she loves sheep. She's more than a little clumsy, but she overflows with love and unconditional acceptance for her children. She's a bit reminiscent of Tohru, but her words and actions make her seem even more innocent.

His first encounter with Tohru. Partly because he thought poorly of her even before they met, he immediately launches into an abusive tirade.

EH--?

DON'T YOU HAVE ANY STANDARDS?

SO IF I TOLD YOU TO SPIN AROUND, YOU'D DO IT? IF I TOLD YOU TO JUMP OFF A CLIFF, WOULD YOU DO IT, TOO?

NO...

I CAN'T STAND PEOPLE WHO HAVE NO INDIVIDUALITY!!

YOUR MAMA IS STURDY.

DON'T JUMP AROUND SO MUCH, DON'T RUN, AND MAKE SURE TO WATCH WHERE YOU'RE GOING!

YES, SIR.

YOU MEAN YOU CAN'T ACT A LITTLE MORE CAREFULLY EVEN THOUGH YOU HAVE A BABY?!

"BECAUSE IT DOESN'T MATTER WHICH IT IS. EITHER WAY, IT WON'T CHANGE THE FACT THAT WE'LL LOVE IT."

Hiro Sohma's Family Tree

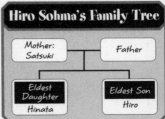

Mother: Satsuki		Father
Eldest Daughter Hinata		Eldest Son Hiro

90

HIS GUILT AND HIS FEELINGS FOR KISA

"I love Kisa." Hiro had no idea what would happen when he told Akito, but the result was that Akito attacked Kisa with enough violence to hospitalize her. After that, Hiro began avoiding Kisa to keep Akito from hurting her again. But because he kept his distance, he was unable to help when she was being bullied.

He is jealous of Tohru's ability to understand and protect Kisa. But his jealousy only increases Kisa's anxiety.

"ONEE-CHAN, ONEE-CHAN"!
WHY DO YOU ALWAYS...
...ALWAYS ...
...KEEP TALKING ABOUT THAT STUPID WOMAN!

I WANT TO BE THE ONLY ONE...
HOW SHAMEFUL.

SO...
...PEOPLE WHO CAN ADMIT THAT...
...HAVE A LOT OF COURAGE, SHE SAYS.
HIRO-SAN...
...YOU CAN DO THINGS.
YOU CAN BE THE WONDERFUL PRINCE WHO PROTECTS KISA-SAN.
BECAUSE INSIDE YOU, HIRO-SAN...
...YOU DO...
...HAVE COURAGE.

Hiro-san, admitting that you're a child is the first step to no longer being one.

"I LOVE HER... I LOVE HER. I WANTED TO BE FREE TO ACT ON MY FEELINGS, AND WANTED THAT PERSON TO UNDERSTAND..."

WHY AM I...
...SO CHILDISH?

Instead of protecting Kisa, Hiro's actions cause her to be injured.

ARE YOU HAPPY ABOUT SOMETHING?
WATCH.

Hiro's face changes as he absorbs Tohru's words.

HIS CONNECTION WITH RIN

Isuzu acts on her own, and never asks anyone for help. Hiro alone knew that she was singlehandedly trying to break the Zodiac curse. He happened to be there when Akito pushed Isuzu, so he heard the whole story... but the two of them have sworn him to secrecy, so he can't tell Hatsuharu.

"THE WAY YOU TALK, RIN, IT'S LIKE IT'S WRONG TO BE LOVED BY YOUR PARENTS."

......
I HEARD...
...THAT YOU'RE ABLE TO LEAVE THE HOSPITAL NOW?
ISN'T THAT GOOD?
IF YOU HADN'T SNUCK OUT SO OFTEN, YOU COULD HAVE LEFT SOONER, THOUGH.

WHAT DO YOU CARE? ARE YOU GOING TO WORRY ABOUT ME FOREVER?
IF YOU'RE WORRIED BECAUSE YOU HAPPENED TO SEE THAT...
...FORGET IT.
JUST GO BACK TO YOUR PEACEFUL LITTLE LIFE...
...WITH YOUR LOVING...
...MOMMY AND DADDY.
!
ARE...
...YOU...
...BLAMING ME?

He worries about Isuzu, so he secretly visits her in the hospital, but...

> "I hope I can say it. 'I was born for you.' It would be nice if I could say that someday."

草摩利津

Ritsu Sohma

Zodiac: The Monkey

A young man with a feminine beauty that rivals Yuki's. He's a walking inferiority complex, constantly ready to take the blame for everything. He's humble with everyone, and the slightest complaint or sarcasm sends him into a fit of apology, complete with crying and shouting. He's the type of person who's more concerned about others than himself, but he's too insecure to believe he could help anyone. He wears women's clothing because it makes him feel calmer (at least, compared to how he feels when he dresses like a man).

He is one of the older Juunishi, but unlike Shigure, Hatori, Ayame, and Kureno, Ritsu doesn't know that Akito is a woman.

Fashion Concept

He sometimes wears chic one-piece outfits (with skirts, of course), but his preference is for kimonos (furisode, naturally). He also dresses like a woman at college, which gives him a certain notoriety. When he does wear men's clothing, it's usually some sort of suit; they might be just a bit more refined than the suits Hatori wears.

(From the 2001 Fruits Basket Character Book)

A third-year student at a private college.
Nickname: Ritchan-san.
His mother is the hostess at a Sohma-run hot springs. He lives on the Sohma "outside". He started dressing like a girl because it calmed him down. Name origin: from a name for the Eighth month: Odakaritsuki
*Rice harvest month

92

Ritsu Quote Collection

"Oh nooooo! Someone I've never seen before knows my name! I was living carelessly, not knowing that the infamy of my name was a burden to so many people! I'm sorry! I'm sorry for all the people who are cursed to endure sharing my pitiful name! I'mmm sorrryyyy!" (->Tohru)

"I thought I would bring fruit, but I didn't know what you'd like, so I brought books about fruit......" (->Shigure)

"Of course...! Someday I hope that I can overflow with confidence, like Aya-niisan...!" (->Shigure)

"...I wonder if I can find it. My reason. I hope I can... someday. I, too... if it's possible... I want to find it in someone else... I hope I can eat takoyaki with them......"

Other People's Words To Ritsu

"The people around you aren't that bothered by you, Ritchan, so even if you apologize, it only causes more problems." (Shigure)

"The people around you aren't blaming you, or criticizing you, as much as you think. So you can have a little more composure." (Hatori)

"...When Ritchan panics, he goes crazy, but he's very nice." (Momiji)

"But as long as you're alive, you have to keep searching for that reason... I'm searching, too. And if I can... if I can, I want to find my reason in someone else..." (Tohru)

Agile

He says he has to work twice as hard as others to keep up in academics or athletics, but he's actually very agile. Being possessed by the spirit of the Monkey, he is able to keep himself from falling off the roof by catching the eaves and lightly swinging back up.

OOF
EH?!
OH...
I TWISTED MY ANKLE...
YOU REALLY ARE SHAMELESS. SERIOUSLY.
I DON'T CARE ANYMORE JUST LEAVE ME OUT OF THIS

To Stop A Rampage, Jab His Side

The most insignificant things send Ritsu into a full-blown panic. In that state, his own earnest apologies deafen him to anything anyone else says. The best way to stop him is to firmly poke him in the lower side--a Ritsu-specific technique invented by Shigure.

Urya!
SINCE RITCHAN WENT TO ALL THE TROUBLE OF BEING BRAVE AND SHOWING UP...
IT'S NOT LIKE I WAS GOING TO BE MEAN.
...BE NICE TO HIM, YUKI-KUN.
AS AN OLD WISE MAN ONCE SAID, "WHEN RITCHAN GETS OUT OF CONTROL, WITHOUT PANICKING OR MAKING A FUSS, PUSH HIS SIDE."

If Shigure pushes his lower side, Ritsu's out like a light.

Ayame is His Idol!

Ha Ha Ha Ha Ha Ha
OF COURSE! SOMEDAY...
...I HOPE THAT I CAN OVER-FLOW WITH CONFIDENCE, LIKE AYA-NIISAN!
AAHH, THAT'S IMPOSSIBLE.

It's impossible for him to be like Ayame, but Shigure and Hatori agree that Ritsu should have more confidence.

Ritsu desperately wants to become a better person. He idealizes Ayame, who oozes confidence and is never shaken. If nothing else, Ritsu reaches for the stars! But the gap between his own timidity and Ayame's innately regal attitude may be too wide.

A Born Airhead?

Ritsu's considerate behavior never ends well. Good manners dictate bringing a gift when paying a visit, but since he doesn't know what kind of fruit they might like, he brings books about fruit. He's also prone to saying exactly the wrong thing, like telling Yuki "You're looking more and more like your brother." Everything he does is just slightly wrong.

I THOUGHT I WOULD BRING FRUIT, BUT I DIDN'T KNOW WHAT YOU'D LIKE...
...SO I BROUGHT BOOKS ABOUT FRUIT...

He is one of those unfortunate people who bases decisions on incorrect assumptions.

IT'S NOT HER FAULT! I'M SORRYYYY!!!

WHOA!!

OH YEAH, YOU'RE STILL HERE TOO...

: ALWAYS HAVE OPEN FLAME FOR BREAKFAST, SO TOFFU-SAN POURED THE MILK THAT WOULD HAVE BEEN YOURS.

: I AM THE ONE WHO DRANK THE LAST OF THE MILK!! I AM THE ONE WHO AM EATEN IN SINS! I AM THE EVIL ONE!! NOW.

PLEASE RENDER JUDGMENT... PLEASE HESITATION, RENDER JUDGMENT!!

Ritsu's discovery that he has used up the milk and left none for Kyo causes quite a scene. As he falls over himself to apologize to Kyo, he escalates past the point of being a nuisance and becomes downright scary.

"I'M SORRY! I'M SORRY! I'M SORRY THAT SOMEONE SUCH AS MYSELF WOULD INTRUDE INTO YOUR HOME! I APOLOGIZE! I APOLOGIZE TO THE ENTIRE WORLD!!"

When Tohru guesses his name on their first meeting, Ritsu assumes it is because his infamy has become common knowledge. He overreacts to Shigure's joking and tries to flee the house, and later goes into a mindless panic after breaking a plate. Finally, when he injures Tohru, he feels he can only atone with his death. Ritsu's overwhelming feeling of responsibility for even the smallest things is mainly due to his firm belief that his very life is a nuisance to the people around him.

I'M SORRYYYYY!!

WHY IS HE APOLOGIZING?

NOOOOO

I'M SORRY I LET YOU SLEEP LATE!!

I'M SORRY I MADE YOU LATE!!

"I'm sorry! You'll be suspended because of being late, and then you'll be expelled!" "Hey! Don't you go deciding the future of my schooling!!" Even Yuki is compelled to comment on Ritsu's early-morning hysteria.

OOHH, I'M SORRY, YOU'LL BE SUSPENDED BECAUSE OF BEING LATE, AND THEN YOU'LL BE EXPELLED! I'M SO SORRY!!

HEY! DON'T YOU GO DECIDING THE FUTURE OF MY SCHOOLING!!

Loving Her Son Too Much?
Or Just Predisposed to Panic?

•Ritsu's Mother, Concubine-san•

Ritsu's mother shares his inclination to panic. She is especially sensitive when talking about her son, because she loves Ritsu deeply. She was originally worried that the Juunishi might be hurt by Tohru, an outsider, learning their secret--but meeting Tohru and seeing her kindness relieved that fear. Because her health is poor, she lives at the hot springs inn for treatment and officially serves as its concierge. She leaves most of the concierge duties to others, though, and runs the place from the shadows. She's got some guts.

YOU'RE THE FRIGHTFUL ONE!!

TO THINK THAT YOU WOULD WANT TO STAY IN A ROOM WITH A GIRL EVEN IF YOU ARE THE CAT : I BELIEVED YOU WERE A GOOD BOY WHEN DID YOU BECOME SUCH A LASCIVIOUS CHILD?! OH, HOW FRIIIIIIIGHTFU-FUUUUUUUUUL!!!!

IS SHE REALLY THAT MEAN?

I WILL APOLOGIZE ON YOUR BEHALF I WILL APOLOGIZE IN THE WORLD'S STEAD I'M SORRY FOR THE LASCIVIOUS-NEEEEEEESS!!

THAT'S NOT WHAT I MEANT!!

FINE! I'LL STAY WITH YUKI!!

Did the son inherit panic from the mother, or did she learn it from him? The mind boggles.

"HE'S VERY PRECIOUS TO ME. DEEP DOWN, HE'S VERY KIND. HE'S MY ONLY CHILD!!"

His mother has taken responsibility for Ritsu countless times, out of love for him.

...BUT MY SON IS A MEMBER OF THE CHINESE ZODIAC TOO, LIKE YUKI-BOCCHAN AND THE OTHERS.

I FORGOT TO TELL YOU THIS EARLIER.

THE SPIRIT OF THE MONKEY POSSESSES HIM.

Ritsu Sohma's Family Tree

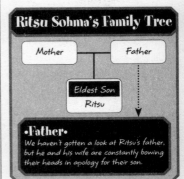

Mother — Father

Eldest Son
Ritsu

•Father•
We haven't gotten a look at Ritsu's father, but he and his wife are constantly bowing their heads in apology for their son.

FOR WHAT REASON, FOR WHOSE SAKE, AM I ALIVE...?

MAYBE... MAYBE IT WOULD BE BETTER FOR EVERYONE IF I CUT SHORT MY EXISTENCE...
BUT NO! I DON'T EVEN HAVE THE COURAGE FOR THAT.
THAT'S RIGHT. I SERVE NO PURPOSE IN LIFE, BUT WHEN IT COMES TO ENDING IT, I AM DOUBLY SHAMELESS.

Even among the Sohma, the members of the Zodiac are special enough to attract attention. Ritsu alone is slower-witted, and needs to exercise and study twice as hard to keep up with even normal people. He grew up being called worthless by adults on the Sohma "inside", and watching his parents bow their heads in apology. He became guilt-ridden, wondering whether his life had any value, or if it was an imposition for him to be alive at all.

There is no merit in the life of such a dull person. Yet I don't have the courage to die. I really am a worthless human being...

EVER SINCE I DISCOVERED BY CHANCE THAT WEARING WOMEN'S CLOTHING HELPS ME CALM DOWN A LITTLE, I'VE DRESSED LIKE THAT.
Kagura-chan... will you give me this dress?
You'd wear it?! More than once?!
BUT THAT JUST ADDED TO THE NUMBER OF THINGS MY PARENTS HAD TO APOLOGIZE FOR.
......

"FATHER AND MOTHER MUST HATE HAVING TO APOLOGIZE FOR ME ALL THE TIME. SURELY THEY WANTED A SON WHO WOULD MAKE THEM PROUD."

Because wearing women's clothes helps him to relax, he even wears furisode to college.

"I HOPE I CAN SAY IT. 'I WAS BORN FOR YOU.' IT WOULD BE NICE IF I COULD SAY THAT SOMEDAY."

THANK YOU.
THANK YOU SO MUCH.
I WANT TO HEAR...
...THOSE WORDS ONE MORE TIME.

Tohru pleads with Ritsu as he considers suicide, and a long-ago memory of her mother surfaces in the back of her mind...

YOU DON'T HAVE TO BE COURAGEOUS!!
WHAT'S WRONG...
...WITH BEING SHAMELESS?!
SOMETIMES LIVING CAN BE HARD, BUT IT'S ONLY BECAUSE WE'RE ALIVE THAT WE CAN MAKE EACH OTHER...
...LAUGH, CRY... BE HAPPY!

Tohru's words help Ritsu to stop questioning the value of his existence. He begins to believe that every life, even his, will touch someone else and strengthen them.

UM... W-WHAT IS... TAKOYAKI POWER?
WELL, THAT IS--! WHEN SHIGURE-NIISAN EATS TAKOYAKI, HE TRANSFORMS INTO A GREAT WARRIOR...
NO I DON'T.

"I want to live for something, for someone..." Ritsu finally meets that "someone".

"What was bad? Where did it go wrong? Should I never have been born?"

Isuzu Sohma

草摩依鈴

Zodiac: The Horse

Isuzu's childhood home was warm and loving, with kind parents who were always smiling. But when she asked one innocent question--"Are you really having fun?"--the illusion was revealed and shattered in an instant. Her parents had been pushing themselves far beyond their limits to maintain their pretense of happiness. After that, they began subjecting her to severe abuse, which continued until Kagura's parents confirmed what was happening and took Isuzu into their home. The trauma affects her health to this day, and she has been hospitalized repeatedly.

She enrages Akito by becoming Hatsuharu's lover, and suffers terrible injuries when Akito pushes her out a window. After that, she begins searching for a way to break the Juunishi curse.

Fashion Concept

Her flashy way of dressing is partially a rejection of the cute outfits she wore as a child. But now that her hair's been hacked off, and one of her major emotional hurdles has been overcome, I think her tastes may start to change a little.

(From the 2001 Fruits Basket Character Book)

A first-year student at a private girls' high school. Nickname: Rin.
After she was abused by her parents, she went to live with Kagura's family. She's in very poor health, and rarely goes to school. She was badly injured when Akito pushed her out a window.
Name origin: from a name for the Sixth month: Isuzukuretsuki *Month of the last cool spring days

Isuzu Quote Collection

"Until the day, someday, when they'll forgive me. You will forgive me, won't you? We can go back to the way things were, can't we?"

"Haru was a strange boy. A kind boy. I felt like I might fall in love with him. Maybe I have fallen in love with him."

"But Haru did want me. There was someone who wanted me, even though I had been told that I was unwanted. I'm happy... What a happy thing."

"From everything that binds you, I want to release you. Haru, your true 'happiness,' see, it's in a bigger world. I'll look for it. I'll find it. Because it's okay for it to end with nothing left in my hands."

"It's too much. Such a person. I feel sorry for her. Kind people are clung to, sought out, taken advantage of, by people like me. That's why I won't get them involved. I can do it on my own. I will keep running on my own." (->Tohru)

Other People's Words To Isuzu

"Are you just stupid? Or is that foolishness part of your plan?" (Shigure)

"I want you, Rin. Do you not want me, Rin? Do you not want to be with me?" (Hatsuharu)

"This is why I hate women. They're cunning. Even that black, trailing long hair...makes me sick." (Akito)

"...you are not needed." (Akito)

"Even now, Haru likes you, Rin. He likes you very much." (Yuki)

Her Relationship With Kyo

I DIDN'T HEAR ANYTHING ABOUT YOU COMING! NOW I'M GONNA BE SICK!
TOHRU, THINK BEFORE YOU LEAP.
YOU'RE NOT TO GLARE AT EACH OTHER TODAY.
I WOULDN'T DO THAT. JEEZ.
IS THAT RIGHT? YOU USED TO HAVE NO PROBLEM GLARING AT EACH OTHER FOR FIVE, TEN MINUTES.
WE WERE JUST KIDS!
ARE YOU TWO ON BAD TERMS?

Growing up hasn't improved their relationship much. As Shishou puts it, "It isn't that they are on bad terms. Only that they are not on good terms." Which makes sense... to him.

When he was younger, Kyo was openly hostile to Isuzu, thinking she would steal his Shishou from him. It used to be normal for them to just sit and glare at each other, but they're not quite that bad anymore.

Her Relationship With Yuki and Hatsuharu

When they were children, Hatsuharu often secretly visited Yuki in his isolated room. Isuzu came with him, but she never did anything but sit silently in a corner.

"I'VE HAD ENOUGH."
"I'M GOING HOME."
I WONDERED...
IF THAT WAS ALL SHE WAS GOING TO DO...
...THEN WHY...
...DID SHE BOTHER TO COME OVER IN THE FIRST PLACE?

Isuzu speaking up was always the signal to leave. From a corner of the room, she kept watch for approaching people.

Eating in Front of People

I'LL EAT IT LATER.
I...
...HATE... EATING IN FRONT OF OTHER PEOPLE.

She never seems to want to sleep, and has very little appetite; it doesn't help that she hates most foods.

Isuzu hates eating in front of other people. She's a bit like a wild animal that's scared of humans. When Tohru brought gelatin for her, it was a big step for her to explain why she didn't eat it right away. Isuzu also doesn't like sleeping. Fundamentally, she doesn't seem to have much energy or will to live.

Her First Friend

Isuzu missed a lot of school due to illness, and kept her distance from her classmates, so Tohru was her first friend. It makes Isuzu so happy she doesn't quite know what to do, but it also embarrasses her, which makes her irritable.

Y-YOU JUST SPRANG OUT OF NOWHERE AND CAME RUNNING!
I'M VERY SORRY.

Becoming friends with Tohru hasn't blunted her sharp edges. When Tohru impulsively tries to hug her during her temporary release from the hospital, Isuzu dodges.

Hatsuharu loses his temper on Isuzu's behalf, when she can't respond to her parents. "Having people take their anger out on us, being made light of... We kids get hurt just like you do." Having someone stand up for her--for the first time in her life--reduces her to tears.

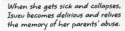

When she gets sick and collapses, Isuzu becomes delirious and relives the memory of her parents' abuse.

"THEY SAID THEY DIDN'T NEED ME. I'M SCARED, HARU. I'M SCARED. I'M SO SCARED I CAN'T TAKE IT."

Isuzu was a happy child whose parents smiled whenever they saw her. But it was all an act: they were forcing themselves to constantly seem like an ideal family, and when she questioned it, they stopped pretending. Her home was broken beyond repair, and her parents began to neglect her. Isuzu silently endured their violence, hiding it from everyone. She is still haunted by their constant rejection, and even now she believes that she is an unwanted child.

Akito tells Isuzu that she isn't needed, just as her parents did. It only reinforces her belief that her life is worthless.

A Mother Who Abandoned Her Child

•Isuzu's Mother•

When it was discovered that Isuzu was injured, she was admitted to the hospital. She tried to defend her parents, but her mother still rejected her. In the end, her parents were incapable of loving a possessed child. They wore themselves out in their efforts to pretend otherwise, for their daughter's sake, but they wound up bearing the brunt of their repressed hatred when she questioned them.

"I DON'T KNOW HOW TO LOVE YOU ANYMORE."

Her mother's stark words have stayed with Isuzu, and still hurt her.

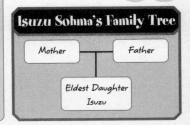

Isuzu Sohma's Family Tree

Mother		Father
	Eldest Daughter Isuzu	

KIND PEOPLE

And so the duo is born, both in name and reality!! Right!!?

AS LONG AS YOU...
...PROMISE ME THAT YOU WON'T WORK TOO HARD...
...BY YOURSELF, ISUZU-SAN.
AND SO, A PARTNERSHIP IS BORN!! AM I RIGHT!?!
I DON'T NEED SOMEONE AS UNRELIABLE AS YOU FOR A PARTNER!!
Keh!
EEEHH?!
AH, UM, BUT I'LL DO MY BEST! I'LL WORK REALLY HARD...!

"I WANTED TO RUN TO HER, FALL ON HER LAP, AND ENTRUST MY HEART TO HER."

BUT AFTER I BROKE UP WITH HARU...
...THAT GIRL WAS THERE.
...THE FIRST TIME I WENT TO GURE-NII'S HOUSE...
AND I FELT...
...THAT BURNING...
...IMPULSE.

When she first met Tohru, Isuzu recognized a kindness as strong as Haru's. She saw that Tohru was someone who would accept her weaknesses and forgive her, and because of that, she kept her distance. She was unwilling to let herself become a burden for someone else.

FREE FROM ALL TIES

When she learns that Tohru is also looking for a way to break the curse, Isuzu breaks down and reveals her true feelings.

THERE ISN'T ONE ANY-WHERE!
NO ONE KNOWS HOW.
AT THIS RATE...!
I'LL NEVER BE ABLE TO RELEASE HIM.
THERE ISN'T A WAY!
I...
I DON'T KNOW...
...WHAT TO DO ANYMORE.

Because she wants Haru to be free from everything binding him, Isuzu decides to try to break the curse. When her attempts at research fail, she approaches Shigure for information, but he evades her questions. After refusing to rely on anyone, Isuzu finally admits that her best efforts have only led to dead ends, and that she can't do it alone.

TWISTED LOVE

DO YOU THINK I'M PITYING YOU?
NO...
NO, I DON'T.
I LIKE YOU.
SO I...
...WANT YOU, RIN.
DO YOU...
...NOT WANT ME, RIN?
DO YOU NOT WANT TO BE WITH ME?
...!
......

Isuzu wishes she could become Haru's heart. He laughs and says, "But then I couldn't even kiss you," but her desire to possess him has become so strong that no degree of physical intimacy satisfies it.

BUT THEN, I COULDN'T EVEN KISS YOU.
BECAUSE THEN I COULD ALWAYS BE WITH YOU.
HARU...
BUT...
...I...
HARU...
IF YOU DIED, HARU...
...I WOULD DIE WITH YOU.

"A 'LOVE' LIKE THIS SEEMS LIKE IT WOULD SOMEDAY CRUSH HARU."

Being with Haru was the only way she could forget her inescapable pain. Isuzu was happy that he wanted her, but it also terrified her. Even as she holds on to him, unable to stop wanting everything about him, she knows she has no right to feel the way she does. She believes that her love will become an unbearable burden for him.

"I alone am free. I can go anywhere, I can love anyone. But, but that's exactly why."

Kureno Sohma

草摩紅野

Zodiac: The Bird

The final Juunishi member to meet Tohru. He is Akito's very favorite, and never strays far from her side. Because she can't endure it when he leaves her, he spends almost all of his time on the Sohma estate. He has become so isolated that he didn't even know how to shop at a convenience store.

He was born possessed by the spirit of the Bird, but his curse broke long ago (which means we've never seen him transformed in the story). Akito alone knows that he has been released. Kureno's instinctive yearning for "God" disappeared with his curse, but he sees and pities Akito's loneliness, and can't bring himself to leave her. He even became her lover when she wanted him to.

Fashion Concept

He doesn't wear white shirts (except when school uniforms used to require them). It's a color he feels an aversion to, and he avoids wearing it because he wants to blend in and not draw attention to himself. Other than that... I don't put him in suits, because it makes him look too much like Hatori-san. (laugh)

(From the 2001 Fruits Basket Character Book)

Akito Sohma's personal aide.
Nickname: Kureno
He lives on the Sohma "inside", very close to Akito. He is the Bird of the Zodiac, but his curse has already been broken. He rarely ventures "outside".
Name origin: from a name for the Third month: Kurenoharu *Late spring

Other People's Words To Kureno

"In that case you should look happier when you smile...!" [Arisa]

"That's a different guy...Kureno-san was totally spacey. He wouldn't even notice if he stepped in dog crap..." [Arisa]

"But...even so, as long as you're alive, things keep happening. As long as you're alive, wishes will keep being made...!" [Tohru]

"That's right. I hate you very much. You should be grateful that I say it so clearly for you. Now you can pretend to be disappointed to your heart's content." [Shigure]

Kureno Quote Collection

"I'm sorry...All I ever do is hurt people...Even so, this is the path I've chosen. I, on my own, decided on this path." [→Tohru]

"I suddenly felt like my field of vision had been opened. Like there was no one inside me but 'me.' And there was nothing to drive me away. The sky was blue. When I thought I'd never be able to fly in that sky again, I was sad, and happy." [→Tohru]

"I won't be seeing Arisa. Because from now on I will continue to be by Akito's side. Only twice...It was only twice that I met Arisa and talked with her. It was a tiny...trivial encounter. If it ends now, without my seeing her, it will be just a trivial memory and someday it will fade into nothing."

"'...It was the first time after becoming human that I, myself, thought I liked someone...!"

Living in His Cage

Kureno is lonely because he's kept apart from the other members of the Zodiac, but he makes no move to go against Akito. He silently submits to her strict boundaries around his life, even though it means getting her permission to even venture outside.

I TRUST YOU DIDN'T CAUSE ANY MISCHIEF OUTSIDE?
BUT I'M SURE
I WON'T EVEN BE ABLE TO SEE YOU AGAIN.
NO. EVERYTHING'S FINE...
...AKITO.

Special Treatment

The other Juunishi distrust Kureno. It may be because Akito singles him out for special treatment, or because the spirits inside them whisper that he's no longer one of them. Shigure seems to have a vague suspicion that he's been freed from the curse.

NEVER MIND.
KURENO! LEAVE.
YOU DON'T HAVE TO SEE ANYONE.

Fearing that Kureno's secret might be exposed, Akito won't even let him see the other Juunishi.

Just Like Tohru...

I'M FINE, BUT IT'S DANGEROUS TO CARRY ALL THAT.
YOU SHOULD PUT THOSE IN A BASKET.
BASKET?
O-OH, OF COURSE. HOW SILLY OF ME.
THANK YOU FOR YOUR KINDNESS.
WAH!

On his first visit to a convenience store, Kureno meets Arisa. She feels an immediate affinity for him because he reminds her so strongly of Tohru. (But the real question is, what did he do with the snacks he bought?)

Kureno bows, even though he's holding too many things to see over. Even his clumsiness is like Tohru's.

Ignorant of The World

Partly because Akito hates him being away from her, Kureno lives a very reclusive life that centers around serving her. As a result, he's become completely disconnected from the rest of the world. He has so little idea of how things work that he doesn't even know to put his items in a basket while shopping at a convenience store.

Arisa is shocked that Kureno has never been in a convenience store before. His world is unimaginably different from hers.

WHAT ARE YOU?! ARE YOU REALLY THE RULER OF SOME KINGDOM OR SOMETHING?!
AH HA HA! NOTHING LIKE THAT.
BUT, WELL, TO HAVE NEVER BOUGHT ANYTHING FROM A CONVENIENCE STORE--AT 26--AND A BEING A GUY--!! HOW?!

Kureno couldn't forget the face of the girl he met late one night at the convenience store. When they met again a few days later, it was because she saw and ran after him, overheating herself to catch him. Kureno is drawn to Arisa, with her intense, genuine emotions: she smiles with real happiness, and she doesn't hold back when she gets angry. She was the first woman he loved with all his heart. But he can't bring himself to abandon Akito to her loneliness, so he chooses to bury his feelings and not see Arisa again.

The woman who ran after him left a strong impression on Kureno's heart.

Hope survives as long as we're alive. Even if wishes aren't granted right away, their time may still come.

"I WANT TO SEE HER... I WANT TO SEE HER... I WANT TO SEE HER, BUT...IT WAS ONLY TWICE, BUT..."

Arisa gets irritated with Kureno, and yells at him for giving up on his own happiness.

Kureno was as in love with Arisa-- the first woman he'd fallen in love with as a normal human-- as she was with him. But he still chooses to return to Akito.

Kureno declares that he won't see Arisa again, trying to persuade himself by saying the words aloud.

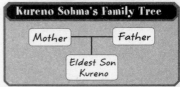

Kureno Sohma's Family Tree

Mother		Father
	Eldest Son Kureno	

BLUE SKY, DISTANT EYES

"I FELT LIKE I HAD BECOME HUMAN, FINALLY."

When his curse broke, Kureno saw the world with his own eyes for the first time.

RIGHT.
BUT I'M NOT LIKE THAT ANYMORE.
I WON'T TRANSFORM.
MY CURSE...
...HAS ALREADY...

IT FELT LIKE MY FIELD OF VISION HAD ABRUPTLY BEEN OPENED.
LIKE THERE WAS NO ONE INSIDE ME BUT "ME."
AND THERE WAS NOTHING TO DRIVE ME AWAY.
THE SKY WAS SO BLUE THAT DAY.
I REALIZED SOMETHING.
I'D NEVER BE ABLE TO FLY IN THAT SKY AGAIN. IT MADE ME BOTH SAD...
IT FELT LIKE...
...I'D FINALLY BECOME HUMAN.
FINALLY.
AND I WAS HAPPY.
...AND ELATED.

Kureno tells Tohru that he was released from the curse when he was only a little younger than her. It happened without warning, and he never figured out what caused it. Akito, being "God", immediately knew he had been freed, and began keeping him abnormally close to her.

BECAUSE THE CURSE IS GONE

Akito sees what's happened as soon as she looks into Kureno's eyes. The curse--the bond that connected them--is gone...

"NO."
"DON'T GO!"
crash

When she felt Kureno's curse break, Akito clung to him and cried. Without her bond to the Juunishi, she would no longer be "God", and she was terrified of losing her reason for existence. Kureno couldn't abandon her to her fear, but Shigure believes he should have walked away from her.

Akito is incredibly fragile. Kureno chooses to live entirely for her, and embraces her. But that decision eventually drives her into a corner.

DON'T ABANDON ME!
KURENO!
...!
PLEASE!
DON'T GO...!
PLEASE...
I'M BEGGING YOU.

FOR THAT CHILD
TIMID...
...AND WEAK.
WEAKER THAN ANYONE.
...THAN ANYONE.
MORE FRAGILE...

"I SWORE I WOULD GO ON LIVING FOR THE SAKE OF THAT GIRL..."

Stricken, Akito wept as if her life was over. She knew the truth: God and the Juunishi are only bound by the power of the curse.

草摩慊人
Akito Sohma

"My 'bond' with everyone! My 'permanence'! No one has the right to negate them!!"

...AS IF IT'S A BAD THING?
OUR WAY OF LIFE IS DIFFERENT FROM YOURS, OUTSIDER.

Akito, the head of the Sohma family, has always been an enigma to Tohru. Tohru once thought that Akito might be the Bird of the Zodiac, but Akito herself revealed the truth: that she is the "God" who rules over the Zodiac. Akito is secretly a woman, whose mother forced her to grow up pretending to be a man. Her mother's reasons are unknown.

Akito tries to bind the Juunishi to her with her authority, and sometimes resorts to violence. She's had violent mood swings since childhood, but they weren't always as extreme as they are now. The change happened overnight; afterwards, she began to deliberately inflict emotional abuse on the Juunishi, doing things like convincing Yuki that he was hated, calling Kyo a monster, and telling Hatsuharu he was a fool.

Fashion Concept

She's the worst when it comes to clothes--she just wears kimonos all the time. When she has to wear Western clothing, she prefers plain garments. Or maybe I should say that dressing up disgusts her, because she hates to have her skin showing...even though you can see it when she's wearing kimonos (laugh).

(From the 2001 Fruits Basket Character Book)

The head of the Sohma family, and the God that rules over the Zodiac.
The fact that Akito is a woman is a closely-guarded secret.
She and her mother, Ren, hate each other.
She seems to be suffering in order to win some sort of victory...

PANIC

Akito feels superior about her special bond with the Juunishi, which Tohru lacks. But their admiration for Tohru begins to stir up a sense of panic...

IN THE END...
...THEY'LL ALL COME BACK TO ME.
BECAUSE...
...WE CANNOT BE APART.
SO STOP...
...TRYING TO DESTROY OUR "HAPPINESS."
STAY OUT OF IT.
BE A GOOD GIRL.
OTHERWISE...
...YOU'LL BE PUNISHED.

DON'T GET CONCEITED...
...YOU LITTLE BITCH.

For the first time, Akito reveals her hostility toward Tohru.

Akito puts Tohru in her place. She believes that the Juunishi can never leave her, but she's still uneasy.

THE DISINTEGRATION OF THE BOND

Akito feels it the moment Kureno's curse breaks, and is terrified out of her wits. She had believed that the curse was an unshakable bond she shared with the Zodiac, and knows that she is only "God" because of them. The thought of losing that bond rips the ground out from under her. She clings to Kureno, begging, "Don't abandon me"; seeing her in that state, he feels something strange.

DON'T GO! DON'T LEAVE ME!
STAY WITH ME! YOU HAVE TO!
DON'T GO ANYWHERE!
DON'T EVER LEAVE MY SIDE!
DON'T LEAVE ME BEHIND!
DON'T...
DON'T...
DON'T...!

It took only a glance to tell her that something was terribly wrong. Kureno was more distant than he had ever been: his eyes, his heart, his soul...Why did the curse break? Why for Kureno? Even Akito doesn't know.

GET AWAY FROM US!
AKITO?!
DON'T LET ANYONE COME UNTIL I SAY SO. DO YOU HEAR ME?!
WHY?
WHY?!
IF ANYONE COMES, I'LL KILL THEM!
I'LL KILL THEM!
AKI...
WHY?!

Without the curse binding them together, there is nothing forcing Kureno to stay at Akito's side. He is suddenly free to go anywhere and love anyone. Akito's youth doesn't blind her to the implications.

Akito Quote Collection

"As long as she's here, she will always be alone...! She needs to realize that she'll beat me. She's no match for me...!"

"Is it fun being with a monster?" (→Kureno)

"Be nicer!! Nicer, nicer, nicer. You used to be much nicer. You looked only at me, as it should be! At me...Her...you do! That woman...you really..." (→Shigure)

"This world, my world, is pitch black. So I have to make my room a fitting color." (→Yuki)

"In the end, they will all come back to me. Because we are inseparable. So stop trying to destroy our 'happiness.' Stop butting in. Be a good girl. ...Otherwise, you'll be punished." (→Tohru)

Other People's Words To Akito

"Akito...It would be nice if he would realize soon, too." (Shigure)

"A love connected by such a bond isn't real. The 'permanence' you've been hanging on to so zealously is a sham. Such a 'permanence' is an illusion." (Ren)

"I wonder if you can win like that." (Ren)

What Akito loves is the reverence the Juunishi offer her. Her love is profoundly different from Tohru's, and completely incompatible with it.

...LOVE YOU ALL.

A HUMAN EQUALING GOD.

THAT IS WHO I AM.
THE ONE WHO CONTROLS THE ZODIAC.
THE MASTER OF THEIR SOULS.

Akito reveals her true identity to Tohru, to make it clear that Tohru can never rival her importance.

HEH
HE SHOULD JUST COME BACK TO ME.
HE SHOULD BE SO LUCKY THAT I GIVE HIM SO MUCH ATTENTION.
A BORING GUY LIKE HIM!!
HEH HEH!
AH HA HA! HE REALLY IS...
...AN IDIOT!!
AKITO...

She looks down on everyone: Kyo (of course), Yuki, and even Kureno, who is widely regarded as her favorite. She sees the Zodiac members as nothing more than servants who exist only for her.

Akito forgets herself in her anger, and strikes Momiji. When Hatori asked her permission to get engaged, and when Yuki said, "I won't make it anyone's fault anymore," rage overwhelmed her. But there was a reason for her violence.

DO YOU WANT TO KNOW WHAT I HAVE TO DEAL WITH?
"SOME-THING"...? "WHY"...?
WHAT WOULD YOU DO IF I TOLD YOU?
DO YOU... WANT TO UNDERSTAND ME?
..."WHY"?
BECAUSE I FEEL SICK!!

"...AKITO. MY CHILD, BORN TO BE LOVED. WE HAVE ALL BEEN WAITING FOR YOU."

Long ago, God and the Zodiac promised to be together forever. Their promise lives on in the hearts of the people possessed by spirits. "God" dwells among the Sohma family, and that God is Akito. The Zodiac and the Cat are incapable of betraying or opposing her, no matter how terribly she treats them. In her presence, their own emotions fade and their bodies cringe in submission; they have no hope of escape, since their hearts ultimately yearn for her. Those uncontrollable emotions, which instinctively drive them, are why the bond is also a curse.

AND THEY'RE NOT ACTING NICE!
WE'RE CONNECTED THROUGH A BOND!
WE'RE IN A WORLD SOMEONE LIKE YOU COULD NEVER BE A PART OF!

Ren dismisses the bond as an artificial love. Akito fights back, but fear lurks in her heart.

AKITO—
APOLOGIZE!

HER CONFLICT WITH HER MOTHER

Ren hates Akito. She mocks the bond that Akito's life centers around, and insists that it isn't real.

YOU'RE STILL SPOUTING THAT GARBAGE?

YOU STUPID CHILD.

AND THAT'S WHY I'M LIVING IN THAT HOUSE.

HOW DARE YOU!!

LISTEN TO YOU!

YOU LEFT WITHOUT RESISTING IN THE SLIGHTEST!

YOU TOLD ME TO GET OUT OF HERE, REMEMBER!

AND YOU ALREADY PUNISHED ME FOR IT.

HOW DARE YOU DO THAT WITH HER!?

Akito can't forgive Shigure for having had a relationship with Ren, but Shigure says it was Akito's fault.

Akito's mother denies the bond between Akito and the Juunishi. Ren tries to drives wedges between her daughter and the Zodiac members, by doing things like sleeping with Shigure to amuse herself, and trying to seduce Kureno. She insists that the bond she shared with Akira was genuine, and that everything else is an illusion. But some mysteries remain unsolved: why does she hurt Akito so much? And why did she have Akito raised as a boy?

A mother who hates and dismisses her child

Ren Sohma

Akito's mother is bewitchingly beautiful, and is deeply attached to Akira, who is deceased. She has some measure of authority among the Sohma family, although not as much as Akito. Akito isn't the only one she treats coldly; her attitude extends to certain members of the Juunishi. She wants a mysterious box that's in Akito's possession, and once used Isuzu to try to get to it.

"THE 'BOND' BETWEEN ME AND AKIRA-SAN IS REAL...!!"

I'LL KILL YOU!

I'LL KILL YOU!

AND THEN I CAN GO TO AKIRA-SAN!

FINE, KILL ME!

I CERTAINLY DON'T NEED SOMEONE LIKE YOU!

IF I DIE, MY SOUL WILL RISE TO HEAVEN.

AKITO'S...

...MOTHER.

Ren's existence is one explanation for Akito's fierce hatred of women, and for why Akito is disgusted by Isuzu's long, black hair.

ANXIETY AND DISTORTION

I CARE ABOUT YOU.

MORE THAN I CARE ABOUT ANYONE.

I LOVE YOU.

AKITO.

AND THAT IS THE HONEST...

...AND UNSHAKABLE TRUTH.

Years ago, Shigure swore to Akito that he would love her for eternity. He still intends to keep that promise.

"SHIGURE, DO YOU LIKE ME?"

YOU'RE JUST MY TOY.

THAT'S AS GOOD AS GETTING ABANDONED!

HA HA HA!

YOUR MOTHER GAVE YOU TO ME.

EVERYONE HATES THE RAT, STUPID!

NO-BODY CARES!

SOON!

NOBODY CARES ABOUT YOU!

DON'T YOU GET IT?

WHEN CAN I GO HOME?

After her mind is twisted, Akito blackens her room with ink. She tells Yuki that he is cursed, and worse: that the Rat is despised, and that even his parents abandoned him.

"God" is a being that was born to be loved, but Akito was still anxious. As a child, she asked Shigure over and over again if he liked her. Yuki has seen Shigure embracing and caressing her--the only reassurances that can really soothe her. And before long, she became twisted...

Akito Sohma's Family Tree

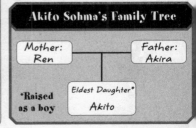

Mother: Ren		Father: Akira
	Eldest Daughter* Akito	
*Raised as a boy		

魚谷ありさ

Arisa Uotani

"I also wanted to change. I'd never felt that way before. 'I'm through being like this,' I thought. I wanted to change."

SHE'S THE ONLY THING IN THIS WORLD

When Arisa was young, her father became an alcoholic after her mother ran out on them. It's not entirely surprising that Arisa took a bad turn, and she debuted as a gang member in fifth grade. It was around then that she heard about Kyoko--the legendary "Red Butterfly", who led a suicide squad despite being a woman--and came to admire her. She began attending middle school after hearing that the Red Butterfly's daughter was a student there. When she met Tohru, she was shocked by the difference between her expectations and reality. But eventually Tohru's acceptance and Kyoko's warmth won her over, and she left her gang. Arisa is now Tohru's close friend, and living as a "normal Yankee".

Fashion Concept

She likes tight clothes. When she was in the gang she covered her skin completely, but since her "reform" she's started wearing things that are more revealing. Uo-chan's style is heavily influenced by Kyoko-san, but she still prefers long skirts (too bad, since she has such great legs...).

(From the 2001 Fruits Basket Character Book.)

A second-year student at Kaibara Public High School.
Nicknames: Uo-chan, Yankee
She lives with her father, in a one-room apartment with a dining and kitchen area.
She joined a gang during her fifth year of elementary school.
Tohru and Kyoko helped her leave that life behind.

Other People's Words To Arisa

"Nope! This one's for Uo-chan!" (Tohru)
"There are feelings that you don't understand unless you get hurt and cause problems. And there are feelings you understand for the first time after falling to the bottom of life." (Kyoko)
"Pain needs kindness, and for darkness to stand out, it needs the sun. You can't make light of either of them. You can't say of them is worthless." (Kyoko)
"I don't...really understand, but you laughed so happily, and it was very pleasant, so...I wanted to look at it forever." (Kureno)

Arisa Quote Collection

"They're so phony! For me to be jealous of that. A town at dusk, the smell of evening supper, houses with lights in them. A house to go home to after saying goodbye to friends. Someone waiting for my return. A kind person who would greet me with a smile. ...Maybe I was lonely. Maybe I've just always been lonely. Precious time to be myself and not have to make excuses...Maybe that's what I've been looking for."
"But any time you feel like being scolded, come and see me." (→no-good middle school girls)
"I can't see Kyoko-san. Not anymore. But she left me something... Her advice, her feelings, and Tohru. They all, all become fertilizer to help me grow."
"...I wanted to see you much, much...muuuch more than I thought. That's why I was happy!!" (→Kureno)

"Yankee" Means...

NOOOOO! STOP!
IT'S LIKE THE SAME FEELING I GET WHEN I SEE AN OLD MAN STILL BUYING HIS LUNCH AT A CONVENIENCE STORE!!
THAT OLD MAN MIGHT NOT THINK ANYTHING OF IT, BUT WATCHING HIM, I CAN'T HELP BUT FEEL AWKWARD AND MISERABLE ON HIS BEHALF!
AND BEFORE I KNOW IT, FOR NO REASON, I START TO CRY! CRY!
THAT'S RIGHT! THE ONE WHO RINGS HIM UP, CRYING, IS ME!

Seeing Tohru in her middle school swimsuit after starting high school makes Arisa tear up. Maybe it's her Yankee past that makes it so easy for her emotions to be stirred up.

Arisa gets depressed about Tohru's swimsuit. She isn't particularly embarrassed, but it gives her the same sad feeling as the sight of an elderly person buying lunch at a convenience store.

Future Plans

When she thinks about the future, she starts with, "I guess I'll get a job"--but that's as far as she's thought. Tohru saying, "You're so tall, you would be a wonderful model" is all it takes for her to decide on it as a career. She may not have been serious, though; she doesn't seem to be taking any steps towards becoming a model.

A JOB I WOULD LIKE...?
You would be a great model, Uo-chan. You'd be wonderful!
WELL THEN, LET'S SAY I WANT TO BE A MODEL.
MAYBE YOU SHOULD THINK THAT OVER A BIT, FIRST.

She wants a career, but doesn't know what she wants to do. She just said the first thing that came to mind.

Max Hunger!

When she gets hungry, her mood turns ugly in an instant. Poor Kyo usually suffers for it, for no real reason. Arisa feels comfortable with him as a friend to fight with, so she doesn't feel guilty about it. The second time she met Kureno was right before lunch, so her temper was a little uncertain.

I'M PISSED BECAUSE I'M HUNGRY!!
BEING HUNGRY PUTS ME IN A BAD MOOD!!
I overslept and had to skip breakfast!!
But...
WHY DID YOU KICK KYON-KYON'S DESK?
Max hunger
BECAUSE IT'S EASY TO KICK!!
YO...

When she needs to vent, Kyo is her favorite scape-goat.

Victim of Hay Fever.

Arisa's hay fever is rather serious. She's allergic to cedar pollen, plus several other kinds. She took too many different drugs (what kinds???) when she was young, so antihistamines don't work for her anymore.

ACHOO!
YEEK!

She has terrible hay fever, but the only precaution she bothers with is a mask.

WH-WH-WHAT'S WRONG? ARE YOU SICK? IS IT A COLD?
AH, IT'S JUST ALLERGIES. I WAS ITCHING THROUGH THE WHOLE DAMN PLAY.

...CALL MY NAME LIKE YOU'RE MY FRIEND!
I HAVE NO BUSINESS WITH YOU ANYMORE.
NOW, BUGGER OFF AND GO CRYING HOME TO MOMMY.
SO STUPID...
YOUR FAMILY MAKES ME SICK!!

When she visits Tohru's home, Arisa is irritated by its loving atmosphere. Or is she...?

That was what she was saying, so Arisa followed up with, "Say goodbye to those pretty teeth...!" (Relax, Arisa.)

IF YOU'RE TRYING TO MESS WITH ME BY SAYING YOU'RE THE RED BUTTERFLY'S DAUGHTER, I'LL SEND YOU TO THE NURSE'S OFFICE...
HONDA?!

WHAT TOHRU GAVE HER.

Seeing Arisa in danger, Tohru risked herself to protect her instead of running away from her.

BUT THERE'S ANOTHER FEELING YOU GET ONCE YOU'VE FALLEN AS LOW AS YOU CAN...
A MOMENT OF TRUE CLARITY.
ALL THIS TIME YOU'VE TRIED TO KEEP AWAY THE BEAUTIFUL THINGS IN LIFE...
...BUT SUDDENLY YOU FEEL CONFUSED.
FOR THERE TO BE PAIN, THERE HAS TO BE KINDNESS.
FOR DARKNESS TO STAND OUT, THERE HAS TO BE THE SUN.
YOU CAN'T HAVE ONE WITHOUT THE OTHER.
WHEN YOU REACH THAT POINT, IT CHANGES EVERYTHING.
YOU BEGIN TO LOVE THE BEAUTIFUL THINGS.
AND BOTH HAVE THEIR USES.

Clinging to Kyoko's back, she cries like a baby. She and Kyoko are very alike.

"I...I... WANT TO BE TOHRU'S BEST FRIEND...! A FRIEND TOHRU CAN BE PROUD OF."

バタン
WHY?
WHY DID YOU HELP ME?
......
ARE YOU TRYING TO MAKE ME OWE YOU?
ぜはーぜはー
!!!
ぜはーぜはー
AH...
YES...
THAT IS...
UM... ARE YOU ALL RIGHT?
Y-YES!
P-PLEASE... COME... IN...

Even at home, Arisa didn't belong--so she joined a gang to have friends to hang around with. Meeting Tohru made her uncomfortable at first, because Tohru and Kyoko had a warmth and love she'd never experienced. But as she realized how lonely she was, and that she wanted that warmth in her life, she began to change. She started wanting to be someone Tohru could think of as a best friend. Now that Kyoko is gone, Arisa has sworn to support Tohru.

Arisa Uotani's Family Tree

•Father•

After her mother ran out on them, he spent his days in a drunken stupor. But Arisa's transformation is affecting him for the better. He's started working again, and even turned up at Arisa's parent-teacher conference.

•Mother•

When Arisa was a first-year elementary student, her mother had an affair and left the family. They haven't heard anything from her since. Her disappearance destroyed their home, and left Arisa in a dark place she couldn't escape on her own.

Mother
Father
Eldest Daughter
Arisa

AN ILL-FATED LOVE?

Arisa gets a different job as a sign of giving up on her feelings for Kureno. Torturing herself for a one-sided love is against her nature.

THIS IS A GIFT, A GIFT, THAT WILL LEAD YOU BACK TO HER! DON'T WASTE GIFTS!
ALL THOSE STAR-CROSSED LOVERS...
...WHO JUST WANNA SEE EACH OTHER...
THINK OF ALL THE STAR-CROSSED LOVERS WHO WOULD KILL FOR THINGS THIS EASY!
OW.

FEELING LIKE THAT... IT'S NOT ME.
I GUESS I'M JUST TIRED...
...OF ABUSING MYSELF.

During the play, she accidentally yells out her true feelings. Tohru is the only one who understands what she means.

COME SEE ME, DAMMIT!
THOUGH HIS FELLOW PRINCE WAS BIASED, PRINCE CHARMING TOOK THE ADVICE.
...SEE WHO?

She was finally able to see Kureno again. But although he said he was happy to see her, he seemed lonely somehow.

BECAUSE, I THOUGHT, MAYBE OUR MEETING MEANT SOMETHING.
BECAUSE ...
...I WAS HAPPY!

A strange man she met late one night at the convenience store: Arisa couldn't get that customer, whose clumsiness reminded her of Tohru, out of her mind. When she saw him from behind as he walked down the street, Arisa impulsively ran after him. He introduced himself as Kureno, and then treated her to lunch. Everything he says melts her heart, and eventually she realizes she is in love with him. But that day was the last time she saw him, despite Tohru's best efforts to make him go see her.

"BECAUSE I WANTED TO SEE YOU MUCH, MUUUCH MORE THAN I THOUGHT."

ARISA AND KYO

Arisa is quick to lose her temper at the best of times, but when it comes to Tohru, she's even more hot-headed. Kyo is just as short-tempered, and the two of them starting fighting at the drop of a hat. But to anyone looking on, it's not hard to read it as playful affection.

YOU...
...LIKE KYO...
...DON'T YOU?!
YOU'VE GOT A LOT OF NERVE!
COMING TO INTERRUPT--THAT'S DESPICABLE!
I WANT TO BE POPULAR!
AAAH!!
ARE YOUR EYES JUST KNOTHOLES
MY, MY... YOU ALL SEEM TO BE HAVING FUN.
EEEEK! EEEEK! I'M SORRY! I'M SORRY!

One girl mistakenly decided that Arisa's arrogant, violent attitude toward Kyo meant that Arisa liked him. "Are your eyes just knotholes !!?" And the idyllic scene explodes into chaos...

DAMMIT! WHAT IS THIS? YOU GOT EVEN BIGGER DURING THE BREAK!!
THAT'S JUST GREAT!! YOU DAMN BOYS JUST KEEP GROWING AND GROWING !!
WHETHER SOMEONE GROWS OR NOT ISN'T REALLY DETERMINED BY GENDER...
IT'S MY GOAL TO CRACK SIX FEET!

Arisa smacks Kyo's forehead when he has the nerve to get taller.

花島 咲
Saki Hanajima

"I thought that some prayers could never be answered, just as some stains that, once there, will never disappear."

...EH.

A second-year student at Kaibara Public High School.
Nicknames: Hana-chan, Demon Lord
When she was in middle school, she transferred to Tohru and Arisa's school.
She had been bullied at her previous school.
She can read people's thoughts by picking up their mental waves, and can also project poisoned waves.

During her second year of middle school, she transferred to the school Tohru and Arisa were attending. She's been friends with them ever since. As a child, she suffered because she was unable to control her powers: as an elementary student, she was cruelly teased and accused of being a witch. One such incident made her angry enough to hate the boy tormenting her--and at that moment, he lost consciousness. He survived, fortunately, but after that her classmates were afraid of her. The bullying she suffered escalated in middle school, and her parents decided to transfer her. Meeting Tohru at her new school gave her a second chance.

Fashion Concept

When not in her school uniform, she only wears black. If you open her closet, its complete blackness is like a work of art. Since middle school, she's kept her nails painted black. She especially likes chic, elegant black dresses, and the black cape that matches her brother Megumi's. (The capes were made by their grandmother.)

(From the 2001 Fruits Basket Character Book.)

Other People's Words To Saki

"...Saki, do you plan to live your whole life as if people exist to punish you...? Is that all you want out of life?" (Megumi)

"So...whoever you are, please come to meet her... If you're in a far-off country, then get on a plane. Hurry. Come to Saki as fast as you can. Please..." (Megumi)

"Hana-chan, I love you. I love you, Hana-chan..." (Tohru)

"You decide. Don't assume that things are a certain way 'cuz that's what people tell you. Do you want to leave? That's all I want to know." (Arisa)

Saki Quote Collection

"It means I'm so stupid I can't make up for it with waves."

"...If Tohru-kun were to die, I...I wonder if I'd be able to smile again one year later? Or if I'd wish that I could forget ever having met her. ...Tohru-kun...has tried really hard..."

"Be quiet...If I'm a witch, what are you? Is it okay for you to do something so terrible?"

"I do...want to be with you...I want to be with you...!" (→Tohru / Arisa)

"I...think that my performance today was a success because he played opposite me. Kyo-kun...Thank you." (→Kazuma)

Lacking Motivation

I HAVE NO USE FOR SUCH A THING...
I DID NOT GET A SINGLE RED MARK.
WHAT DID YOU SAY?!

Because it was so hot in the supplementary summer classes, she didn't get a single red mark the next year. With the proper motivation, she can make high enough grades to avoid supplementary classes. It's also possible that she deliberately takes make-up tests because they're easier.

She is basically lethargic and unmotivated, and has been known to have her parents called in after receiving red marks in every subject. Before she picks a career, she might want to put more energy into trying to graduate.

Black Nails: The Sign of A Sinner

IT'S BECAUSE THE UNIFORM ISN'T BLACK. ...
WHAT NONSENSE ARE YOU TALKING ABOUT?!
ARE YOU TELLING ME TO LOSE THE PROOF THAT I'M A SINNER...?
WHAT A STRANGE ADULT...

After she accidentally attacked a classmate with poisoned waves, she began to wear nothing but black, thinking that it showed she was a sinner. Since the uniform at Tohru's school wasn't black, she painted her nails black to reproach herself.

AT THIS POINT, IF EITHER OF US WORE YELLOW OR PINK, THE WHOLE TOWN WOULD BE IN AN UPROAR...
THEY WOULD, WOULDN'T THEY...?

Even when it gets her in trouble with teachers, she stubbornly keeps her fingernail color. And her younger brother, Megumi, began wearing black clothes to support her.

Kyo-Kun's New Mother?

SHISHOU! WHY'RE YOU... HOW...!
HELLO, KYO. GOOD WORK IN THE PLAY.
YES, GOOD WORK.
I THINK MY PERFORMANCE TODAY WAS A SUCCESS BECAUSE HE PLAYED OPPOSITE ME.
KYO-KUN... THANK YOU VERY MUCH.

When she sees Kazuma at the Cultural Fest, she greets him with one of her rare smiles. That smile terrifies Kyo. Can she really intend to become his mother?

At the parent-teacher conference, Saki takes one look at Kyo's Shishou, Kazuma, and decides he's wonderful. Kyo is deathly afraid, not knowing how serious her attraction might be.

A Strange, Mysterious Person

Surprisingly, Saki can't stand ghosts. She thinks they're creepy because they're strange and mysterious. Aren't her poisoned waves "strange and mysterious"...?

IS IT THAT SURPRISING ...?
OF COURSE IT IS!!
WHY THE HELL DON'T YOU LIKE THEM?!
......
IT'S CREEPY HOW THEY'RE...
...SO STRANGE AND MYSTERIOUS...

Saki matter-of-factly explains her fears. It's hard to tell when she's scared, because it doesn't show on her face.

Saki can hear the waves of people's thoughts, and can project poisoned waves. At her previous middle school, she silently endured bullying that endangered her life--until she almost killed one of her tormentors with a curse. She never forgave herself, and even after transferring to a new school, she continued distancing herself from others. Tohru and Arisa were willing to approach her, though, and their acceptance of her dangerous power allowed Saki to heal a little.

SAKI-CHAAAAN!
COME ON! HURRY UP!
SHE SAID...
...SHE DOESN'T... FEEL GOOD...
!
IT'S ALL RIGHT, HONEY.
LET'S GO HOME, OKAY?
SAKI!
SAKI-CHAN!
I'M SORRY. WE THOUGHT YOU MIGHT BE OKAY IN A PLACE LIKE THIS.
SO NOISY...

AN UNFORGIVABLE SIN, AN UNFADING STAIN.

Hearing people's inner voices is painful. Her parents thought she might be okay in an open place like a park, but even that was too much to bear.

I DO...
...WANT TO BE WITH YOU...
I WANT TO BE WITH YOU!

NOW THAT YOU MENTION IT, I DON'T KNOW IF ANYTHING GOOD COMES FROM ASSOCIATING WITH ME, EITHER...
IN MY CASE, IT MIGHT BE TWO HUNDRED HURTS AND NO GOOD THINGS!
I WASN'T JOKING, AND I DEFINITELY DIDN'T WANT TO MAKE ANYONE DEPRESSED...
Are you listening...?

"THERE WASN'T JUST ONE SHADOW ANYMORE..."

Tohru has tears in her eyes when she asks Saki not to leave her. Arisa tells Saki that she has to be the one to decide what she really wants to do. In response, Saki reveals her true feelings for the first time.

I REALLY...
...THOUGHT THAT I HAD... KILLED HIM...
IF IT HAPPENS AGAIN...
...I MIGHT KILL HIM FOR REAL...
I'M SCARED...
NO MORE
I DON'T WANT TO WISH...
...FOR ANYONE'S DEATH EVER AGAIN.

Saki is afraid of the sin she commited --and afraid of how easily she could hurt others.

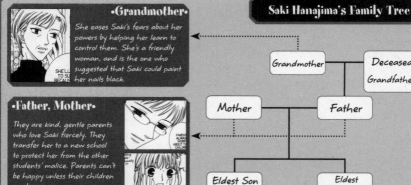

Saki Hanajima's Family Tree

•Grandmother•

She eases Saki's fears about her powers by helping her learn to control them. She's a friendly woman, and is the one who suggested that Saki could paint her nails black.

•Father, Mother•

They are kind, gentle parents who love Saki fiercely. They transfer her to a new school to protect her from the other students' malice. Parents can't be happy unless their children are happy.

Grandmother
Deceased Grandfather
Mother
Father
Eldest Son Megumi
Eldest Daughter Saki

WAVES ARE...

Saki can read other people's waves, which are basically their mental vibes. Rather than hearing them with her ears, she hears their echo inside her head. She can also project bad waves to people, and since meeting Tohru and Arisa, she's learned how to control her ability.

Guhaa!
SOME-THING'S HERE!!
IN THAT CASE...

After this, Minami keeps hearing things, and is bedridden for a week.

DENPA WAVES ARE LIKE PEOPLE'S FEELINGS...
RATHER THAN HEARING WITH MY EARS, THEY COME DIRECTLY INTO MY BRAIN LIKE WAVES...
I DIDN'T ASK FOR A FRICKIN' DISSERTATION.

Reading waves and sensing things spiritually are apparently different, but Saki's explanations aren't terribly enlightening.

Saki senses that Yuki and Kyo have unusual waves, but even she can't tell what they are.

...YOUR WAVES ARE ECHOING...
WHY ARE YOU...
...STANDING BEFORE A GRAVE WITH SUCH FEELINGS OF REGRET...?
EVEN NOW, IT'S THE SAME...
EVEN NOW...

MY MIND!!
DID YOU READ MY MIND!?!
And that laugh!!!
YOU CAN'T READ MINDS WITH WAVES... I LAUGHED BECAUSE I REMEMBERED SOMETHING...

She probably can read people's mind with waves, judging by her behavior...

RESPECTING OTHERS' FEELINGS

ACTUALLY,
...I WAS A LITTLE...
...JEALOUS, TOO...
BUT...
RESPECT THE OTHER PERSON'S FEELINGS.
IT FELT LIKE THE SOHMA FAMILY HAD TAKEN TOHRU-KUN FROM ME.
IT LEFT ME FEELING...
...LONELY.
YOU ARE RIGHT.
THAT'S WHY I CANNOT BE SELFISH...
I MUSTN'T BE LIKE THOSE THREE...
YOU CAN LEARN FROM THEIR BAD EXAMPLE...

Megumi always helps her realize what's important. Saki has relied on his advice countless time.

"WHEN YOU TREASURE SOMEONE, IT CAN BE A LITTLE PAINFUL, AND SOMETIMES YOU MAY GET LONELY, BUT IT CAN ALSO MAKE YOU HAPPY."

After Tohru started living with Yuki and the others, Saki felt like the Sohmas had taken her away, and was a little jealous. She rebukes herself with Megumi's reminder: that other people's feelings should always be respected, and forcing unwanted love on someone burdens and hurts them. Being friends with Tohru and other people helps Saki understand feelings that are vital to the human experience.

A Brother Who Wished For His Sister's Happiness

•Megumi Hanajima•

Saki's younger brother, and the person who understands her best. He's a middle school student, but he's very mature and perceptive. He has a knack for seeing to the heart of things, and for making his way in the world. He doesn't have powers like Saki's, but he can curse people if he knows their names. He's proud that he's mastered a complicated spell that lets him reflect any curses directed at him back at their sender.

...IN THIS WORLD...
THEN...
...I WILL PRAY.
...IN THIS WORLD, OVER-FLOWING WITH PEOPLE...
BECAUSE THERE'S NO WAY...
...THAT SAKI IS MEANT TO BE ALONE HER WHOLE LIFE...
SO, WHO-EVER YOU ARE...
I CAN'T BELIEVE THAT THERE'S NOT ONE PERSON OUT THERE...
...PLEASE COME TO MEET HER...
...WHO WOULDN'T LOVE SAKI.

In front of Saki, he prays that someone will enter her life and love her--even if they are so far away that they'll have to fly to her.

He says he doesn't have any powers, but... he has plenty.

...IS CURSE PEOPLE...

"THEN I WILL PRAY. BECAUSE THERE'S NO WAY THAT SAKI IS MEANT TO BE ALONE HER WHOLE LIFE."

Classmates

CLASS REPRESENTATIVE

She's served as class representative with Yuki since their first year. When Yuki is busy with the student council, she organizes their class in his place.

"CINDERELLA" SCRIPT WRITER

I GUESS YOU CAN'T REALLY FIX A CASTING MISTAKE.
I'M SORRY!

Because the entire play is horribly miscast, she decides to adapt the script to fit the cast. She makes it into a brilliant comedy.

WHA ...?!
WHAT ARE YOU GUYS DOING HERE?!
YOU HAVE TO TREAT GIRLS MORE GENTLY!!
That's right!
IF YOU CAN'T BE GENTLE, YOU'LL NEVER BE A REAL MAN!!
WHY ARE YOU TALKING LIKE GIRLS?

I WISH I COULD SAY THAT!
I WISH I COULD FEEL THAT WAY, TOO!
WHAT'S YOUR GUYS' PROBLEM ...?

IEND-FRAYS

Classmates who have become regular characters. But they don't have names. They're a lively, mischievous duo who like to have fun.

The Delinquent Trio

ゴ゙ ゴ゙ ゴ゙ ゴ゙
COME WITH US, PUNK.
AND COME ALONE.

A trio of Yankees who were after Arisa. They wanted people to be afraid of their gang, so they tried to beat Arisa up because of her tough reputation. They hit her with their best attack, but she shrugged it off and chewed them out. She won their admiration, and they now call her Ane-san. They like handsome men, and cave when they're offered things they want.

The "old-fashioned Yankees" challenge Arisa as threateningly as they can. (Very clever of them, reminding her to come by herself.)

ANE-SAN*...
ANE-SAN?!
ANE-SAN?!!

One word from Arisa stops them cold. They now dutifully attend middle school, and follow Arisa's instructions to the letter. Sometimes, they come to hang out at Kaibara High.

Arisa Uotani's sempai

NOTHING TO GAIN FROM GOING.
......

She went to tell Kyoko when Arisa was being swarmed. She's since moved far away.

Mayuko Shiraki's Mother

HEY, MAYUKO.
WHY WON'T YOU MARRY SHIGURE-SAN?

She runs a used bookstore. She worries that her daughter, who's not getting any younger, will never get married. (Mayuko's father is currently in the hospital.)

The Sohma Family Head's Personal Maid

WHERE HAVE YOU BEEN?
AKITO-SAN HAS BEEN CALLING YOU FOR A WHILE.
YOU MUSTN'T KEEP HIM WAITING ANY LONGER.

She manages the Sohma servants. She believes Akito is beyond reproach, and looks down on everyone else.

Chapter 3: The Banquet

SCHOOL LIFE KNOWLEDGE GALLERY

This section is packed with all sorts of information, like info on the Student Council and the routines of Kaibara High, as well as trivia that's common knowledge among the Furuba cast. There's also a gallery of the artwork from various chapter introduction pages, with commentary by Takaya-sensei!

Operations of the Student Council (also known as the School Defense Force)

Kaibara Public High School Student Council Organization Chart

Members of the Kaibara Student Council are appointed, not elected. In other words, all of the current members of the student council were chosen by President Takei. Yuki was his first and only choice for the next president, but Yuki refused the appointment for a long time.

I AM YOUR STUDENT BODY PRESIDENT, MAKOTO TAKEI!!
ALSO KNOWN AS THE LEADER OF THE SCHOOL DEFENSE FORCE!!

He loves Yuki as much as Motoko does. His behavior is so over the top that he can seem like an idiot, but he's probably one of the school's best students.

Kakeru asks Ayame to become the "commander" and Ayame agrees. Machi is so scared by the ruckus that she backs up against the wall (laugh).

YOU GOTTA BE OUR COMMANDER!!
WELL, I CAN THINK OF NO REASON WHY I SHOULDN'T BECOME YOUR COMMANDER!!
THEY'VE BEEN LIKE THAT FOR A WHILE...
YOU WERE BORN TO BE THE COMMANDER OF THE SCHOOL DEFENSE FORCE!!
Whoooa!! You're so cool!

FORMER ASB PRESIDENT
Leader of the School Defense Force
Third-year, Makoto Takei

▼

Commander of the School Defense Force
Ayame Sohma

▼

CURRENT ASB PRESIDENT
Leader of the School Defense Force
Second-year, Yuki Sohma

▼

ASB VICE PRESIDENT
School Defense Force Second-in-Command
Second-year, Kakeru Manabe

▼

SECRETARY	SECRETARY	TREASURER
First-year, Naohito Sakuragi	Second-year, Kimi Todo	First-year, Machi Kuragi

SCHOOL LIFE

MEETING TO DECIDE COLORS

I'M SORRY!! THAT'S RIGHT!! I WAS THE ONE WHO BROUGHT IT UP!!
DON'T YOU THINK THAT THE VERY FACT THAT WE'RE DISCUSSING COLORS AT ALL...
...IS COMPLETELY STUPID?!
OUR WHITEBOARD!
OUR BRAND NEW WHITEBOARD IS BEING BURIED IN MORONIC WORDS!

The most pointless meeting in the world. The outcome: Yun-Yun is represented by red, Kakeru by black, and Naohito by blue.

A SCHOOL DEFENSE FORCE THAT FIGHTS AGAINST EVIL

A MISUNDERSTANDING

WE DO HELP THEM.
WE'RE THE SCHOOL DEFENSE FORCE THAT FIGHTS AGAINST EVIL, YOU KNOW?
LOOK, YOU...
WOULD YOU STOP SAYING THAT WITH A STRAIGHT FACE?
It makes me nervous.

Kakeru originally became the vice president after the previous president, Takei, told him that the student council is the School Defense Force.

Main Operations of the Student Council

The student council has a variety of responsibilities. In addition to creating budgets and assigning responsibilities, the president personally talks to the student clubs to get feedback and input. Yuki believes that there's no point to the Council's existence if they don't help everyone, but...?

I REFUSED THIS TROUBLESOME JOB AT FIRST...
...BUT ACQUIESCED WHEN I LEARNED YOU WOULD BE PRESIDENT.
I'D LIKE YOU TO REMEMBER THAT.
BECAUSE YOU ARE MY...

Naohito says he agreed to be secretary after he found out that Yuki would be the president. He informs Yuki that they are rivals.

Naohito Sakuragi

Since meeting Yuki face to face, Naohito has always been irritated about something or other. He's efficient in his duties, but grumpy about it. It's usually Kakeru's idiocy or Machi's habit of messing things up that gets under his skin, but he may also have real issues with Yuki.

WHAT DO YOU MEAN BY THAT RIDICULOUS SIGN?!!
IT'S BLATANT STUPIDITY!!
AND HOW COULD YOU GUYS HAVE MESSED UP THIS ROOM ALREADY? I JUST CLEANED IT UP!! MY HEAD HURTS...

The "ridiculous sign" is the one that says "School Defense Force". Naohito gets so angry that he throws it out. (But Kakeru just produces a new one.)

Kimi Todo

A devilish girl who beguiles men with her beauty. She claims that half of the male students are in love with her, and if she flirts with a boy who already has a girlfriend, the relationship ends over her. But Yuki and Kakeru are immune to her charms.

HE'S A GENTLE FLOWER, AND YOU SHOULD TREAT HIM ACCORDINGLY.
OH! That's right!
THANK YOU FOR THE CANDY THE OTHER DAY!
Yun-Yun and I...
...ENJOYED EATING IT TOGETHER.

Kimi selfishly eats the candy that Motoko and the others selected so carefully--and she eats it with Yun-Yun! Yuki doesn't understand why she seems to be trying to get people to hate her.

Under the smiles, she's violent. She's punched Kakeru in the stomach countless times.

And you've been hoping to take Kimi there, haven't you?
HERE COMES MISS DEMURE.
HAVE WE.

KIMI MAY BE ACTING LIKE THIS, BUT REALLY, SHE'S JUST--
SHUT UP! HE DOESN'T NEED TO KNOW THAT!!

She acts cute and innocent in front of boys, but...

PATROLLING THE SCHOOL

O-OW!
WHAT ARE YOU DOING HERE?!
WHAT DO YOU MEAN, "WHAT"? I'M ON PATROL.
WE'VE DISCOVERED THE SCENE OF THE BULLYING!
OR HAVE WE?
...WHILE EATING YAKISOBA?
I CAN EAT WHILE I PATROL.

Yuki stumbles across some students bullying Machi. When he gets upset and wants to help her, Kakeru stops him and says it's her own fault for not fighting back. Instead, Kakeru intervenes in a less obvious way.

PREPARING FOR THE CULTURAL FESTIVAL

IT'S IRRESPONSIBLE!!
I WISH I COULD SEE THE FACE OF WHOEVER'S BEHIND THIS.
HEY, YUN-YUN! ABOUT THE PLAN FOR THE CAMPFIRE AND FIREWORKS THAT I SUGGESTED...
OH!
DID IT NOT GO THROUGH?!

SO IT WAS YOU, YOU BASTARD.
AGAH!

Kakeru Manabe: the man who spread idiotic rumors about this year's Cultural Fest featuring a campfire and a hundred fireworks.

MEETING PREPARATIONS(?)

I found you, Yun-Yun! ♡
HURRY TO KAKERU. OOPSIE! DID I MAKE A BOO-BOO? ♡
GRR... I AM SERIOUSLY REALLY PISSED!

Even though there's still plenty of time before the meeting, Kimi uses the PA system to call Yuki. And she does it in the most provocative possible way, as if she were the "other woman".

真鍋翔
Kakeru Manabe

But...
DON'T LET THAT AFFECT YOUR OPINION OF ME. LET'S BE FRIENDS!
THANKS FOR SEE- ING ME

...WELL?

"WE DON'T REALLY NEED TO GO BACK IF WE LOOK COOL WITH THE WRONG BUTTONS PUSHED."

Other people's words to Kakeru

"There's something about him. Something about Manabe's manner that reminds me of someone. This manner that causes every fiber of my being to scream out in rejection...He's oblivious to the fact that his words and actions grate on others... Agh! He's just like him!!!" [Yuki]
"To be honest...it's exhausting working with him. He acts a lot like Nii-san. But also, to some degree, he resembles him [Kyo]." [Yuki]
"Is it because he's actually very nice?" [Yuki]

Kakeru Quote Collection

THAT ...ADE ME ...HAPPY.

"Where should I stand so I can see the same thing? If I could make myself see from their viewpoint, maybe I could understand other people's feelings before I hurt them?" [→Yuki]
"If you're not going to be nice all the way or comfort her all the way, I think it would be much friendlier to leave her alone from the beginning. Anyway, if someone says something mean to you, you could just say something back. Not being able to say anything back puts you at fault, too." [→Yuki]

An irrepressible character who says he joined the student council because he liked the sound of "School Defense Force". It's impossible to tell if he's serious or irresponsible. His pushy, overwhelming personality is a lot like Ayame's.

He has a girlfriend?!

Oh
YOU HAVE A GIRLFRIEND...?
I DO. I DO.
JUST ONE GIRL. SHE'S AWFUL CUTE.
I REALLY LOVE HER!

He doesn't seem like the romantic sort, but he actually has a girlfriend. He describes her fondly to Yuki, and seems to only have eyes for her.

Perpetrator of a nickname

He's the affable sort who will cheerfully talk to anyone. He quickly warms up to Yuki, and is responsible for Yuki's "lovely" nickname.

Oh!
THERE YOU ARE...
YUN-YUUUUN!!
OF COURSE HE'D BE THE ONE...

A HISTORY WITH TOHRU

SO YOU HAVE NOTHING TO WORRY ABOUT. I'M NOT AFTER HONDA-SAN.
I HAVE A DIFFERENT REASON FOR ASKING ABOUT HER, I GUESS...
EH?
BUT I'M SURE I WON'T BE THE LAST PERSON TO ASK ABOUT HER.
AS FOR THE REASON, I'LL PUT OFF TELLING YOU...
...A LITTLE LONGER.
IS THAT BAD?

Kakeru is curious about Tohru, but he's not ready to explain why. His side of the story isn't the only one that needs to be told.

Kakeru says he's met Tohru before, and that meeting weighs on his mind. But he still won't talk about the circumstances of their meeting. Saki remembers him, so it must have happened during or after middle school, but Tohru herself doesn't remember it.

INDEPENDENCE FROM HIS PARENTS

Kakeru is his father's eldest son, but is the child of a mistress; Machi is the child of his father's legal wife, but she's a girl. Their mothers raised them very strictly, focusing on the issue of the succession. But Kakeru washed his hands of the whole mess and struck off on his own. That kind of strength is something Yuki has always wanted.

AFTER THAT...
...I THINK MY MOTHER CAME TO HER SENSES, TOO, BECAUSE SHE PULLED OUT OF THE SUCCESSION DEBATE.
AND I WAS OFFICIALLY FREE!
AND SO, THAT BRINGS US TO THE PRESENT.

Realizing he'd been placed in an untenable position, Kakeru chose to opt out altogether.

IF I LOOK COOL WHEN I PRESS MYSELF HERE...
UNCOOL!!

When Yuki says that his relationship with his parents is one where they all push each other's buttons the wrong way, Kakeru laughs and says it's fine as long as they look cool. It helps if you can laugh off what can't be changed.

"I SEE...IT MIGHT BE THAT MACHI'S NOT 'FREE' YET."

He is impressed and exasperated by the serious way Yuki thinks and worries about his parents, and about love.

WHERE SHOULD I STAND...
...SO I CAN SEE THE SAME THING?
IF I COULD MAKE MYSELF SEE FROM THEIR VIEWPOINT...
...MAYBE I COULD UNDERSTAND OTHER PEOPLE'S FEELINGS...
...BEFORE I HURT THEM?

Kakeru infuriates Yuki by saying that Kyo seems happier than he does. The fight helps Kakeru recognize his own faults, and he envies Yuki's kindness.

YOU REALLY ARE A GOOD GUY.

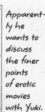

Apparently he wants to discuss the finer points of erotic movies with Yuki.

"......YOU'RE LUCKY. YOU'RE LUCKY, YUKI...YOU UNDERSTAND."

FRIENDS WHO CAN BE HONEST WITH EACH OTHER

OH MY GOD, NO WAY, YUN-YUN!
SOMETHING DIRTY?
NO!! I MEAN EMOTIONALLY PAINFUL!

Kakeru is always open about his emotions with Yuki. That honesty draws Yuki's real feelings out in return, and eventually Kakeru becomes a friend Yuki feels comfortable discussing his fears with.

倉伎真知

Machi Kuragi

"IS THE ONE NOT PARTICIPATING IN THIS WORLD ME? AM I NEEDED? AM I A NECESSARY BEING?"

......っ

Other People's Words to Machi

"Saying you won't do it anymore doesn't solve the problem. Both parties have to understand why you do it." [Yuki]
"Really, what are you thinking...? You don't change, do you, Machi? It's because you're like that that everyone thinks your dull and won't talk to you." [Machi's Mother]
"That surprised me...That was the first time I've seen Machi like that. She got all red and mad." [Kakeru]
"But I see. So Machi...likes red huh~~" "Eeehh~? What? Machi, could it be..." [Kakeru/Kimi]

Machi Quote Collection

"No, I don't. The president isn't at all like a prince."
"'What color do you like?' The moment he asked me that, I suddenly didn't understand what I was being asked, who the person in front of me was, what I' was."
"I thought you wouldn't like being alone and discouraged in there."
"I don't really understand 'this word.' I don't even understand 'me.'"

Kakeru's younger half sister, and the Council's treasurer. Growing up, her mother's competition with Kakeru's mother put her under a lot of pressure. Her mother required such compliance from her that Machi grew unable to assert herself--she even has trouble naming a favorite color. She now lives alone in an apartment.

Obstinacy

A difficult girl who can't express her emotions. If anyone manages to guess what she's feeling, she automatically tells them they're wrong.

HUNH.
I KINDA, WANNA ASK. BUT I ALSO KINDA DON'T.
ASK.
TAKE THE RISK.
THE SHORT VERSION HERE...
...IS THAT MACHI IS BEING INFLEXIBLE!
THE SHORT VERSION TELLS ME JACK.
WAIT A SEC.
IS THAT THE LEAF YUN-YUN GAVE YOU?
IT'S NONE OF YOUR BUSINESS, MANABE!
IT'S NOT!
YOU'RE WRONG--BUT YOU'RE NOT, ACTUALLY!
WHICH IS IT, MACHI?

A chaotic room

Machi reacts badly when things are too orderly. Perfection reminds her that she was expected to be perfect. She also can't handle brand new things.

...NO.
NOTHING'S CHANGED.
HAVE YOU MADE ANY FRIENDS?
HOW'S KAKERU-KUN DOING?
ARE YOU GETTING ALONG?

A ME WITH NOTHING

Machi exhausted herself studying, trying to meet her parents' expectations, but they lost interest in her after her younger brother was born. She loved her brother dearly, but her parents believed that she hated him...so they drove her out of the house.

"WHAT COLORS I LIKE, WHAT PLACE I LIKE--I DON'T KNOW. I HAVEN'T EVEN THOUGHT ABOUT IT. I'M ONLY DESPERATE TO ANSWER PEOPLE'S EXPECTATIONS. BUT I WAS ABANDONED."

IT'S TRUE, I GUESS.
"I AM "DULL."

When her mother tells her she's dull, she doesn't argue.

SAYING YOU "WON'T DO IT ANYMORE"...
...DOESN'T SOLVE THE PROB-LEM.
BOTH PARTIES HAVE TO UNDER-STAND...
...WHY YOU DO IT.

When Machi mechanically apologizes and says she won't do it again, Yuki offers to help her figure out her reasons and solve the problem.

...NEEDED IN THIS WORLD?

Machi feels like an incomplete doll, as if she is totally disengaged from the world.

WHAT FREES AN IMPRISONED HEART.

YUKI!
YES.
LONELY.
AND HE MAKES THINGS...
HE'S ALWAYS SURROUNDED BY PEOPLE.
AND HE'S KNOWN AS "PRINCE CHARMING."

WHEN YUKI'S FANS HARASS HER, MACHI SAYS THAT YUKI ISN'T LIKE A PRINCE AT ALL.

"Every time he was treated like a prince, 'loneliness' would eat away at him, it seemed."

clank
!
ARE YOU ALL RIGHT?

Machi and Yuki are fundamentally alike, so she was able to recognize his loneliness before they even got to know each other. But Yuki is trying to change, and watching his efforts slowly attracts her to him.

Machi rescues Yuki when he gets locked in the equipment room, because she knows how lonely and frightened he must be.

......!
I...
I'M NOT TAKING CARE OF IT!
HUH?

Machi is so embarrassed when Yuki finds out she's carefully preserved the maple leaf he gave her that she tries to insist on returning it.

Prince Yuki Club Operations

Rumor has it that half of the female students are members of the Prince Yuki Club. On the surface, it looks like a Yuki fan club...but it's really a group that exists so the members can keep an eye on each other and make sure no one steals him.

FOUNDER AND PRESIDENT
Third-year, Motoko Minagawa

ANYTHING!?
NO, NOTHING!

A classmate of Tohru's who constantly picks fights with her, and has been on the receiving end of Saki's poisonous waves. She played the Wicked Stepmother during the Cultural Festival.

SECOND-YEAR REPRESENTATIVE
Second-year, Minami Kinoshita

A simple soul, who hasn't yet caught on that Yuki will no longer be at the school by the time she's president. She's very self-absorbed.

MORE IMPORTANTLY ?!!
WHAT DID YOU DO FOR YOUR SUMMER VACATION?

FIRST-YEAR REPRESENTATIVE
First-year, Mio Yamagishi

THIRD-YEAR MEMBER
Third-year, Rika Aida

THERE'S NO LOCK IN THE SCHOOL...
...THAT I CAN'T OPEN!!

Motoko's friend, who has mastered the impressive technique of opening any lock in the school with just a single pin.

The Prince Yuki's Club's unspoken, unbreakable rule is, "Don't steal him, bitch!!" Because of that, their written rules are very strict: 1) Do not steal Prince Charming's private property. 2) Do not go inside the Prince's house. 3) When you talk to him, you must have someone with you. Living with him is beyond inexcusable!

Main Operations of the Prince Yuki Club

SCHOOL TRIP BODYGUARDS

During the school trip, which is traditionally a chance for people to confess their love to each other, Yuki was unmolested because club members were protecting him from the shadows.

...We, the Prince Yuki Club, are protecting you!
If we give into our feelings and confess our love, then none of us win, so we remain vigilant!
Oh... But I want to beat everyone to him, really...

GATHERING INFORMATION ON THE STUDENT COUNCIL MEMBERS

After it's established that Yuki will be the next ASB president, Motoko and the others start worrying that there will be girls in his student council. They pester Takei about it every day.

ALL I'M ASKING IS IF THERE ARE WOMEN ON THE NEW COUNCIL.
THAT'S THE ONLY POINT THAT WE ARE CONCERNED WITH!!
I SEE...

TOHRU EXTERMINATION POLICY

Their first plan of attack for exterminating Tohru, who has suddenly become very close to Yuki-kun, is to eliminate Saki Hanajima's protection of her. They begin by trying to learn Saki's weaknesses.

NO MATTER WHAT IT TAKES, WE MUST FIND THE DEMON'S WEAKNESS...
...AND USE THAT WEAKNESS TO SEAL HER POISONOUS WAVES!!

Enemies of the Prince Yuki Club

BUT THE WITCH IS PROTECTED BY A DEMON LORD WITH TREMENDOUS POWERS...
YES...
A DEMON WHO CONTROLS ELECTRO-POISON DENPA WAVES!!

THE DEMON LORD (SAKI HANAJIMA) AND THE WITCH (TOHRU HONDA)

Tohru Honda may be a witch who has deceived Yuki-kun, but at least she's human. The truly terrifying one is Saki Hanajima, a demon lord who protects her with inhumanly powerful wave attacks!

WH-WH-WH-WH-WHAT THE HELL IS THIS?! WHO DO YOU THINK YOU ARE?!
UM...
YOU SHOW UP ALL OF A SUDDEN AND, INSTEAD OF ADDRESSING YUKI BY HIS PROPER NAME, YOU CALL HIM YU-YU-YU--!!
DON'T YOU KNOW IT ANNOYS HIM TO BE CALLED STRANGE THINGS?!
OR MAYBE YOU'RE JUST TRYING TO MAKE US JEALOUS?!
AH...OH NO. I'M SCARED.
YOU SAW RIGHT THROUGH ME, DIDN'T YOU?

KIMI TODO

Almost every boy with a pulse is entranced by Kimi, whose lovely face and voice drive them mad. It's unbearable to imagine a woman like that being part of the new student council, and seeing Yuki-kun every day...!

Prince Charming Mode
"Prince Yuki" is the name for the Yuki Sohma fan club that exists within Kaibara High School.
They say its membership includes more than half the female student body!
And so the club rules are strict and absolute.
Anyone who disobeys (even if they're not in the club) may or may not receive harsh punishment!!
Their club mission statement is "Let us all extol, love, and protect the Prince who has graced our school with his presence"...
...but what they really mean is, "Don't steal him, bitch!!"
OUR CLUB CAN NO LONGER TURN A BLIND EYE TO THESE COUNTLESS TRANSGRESSIONS. NOW THAT MY SENIORS HAVE GRADUATED, I CAN FINALLY ENFORCE THE RULES PROPERLY...
TOHRU HONDA MUST BE PUNISHED!

CLUB MISSION STATEMENT:

"LET US ALL EXTOL, LOVE, AND PROTECT THE PRINCE, WHO HAS GRACED OUR SCHOOL WITH HIS PRESENCE."

LOVE THAT MAKES A HEART UGLY

Motoko loves frilly things like lace and ribbons, rattles off poetry when she's excited, and lives at the Minagawa Vegetable Shop.

NO, IT'S SOMETHING ELSE.
THAT IS THE SPARKLE OF A PRINCE.
IT'S YUKI'S NATURAL LIGHT.

"...MY FOOLISH, SELFISH, ARROGANT RIVALS. BUT THE FLAWS I SEE IN OTHERS ARE REALLY JUST REFLECTIONS OF THE FLAWS I SEE IN MYSELF."

MOTOKO MINAGAWA

Motoko, the president of the Prince Yuki Club, seems lighthearted at first glance--but she loves Yuki more earnestly than anyone. She doesn't know the real Yuki, or how much he's suffered, but even she realizes that Tohru's influence has changed him dramatically.

STAY AWAY FROM YUKI.
STOP MEDDLING!!

Yuki tells Motoko that her polite manner of speech is cute. But she understands who he's thinking about when he says it.

School Functions

WE'VE SEEN TWO MAJOR FUNCTIONS AT KAIBARA HIGH: THE CLASS TRIP AND THE CULTURAL FESTIVAL. BOTH THE FIRST- AND SECOND-YEAR CULTURAL FESTIVALS ARE IMMORTAL-IZED HERE.

Class Trip

TYPICAL DESTINATIONS: KYOTO AND NARA

Instead of going everywhere with the entire class, students can wander around freely with their friends. But they're not allowed to stop and buy food.

1

DISAGREEMENTS ABOUT PREPARATIONS AND GROUP MEMBERS

AAGH! DAMMIT, NOW I DEFINITELY REFUSE!
KYO, YOU DUMMKOPF!!
rub rub rub
rub
rub rub
YOU GET TO GO WITH TOHRU. YOU SHOULDN'T BE SO SELFISH!!
I WISH I COULD GO WITH TOHRU!
HEY...
I WANT TO EAT DEER SENBEI* WITH HER!
YOU SHOULDN'T EAT THOSE.
DON'T YOU WANT TO, KYO? OR DO YOU EVEN HATE BEING WITH TOHRU?!

After Arisa tells Kyo, "It's more fun with you there. That way I can mess with you," he gets dragged into their group.

2

A CLASS TRIP MEANS...(PART 1)

A CLASS TRIP IS A ROMANTIC EVENT!! I MEAN, THAT'S THE ONLY REASON ANYONE GOES ON THOSE TRIPS, RIGHT?! ROMANCE!
YOUNG PEOPLE LEFT ON THEIR OWN CONFESS THEIR LOVE AND ARE CONFESSED TO, AND EXPERIENCE THEIR FIRST--
HEY, LISTEN TO ME!!
AND SO, WITH SHIGURE-SAN'S ENCOURAGE-MENT...

Shigure claims that a class trip is a series of romantic escapades. On his high school class trip, some of his classmates caused trouble by sneaking out of their hotel and going to the red light district.

3

A CLASS TRIP MEANS...(PART 2)

OUR CLASS TRIP HAS BEGUN!
...THIS ISN'T REALLY THE TYPE OF PLACE TO VISIT IN LARGE GROUPS?
IT KINDA KILLS THE ATMOSPHERE.
MAYBE SO, BUT THIS IS A CLASS TRIP--THERE'S NOT MUCH WE CAN DO ABOUT IT.
DON'T YOU THINK...
IT PAINS ME THAT I CANNOT FREELY TRY THE FOOD AT VARIOUS RESTAURANTS
I want to eat nishin soba*
YOU'RE HUNGRY?

Arisa insists that places like temples should be visited in smaller groups, while Saki complains about not being able to stop and snack. These valuable insights strike at the roots of the school trip.

4

THEY INCORRECTLY RECITE HAIKU.

LET US MAKE A FINE COUNTRY THE KAMAKURA SHOGUNATE...
THAT'S NOT A HAIKU.
THIS ISN'T KAMAKURA.

An elegant setting calls for poetry recitation, but this isn't Kamakura. And the second attempt--"Sing, nightingale, in the Heian capital."--isn't haiku, either!

5

LOVE CONFESSION TIME!

IF YOU GO OUT WITH ME, YOU MIGHT GROW TO LIKE ME!
YOU CAN LEARN MY NAME NOW!
THEY'RE REALLY GOING AT IT!
A FIGHT SCENE?
THAT KYON IS CLEARLY MAKING A FACE LIKE HE DOESN'T LIKE HER.
I TOLD YOU...
I DON'T EVEN KNOW YOUR NAME.
I DON'T LIKE YOU OR ANYTHING.

A girl takes Kyo aside and tries to force her love on him. He almost flies off the handle at her for insisting she loves him when she knows nothing about him.

Intermission for Buying Food

6

ALONE WITH KYO-KUN...

...YOU WANNA KILL SOME TIME...
...WITH ME?
OKAY ...!

During some free time, Tohru and Kyo are able to be alone. Tohru is worried that he might push her away someday, but his casual words and smile make her feel better.

7

DAY TWO: YUKI'S AWAKENING

SNAP
YOU WERE PROBABLY BROUGHT UP AS A SPOILED LITTLE RICH GIRL...
Good grief.
YUKI'S AWAKE!!
GOOD JOB, NABE!!
NABE, YOU'RE THE BEST!!
GO EAT BREAKFAST NOW, ALL OF YOU!
OW! OW!! I'M SORRY, I WAS WRONG!! I MEANT "BOY"! "SPOILED LITTLE BOY"!!
EITHER WAY, YOU'RE MAKING FUN OF ME.

Yuki-kun doesn't deal well with mornings. In his stupor, he alarms his classmates by walking face-first into a sliding door. But it's also possible that he's even stronger when he's half-asleep...

8

FAILING TO FEED THE ANIMAL

Here, deery deery deery...
WHEN YOU FEED ANIMALS, YOU HAVE TO BE PATIENT...
YEAH...
"YEAH" MY BUTT!
HEY...
I DON'T REALLY WANT TO ASK, BUT WHAT ARE YOU DOING, YANKEE?
OH NO!

A new approach to dealing with Kyo: they take a hint from how friendly the Nara Park deer are with humans. But ume-konbu probably isn't the best bait to use on him.

9

A SOUVENIR.

IT'S A SOUVENIR FOR MYSELF.
I RAN OUT AND BOUGHT IT A WHILE AGO.
I'll do my best!
IF I BUY SOME PAPIER-MACHE, IT WILL BE ALMOST COMPLETE!
PAPIER-MACHE?
YUKI-KUN, HAVE YOU THOUGHT OF WHAT YOU'RE GOING TO BUY FOR YOURSELF?
FOR MY-SELF?
I... HAVEN'T...

The souvenir that Tohru bought was a set of Zodiac ornaments. She adds to it by making a Cat ornament out of paper mâché, and winds up with a Juusanshi collection.

10

SOUVENIRS FOR THE STUDENT COUNCIL

FOR YOU, MACHI.
HERE.
A SOUVENIR.

For the student council, who said they didn't need souvenirs, Yuki brings back red maple leaves. Machi makes hers into a bookmark.

Intermission for Buying Food

Cultural Festival

PROGRAM: CLASS 2 - D, PERFORMING "SORTA CINDERELLA"

Class 2 - D won the use of the stage in a draw, so they decided to put on a play. They held another draw to choose the play, and wound up with "Cinderella". But they voted on the casting--and the result was the unlikely pairing of Saki as Cinderella and Kyo as Prince Charming. But the strangest thing was the decision to cast Tohru as the wicked stepsister.

◆THE "SORTA CINDERELLA" STORY

Once upon a time, there was a self-important girl named Cinderella, who loved pure black dresses. She has a fairy...guardian make dresses so she can get her beloved stepsister back from her stepmother. And then, for no reason other than to advance the plot, she finds that she has to go to the palace...

1

PREPARATION: REWRITING THE SCRIPT

A JAPANESE CHARLIE'S ANGELS...!
FULL THROTTLE.
I DOUBT IT WOULD GET PAST THE BOARD OF EDUCATION.
SO IS THERE A BATH SCENE WITH CHARACTERS OTHER THAN OGIN-SAN IN IT?!

Since rehearsals are going nowhere fast, they decide to rewrite the story. (The class that's doing "Mito Koumon" also did some heavy adaptation, so that Koumon-sama and company were all women.)

2

PREPARATION: MAKING THE COSTUMES

Please, make my dress pure black.
PURE BLACK?!
IT'S "PURE WHITE"!
NOT THAT IT MATTERS... BUT YOU CAN'T, CINDERELLA!

Ayame and Mine are in charge of costumes. When Mine arrives at the school, Saki asks her to make Cinderella's dress pure black.

3

CULTURAL FESTIVAL--ENTRANCE GATE

Kaibara Public HIGH SCHOOL Cultural Festival
Women
Delicate
Men
...IS THAT SUPPOSED TO LOOK LIKE A RANSOM NOTE?

The entrance alone makes Hiro suspicious: its cut-out letters make him think of a ransom note, and the signs reading "men", "delicate", and "women" are just...weird. It's hard to say who thought that was a good idea, or whether the student council even approved it.

4

THE CURTAIN RISES ON "SORTA CINDERELLA".

YOU CAN'T POSSIBLY EXPECT AN AMATEUR TO MAKE A DECENT DRESS.
BUT IF YOU'RE WILLING TO BE A LAUGHINGSTOCK, THEN I ACCEPT THE JOB.
I HAVE TO ADVANCE THE STORY, YOU LITTLE BRAT! BUT DON'T YOU DARE EMBARRASS ME!
MORE IMPORTANTLY, ONEE-SAMA... WOULD YOU LIKE SOME TEA?
May I?
NO MORE FRIVOLITIES FOR YOU!
THAT'S AN... INTERESTING CINDERELLA.

A Cinderella with an attitude, talking back to her stepmother--this is no meek fairytale heroine! (The stepmother's reaction is a little unexpected, too.)

5

CINDERELLA'S WISH (PART 1)

When her fairy guardian offers her a wish, Cinderella makes a shocking request. Apparently her dear stepsister and yakiniku are the only things on her twisted little mind.

SHLOCK
BURN THE PALACE DOWN.
I'M AFRAID THAT'S A CRIME. PLEASE WISH FOR SOMETHING SOFTER, MORE PURE.

I WISH FOR DELICIOUS YAKINIKU.
THAT'S NOT WHAT I MEANT.

6

A MOODY PRINCE CHARMING

WHAT ARE YOU BROODING ABOUT, SUNSHINE? WE THREW THIS GIANT THING FOR YOU.
NOW GO PICK A LADY.
SHUT UP, WILL YOU? I ALREADY SAID I'M NOT INTERESTED.
NO WONDER YOU'RE A VIRGIN.
TAKE A TRIP TO THE STORE AND BUY YOURSELF SOME DIGNITY!
What was that?
I'M WORRIED ABOUT YOU, YOU STUPID LUG, AND THIS IS MY THANKS? GO BUY YOURSELF SOME COURTESY!
YOU'RE SHAMELESS, YOU INFURIATING SACK OF SKIN!
DESPITE THE GENTLE PERSUASION OF HIS FELLOW PRINCE, PRINCE CHARMING COULD NOT BE CONVINCED TO DANCE.

Prince Charming's total lack of interest in looking for his bride leads to some crude commentary by his friend, played by Arisa.

7

THE STEPSISTER'S INVITATION

PRINCE CHARMING? WOULD YOU DANCE WITH–
NO!
THEN MIGHT YOU BE BOTHERED TO SHARE A DANCE WITH–
I SAID NO! FIND SOMEBODY ELSE!
–ME? IGNORE HER.
OH...
I SEE.
I BEG YOUR PARDON.
PRIN–
I'M NOT DANCING, DAMMIT!
WAI–
HE ALSO, OF COURSE, REFUSED TO DANCE WITH THE STEPSISTER.
REFUSED TO DANCE WITH THE STEPSISTER...

When the stepsister timidly asks him to dance, Prince Charming automatically turns her down. When he realizes what he's done, he gets really depressed.

8

CINDERELLA'S TRUE LOVE

I'M VERY BUSY RIGHT NOW.
DID YOU JUST COME HERE FOR THE MEAT?
On bottle: I live for meat.

Cinderella has arrived at the Ball, but she shows no interest whatsoever in Prince Charming or in dancing. All she wants to do is eat yakiniku.

9

HANDING OFF THE GLASS SLIPPER

NOW YOU CAN'T SAY I NEVER GAVE IT TO YOU.
UH... RIGHT. NO OFFENSE...
...BUT YOU HAVE NO EMOTIONS.

When the clock strikes twelve, Cinderella gives the prince her slipper and leaves--but only because the script says so.

10

A...MARRIAGE PROPOSAL?

ARGH!
WHY WOULD I... SHE'S NOT... ARE YOU STUPID?! OF COURSE NOT!
BUT I...NO! THAT'S NOT...
THAT IS KINDA WHY WE'RE HERE, PRINCE.
THEN YOU'RE HERE FOR ME? THAT'S RATHER NIGHTMARISH.
THAT'S MORE LIKE HELL THAN A NIGHTMARE TO ME!
And stop looking like you'd be the one put out!

Prince Charming sets out to find Cinderella, using the glass slipper. But the two of them wind up fighting about which of them is more horrified by the idea of their marriage!

11

CINDERELLA'S WISH (PART 2)

Cinderella's dearest wish is to manage a yakiniku shop with her stepsister. Right to the end, meat is on her mind.

SO I WILL ASK ONE MORE TIME.
WHAT IS IT YOU TRULY WISH FOR?
I WANT TO MANAGE A YAKINIKU SHOP WITH ONEE-SAMA.
SHE'LL NEVER LET THAT DIE.
MEAT...

MORAL

Women Don't Need To Get Married To Live Fulfilled Lives!

Cultural Festival

PROGRAM: CLASS 1 – D RAN AN "ONIGIRI SHOP"

Class 1 - D follows Yuki's suggestion of running an onigiri shop with "surprise" onigiri! Since Tohru is good at cooking, she is one of the people in charge of making the onigiri. She tackles it with enthusiasm, and even spends time at home researching the surprise ingredients.

1

PREPARATION: CHOOSING INGREDIENTS

Tohru suggests three-flavored onigiri, but Minami rejects the idea. Next, Kyo comes up with Battle Onigiri: combat to defend the right to eat onigiri! ...or something. His idea is also shot down, for some reason.

HOW ABOUT WE HAVE BATTLE ONIGIRI!
BATTLE?!
A ONE-ON-ONE MATCH.
WEAPONS ARE ALLOWED, BUT NO KILLING...
...DELIBERATE BLOOD-SPILLING OR TRYING TO CUT OFF SOMEONE'S ARM.
NO.
DEFENDING HONOR AND YOUR RIGHT TO EAT ONIGIRI IN ONE GLORIOUS FIGHT!

2

CULTURAL FESTIVAL: GRAND OPENING

ALREADY, THE DAY OF THE FESTIVAL IS HERE.
THIS IS GREAT!
WE'RE REALLY SELLING A LOT!
WE MIGHT TAKE FIRST PLACE IN THE FOOD DIVISION.
THANK YOU VERY MUCH!
BECAUSE ONIGIRI ARE EASY TO EAT.

The cheap and convenient onigiri are very popular! The class sells so many that they think they might win first place in the food division.

3

CAT ONIGIRI = SUPER POPULAR

Tohru's Cat onigiri are popular, too. She considered making Rat-san onigiri as well, but that idea was thrown out.

THE ONIGIRI YOU MOLDED TASTE GREAT, HONDA-SAN.
EH?!
TH-THAT'S NOT...
THIS CAT ONIGIRI IS ADORABLE.

4

A WAY TO ATTRACT CUSTOMERS (?)

......
CAN'T YOU TELL YUKI-KUN DOESN'T LIKE IT?
WELL, YEAH, BUT HE'S...
THAT'S RIGHT.
OHMA-KUN, NABLE TO EFUSE A QUEST OF HE THIRD-YEAR TUDENTS...
IT'S ALREADY CAUSED AN UPROAR.

The third-year girls somehow talk a reluctant Yuki into wearing a pink dress. The sight attracts paying customers in droves, but Yuki himself is thoroughly unimpressed.

5

MOMIJI AND HATORI INVADE

Hatori and Momiji make a surprise appearance, and the class goes into a small uproar. It was Tohru's first meeting with Hatori.

...I SEE.
HATORI...
HEY!
?
YOU REALLY ARE A "NORMAL" GIRL...
DON'T CLIMB ON THE BOOTH!
WHAT ARE YOU DOING, YOU IDIOT?!

6

A PHOTOGRAPH OF YUKI IN A DRESS.

Hatori takes a picture of Yuki wearing the dress, because Akito asked for a photo of him.

MY LIFE IS OVER...
......
WHAT WILL AKITO SAY...
...WHEN HE SEES ME IN THIS OUTFIT?
Kya aaa ahh!
SOHMA-KUN, YOU'LL CATCH COLD!
YOUR TRACTOR- I MEAN, TRACHEA!

K N O W L E D G E

Furuba Trivia

WE'VE PUT TOGETHER SOME MISCELLANEOUS FACTS ABOUT THE WORLD OF *FURUBA*! (THEY MAY NOT BE ALL THAT USEFUL IN REAL LIFE.)

The Character Section

- **ONCE TOHRU FALLS ASLEEP, IT'S HARD TO WAKE HER UP.**
  She also talks and laughs in her sleep.
- **SHIGURE PICKED OUT TOHRU'S BED AND BOUGHT IT FOR HER.**
  When Uo-chan saw the fluffy--and expensive--double bed, she was so shocked that she blurted out, "He's acting like an old man with his first grandkid..."

The General (?) Knowledge Section

- **SAKI SAYS THAT THERE ARE NO RULES IN BADMINTON: YOU JUST HIT THE BIRDIE BACK AND FORTH AS HARD AS YOU CAN.**
- **TOHRU AND KYO DON'T KNOW WHO "JASON" IS.**
  Jason came up at the summer lake house, and was described as a "new type of bear". When Yuki tries to explain, Kyo doesn't listen--"Who gives a damn if some bear shows up in a horror movie?!!" (But if you'd listen, you'd know he's not--oh, well.)
- **HATSUHARU SAYS FAIRIES REALLY DO EXIST.**
  The "fairies" were actually the girls in his class.
- **HARU ALSO SAYS THAT YOU CAN DEAL WITH A SCARY HAUNTED HOUSE BY MAKING UP YOUR OWN STORIES ABOUT THE GHOSTS.**
  He explains that ghosts stop being scary if you feel like you know them.

Furuba Characters As Children

Tohru

Tohru hasn't changed since she was little. Kyoko once accidentally hit her in the face with a cabinet door, and Tohru only smiled--while blood dripped from her nose. (Kyoko fainted.)

I BONKED TOHRU IN THE FACE! I'M SO SORRY, TOHRU!
WHA?
DOES IT HURT? IT'S GOTTA HURT! MOMMY'S SORRY, BABY!
たらり。

TOHRU.

Yuki

Yuki was forced to attend an even more prestigious elementary school than the other Sohma children, because he was possessed by the Rat. It made him unbearably lonely.

THE BIRTH OF A CHILD SSESSED BY THE RAT...

Kyo

Kyo still went through hard times after Shishou took him in, but he smiled a lot more.

SHISHOU HELPED ME SO MUCH.

Shigure/Ayame/Hatori

The Mabudachi Trio were stars even in high school--especially Ayame, who had fun reforming the school during his tenure as ASB president. Along the way, he caused plenty of trouble for Hatori, his vice president.

LOOK!
TORI-SAN'S THERE, TOO.

Hatsuharu

Haru helped Isuzu after she collapsed in the street. After that, the two of them quickly became close.

HM...

- **YUKI'S FAVORITE FLAVOR OF NATTOU IS GROUND BARLEY.**
- **SHIGURE'S WHITE DAY GIFT TO TOHRU WAS ONE OF AYAME'S MAID OUTFITS.**

  She accepted it graciously, but Kyo and Yuki protested so much that she doesn't wear it. It's tucked away in her chest of drawers.
- **LIKE YUKI, SHIGURE ISN'T MUCH OF A MORNING PERSON. HE DOESN'T WAKE UP UNTIL LATE IN THE DAY.**

  Shigure became a novelist so he wouldn't have to stick to normal people's schedules. Oh, and Ayame is the kind of person who sleeps and wakes up whenever he wants to.
- **WHEN KYO FIRST MET KAGURA, HE WAS DRAWING FRIED EGGS BECAUSE HE'D HAD THEM FOR BREAKFAST.**
- **WHEN KYO AND HATSUHARU WERE IN ELEMENTARY SCHOOL, HARU COULDN'T EVEN FIND THE BATHROOM ON HIS OWN. KYO HAD TO TAKE HIM.**

  In the Sohma estate, you don't need to have Haru's sense of direction to get lost--Tohru got lost, too.
- **SHIGURE (PROBABLY) HAS A LICENSE**
- **THE SUIT SHIGURE WORE TO TOHRU'S PARENT-TEACHER CONFERENCE WAS HATORI'S. IT'S WORTH 300,000 YEN, OR ABOUT $2800.**

  When he wore it back to Hatori's to return it, Hatori told him to burn it. So Shigure cheerfully kept it (and hopefully got it cleaned).
- **SHIGURE WRITES BELLES LETTRES UNDER HIS REAL NAME, AND PUBLISHES A VARIETY OF OTHER BOOKS UNDER ASSORTED PEN NAMES.**

  A story from one of his scarier books plunged Yuki, Kyo, and Arisa into the depths of terror. It was about someone who found a cup of brown juice in the kitchen and drank it, before realizing what was inside..."Whoa, scary!"
- **HATSUHARU DRAGGED PRESIDENT TAKEI INTO THE BATHROOM TO PROVE THAT HE DOESN'T DYE HIS HAIR.**

  Once inside, Haru showed him hair that should only be seen in a bathroom, or--well. (We'll restrain ourselves from that train of thought.)
- **AYAME ONLY MAKES TEA FOR TWO PEOPLE OTHER THAN HATORI. EVEN IF HE MADE TEA FOR YUKI, IT WOULD GO TO WASTE.**

  The other two are probably Akito and Mine.
- **TO PROTECT HIMSELF FROM THE SUN, AYAME WEARS LONG SLEEVES IN THE SUMMER. HE BURNS EASILY.**
- **AYAME HAS HAD LONG HAIR SINCE HE WAS IN HIGH SCHOOL. WHEN A TEACHER GOT MAD ABOUT IT, AYAME DISTRACTED HIM BY ANNOUNCING THAT HE WAS A KING AND THAT HIS POSITION REQUIRED LONG HAIR.**

  He explained why the royal family kept their hair long: "The first king, the honorable Rurubara-sama, received a message when he reached the age of four."

Laugh your way through a haunted house!

LAUGHTER WILL BLOW AWAY MY FEAR!!
I'M L-L-LAUGHING, SEE... HA HA HA...!!
SHE'S REALL Y PUSHING HERSELF...
IF IT'S TOO MUCH, YOU CAN JUST LEAVE! HEY!!
HYAAAH!!
I'M...
I'M SCARED!!
YOU'RE WHAT'S SCARING ME...

Tohru, who can't handle her fear of haunted houses, thought of a way to survive the experience. It didn't work all that well.

A dangerous event: bare-handed watermelon smashing

GO FOR IT, HIRO. IT'LL BE A GOOD STORY FOR WHEN YOU'RE A BIG BROTHER.
I HAVE NO IDEA WHAT YOU'RE TALKING ABOUT...
DON'T SMASH IT WITH YOUR BARE HANDS AND THEN EAT IT!!

ONG ONG ONG
ARE YOU CRYING BECAUSE YOU COULDN'T BREAK IT, OR BECAUSE YOUR HAND HURTS?
CONGRATULA... TIONS...

A new tradition for celebrating pregnancy: smashing watermelons with your bare hands! "Go for it, Hiro. It'll be a good story for when you're a big brother!" (Shouldn't that be "bamboo"? Haru's playing with words.)

KNOWLEDGE

When there's something you want to say...

WHAT'S WRONG, KYO?
IS THERE SOMETHING YOU WANT TO TALK ABOUT?
EEP!
WHAT?! WHY DO YOU ASK?!
WHA?!
...STARING AT ME FROM BEHIND IF YOU WANTED TO TELL ME SOMETHING. SO...
SINCE YOU WERE LITTLE, YOU'VE HAD THE HABIT OF...
Play with me! Play with me!

When Kyo wants to talk to someone about something, he tends to stare at them from behind. Cats are like that.

The creepy stain that looks like a person.

I CAN SEE WHY YOU WERE SCARED. IT ALMOST LOOKS LIKE A FACE.
AH! I'M SORRY. MAYBE YOU'RE STILL SCARED OF IT...
OF COURSE I'M NOT!!
How old do you think I am?!

When Kyo was a little boy, he was so scared of a spot on Kazuma's kitchen wall that he cried. He thought it looked like a human face. The spot remains to this day.

Eating lunch in front of a grave

WH-?
DON'T EAT LUNCH IN FRONT OF A GRAVE!!!

When visiting the grave of someone like Kyoko, who liked lively surroundings, you bring boxed lunches. If you get in trouble, you can always apologize! However, this isn't normal behavior.

A suicide squad outfit is appropriate for visiting a grave.

To visit Kyoko's grave, Arisa wears the "Red Butterfly" suicide squad leader coat Kyoko gave her. Yuki, who still doesn't really understand who Kyoko was, is troubled.

I GOT THIS FROM KYOKO-SAN.
THE COAT OF THE LEADER OF THE RED BUTTERFLY SUICIDE SQUAD.
R-RED... BUTTER-FLY?

...It was from Kandora-sama, who illumines the four directions with gold and red light. When Kandora-sama chanted 'Ma rudu mani,' his forehead shone with a blue light and, like a pony struck by a whip Rurubara-sama's honorable person was liberated. With a wave of warm compassion, his..." (We don't want to waste the page, so we'll stop there.)

- **AYAME AND KAKERU ARE EMAIL BUDDIES.**

  They met each other at the high school, and hit it off right away.

- **ARISA GETS HAY FEVER.**

  It's pretty serious, since several pollens (not only cedar) trigger it.

- **KYOKO'S NICKNAME, "THE RED BUTTERFLY OF KANNANA", COMES FROM THE WAY HER BIKE'S RED TAIL LIGHTS DANCED LIKE BUTTERFLIES.**

  Uo-chan tried explaining it to Kyo, but he never quite got it no matter how she phrased it.

- **THE PROTOTYPE FOR OKAMI-SAN IS A GHOST WOMAN WHO APPEARED IN *TSUBASA O MOTSU MONO.***

  She made such an impression that it would have been a shame to not use her again, so she was revived.

- **HATORI IS THE TALLEST CHARACTER IN *FURUBA.***
- **MOST OF THE JUUNISHI'S NAMES COME FROM THE NAMES OF MONTHS.**

You can catch stag beetles in department stores

WHERE CAN YOU CATCH STAG BEETLES OTHER THAN AT A DEPARTMENT STORE?
......
ARE YOU FOR REAL?

At least, that's Momiji's theory! "Where can you catch stag beetles other than at a department store?" (Stag beetles are often found in kunugi trees.)

When three women set out, a murder mystery is sure to unfold.

Three women set out on a trip through Kyoto: home of hot springs, gourmet food, and murder... ("I think they've watched too many TV dramas...", Yuki notes.) The mystery's climax will happen on the edge of a cliff, while a strong wind blows. Tune in next time!

AND THEN, A MURDER MYSTERY WILL OCCUR...
EHH ?!!
I THINK THEY'VE WATCHED TOO MANY TV DRAMAS...
GOING ON A TRIP WITH EVERY-ONE

Stories within Furuba

Mogeta (animated TV series)

Today is the day, once again. Yes it's true! Ari's taking a walk with Mogeta!
(Aritamis Donpanina Taios is long, so it's always abbreviated)
Today is the day, and you know he can't lose! That mysterious creature, Mogeta!*
Sometimes--well, rarely--when they remember--they fight scaaaary enemies.
Today's enemy
*This is the Mogeta anime theme song...more or less...

The mysterious Mogeta and Ari have a startling backstory! Aritamis Donpanina Taios (Ari for short) is a miser, and--shockingly--Mogeta is a girl!

MOGETA: THE LAST CRUSADE
RIGHT ABOUT NOW, THEY SHOULD BE ENJOYING A MOVIE...
Only WE can save the world!
MOGETA, NO!!
DON'T GIVE IN TO THE FORCES OF EVIL!!
MOGET...
...TAAA!!

*There is a simple version of the story in the written interview.

An anime that has appeared several times within Furuba. It's so popular that it's been made into a movie--Tohru and Yuki, and Kagura and Kyo, went to see the movie on their double date. Kisa and Hiro are fans, too. The storyline is...let's say it's kind of surreal.

Summer-Colored Sigh (novel)

Summer-Colored Sigh has a sequel! Shigure releases other kinds of books that annoy people under different names.

YOU LIKE?
IT MAKES ME SICK.

A novel Shigure published through Hanajiro Novels, under the name Noa Kiritani. He writes his main work, which is more literary, under his real name. His titles include *Heartthrob* and *In the Moonlight*.

The Most Foolish Traveler in the World (short story)

Found in *A Collection of Funny Stories*. Momiji's classmates all laughed when a boy brought the story to class, but....

AS THE MONSTER MUNCHED ON HIS EYES...
...HE SAID, "THANK YOU, THANK YOU. I'LL GIVE YOU THIS IN RETURN." AND LEFT HIM.
"THANK YOU, THANK YOU."
BUT THAT WAS A LIE, TOO.
"THIS IS THE FIRST TIME ANYONE'S GIVEN ME ANYTHING. I'M SO HAPPY. THANK YOU, THANK YOU."
Fool
HIS GIFT WAS A SINGLE PIECE OF PAPER THAT HAD "FOOL" WRITTEN ON IT.

A short story Momiji read. In it, a foolish traveler loses all of his possessions because he believes the clever lies of the people he meets. Eventually, even his body is stolen. But the traveler never begrudges anything to anyone.

Bonus: The face of someone seeing something they hate

......
THAT'S IT!!
GIVE IT TO ME, MAYU-CHAN!! NICE DISGUSTED FACE!!
CLENCH

Shigure decides to attend Tohru's parent-teacher conference. His reason for taking her grandfather's place? He wants to see Mayuko-sensei make that very face!

Take care not to annoy people who give injections!

HAA-SAN......!
TAKING ADVANTAGE OF YOUR POOR, HELPLESS PATIENT... YOU'RE SO SADISTIC!
I KNEW YOU WERE DOING IT ON PURPOSE!
IT'S YOUR FAULT FOR COMPLAINING SO MUCH.

Hatori has been known to deliberately give Shigure injections in painful spots, because Shigure was too loud and obnoxious. Haa-san's scary!

It's not safe to say your real name

FOR YOUR SAFETY, I SUGGEST YOU DO NOT SPEAK YOUR REAL NAMES IN THIS HOUSE.

For your own safety, it's better not to casually say your real name inside the Hanajima house. Knowing your name gives Megumi the power to curse you. His curses take effect after three days.

GALLERY

Monochrome Chapter Intro Page Gallery

[WE'VE COLLECTED SOME OF THE CHAPTER INTRO PAGES THAT LOOK AS IF THEY'RE TELLING A STORY!]

GALLERY

Chapter 52 intro page. This was the chapter when Kazuma invites Tohru and Kyo-kun to have lunch at his house.

ARTIST'S COMMENT

In this picture, Kyo wants to play in the snow; Shishou-san is being motherly and making him wear a scarf so he won't catch cold.

ARTIST'S COMMENT

I remember my editor asking me, "What are they doing?" (laugh). The two of them are weeding the garden.

Chapter 50 intro page. Arisa meets Kureno again in this chapter-- and Yuki and Kyo aren't in it at all. So this intro page has a lot to do with fan service.

第50話

The intro page for chapter 53, when Momiji invites Tohru to the summer beach house. When he said, "We have to catch some!" he meant stag beetles, but they wound up catching kabuto beetles.

ARTIST'S COMMENT

The truth is, I can't stand bugs at all. I used an encyclopedia for reference while I drew this cicada, and it almost made me cry while I was drawing (laugh).

第55話

Chapter 55 intro page. This is the chapter where Hiro tells Tohru she has a mother complex, and shakes her to the core. Her happy expression in this picture is painfully tragic.

ARTIST'S COMMENT

Mother and child watching the stars together. I remember not being able to make their sitting positions look natural, and drawing it again and again.

The intro page for chapter 61, when Isuzu (the Horse) and Tohru first meet. Fans were shocked that Isuzu was shown completely naked.

ARTIST'S COMMENT

Two of the characters who very suddenly gave Furuba a more mature atmosphere (I think). They have a very delicate relationship.

第61話

Chapter 58 intro page. This was when Akito comes to the beach house, and Tohru tries to smash a watermelon with her bare hands.

ARTIST'S COMMENT

It's kind of Haru to give away the most delicious part of his cake, but it's bittersweet, too. That's what was on my mind as I was drawing.

The intro page for chapter 56, which looks back at Mayuko and Kana's past happiness, and the sad way things turned out.

ARTIST'S COMMENT

I wanted the lines to look more tucked in, but it wasn't meant to be. Oh, and Kana's hand isn't on Mayu's chest (laugh).

Chapter 64 intro page. This was the chapter where Akito flies into a rage and injures Tohru; Tohru also learns that Kyo is going to be confined.

ARTIST'S COMMENT

And Shigure is the third character...(laugh). Hatori-san has it rough. Thanks to Shigure-san, he does nothing but worry. Do your best (laugh)!

第64話

The intro page for chapter 83--the momentous chapter when "Sorta Cinderella" was born! Yuki also went through a significant change.

ARTIST'S COMMENT

For this intro page, the image came to me first. While I was drawing it, I thought, "I wonder if I can't express Yuki's emotions?"

Chapter 94 intro page. This chapter delves into Machi's suffering, and the ways she's changing. So Machi "likes red, huh~?" (laugh)

ARTIST'S COMMENT

It kind of matches Yuki's intro page: Japanese style and Western style. You get the impression both of them spent their childhoods in dark places, looking out at the world.

Chapter 4:
Fun and Games

CONTEST
MENTAL GAME
QUIZ
FORTUNE
GAME OF LIFE

We're presenting the results of the reader contests held by Hana to
Yume magazine, along with a personality test, quizzes, fortune-telling,
a Game of Life, and other fun activities!

PRESENTING THE RESULTS OF THE CONTESTS HELD BY HANA TO YUME MAGAZINE! THANK YOU FOR ALL YOUR ENTRIES!

Furuba-themed Contest Results

You chose: Most Touching Lines

The series' most touching lines, according to your postcards!

(Volume 6) Tohru reaching out to Kyo, and easing his lifelong suffering, was the winner in this category!

"TOGETHER
I WANT US TO LIVE...
...EAT MEALS, STUDY...
...SHARE OUR TROUBLES...
...LIKE WE DID BEFORE...
TOGETHER.
I WANT TO STAY TOGETHER!!
I'M BEING...
...SO SELFISH.
BUT DIDN'T...
...KYO-KUN TELL ME--

"TOGETHER. I WANT US TO LIVE...EAT MEALS, STUDY... SHARE OUR TROUBLES, LIKE WE DID BEFORE... TOGETHER. I WANT TO STAY TOGETHER......!!"

•READERS' COMMENTS•

"Tohru's feelings for Kyo really come through, especially when she says, 'I want us to live together.' She may not have meant much by it, but I don't think there's anything else she could have said at that moment that would have meant more to him." (P.N. Chie Yagata)

"This chapter conveys Kyo's whole spectrum of emotions, Tohru-kun's kindness, and Shishou-san's love. Kyo is so heartsick, and he's lost all hope; when Tohru-kun clings to him and cries, it really makes an impression." (P.N. Sarayo)

"Y...YOU...DON'T HAVE TO...LOVE EVERYTHING. IT'S OKAY IF YOU WERE SCARED. IT'S OKAY...THIS IS WHAT I WANTED ALL ALONG. TO HAVE SOMEONE TO SHARE MY WORRIES WITH. WHO WOULD SAY LET'S GO ON LIVING TOGETHER."

•READERS' COMMENTS•

"It made my heart ache--all I could think was, 'Kyo-kun, Kyo-kun, Kyo-kuuuun.'" (P.N. Kyo-kun LOVE ♥)

"There had been some scenes where Kyo treated Tohru coldly, but those words showed how he really felt. I cried!!" (P.N. Kanami Yuzuki)

Y...
YOU...
YOU DON'T HAVE TO...LOVE EVERYTHING.
IT'S OKAY...
...IF YOU WERE SCARED.
IT'S OKAY...

(Volume 6) In this touching scene, Kyo opened his heart to Tohru, who wanted to be with him even though she'd seen his monstrous form.

"YOU DON'T KNOW HOW SCARED SHE WAS THEN. SO HOW CAN YOU SAY THOSE THINGS...?!"

•READERS' COMMENTS•

"I felt like those words overflowed with Kyo-kun's emotions. There are other scenes where I cried, but this one made me cry hardest. I liked Kyo-kun even more." (P.N: Rumua Ma)

YOU DON'T KNOW HOW SCARED SHE WAS THEN!
SO HOW CAN YOU SAY THOSE THINGS?!

(Volume 11) When Akito belittles Tohru, Kyo-kun desperately contradicts her. But nothing he says reaches her.

(Volume 4) His mama got better after forgetting him. But Momiji doesn't hold it against her, and is moving on with his life.

•READERS' COMMENTS•

"I used to think that if someone I loved passed away, I would have been spared the pain by never knowing them at all. But when I heard these words, I realized it was better to face it without running away." (P.N. Gachapin)

I WANT TO...
...BELIEVE THAT.
BECAUSE I WANT TO THINK...
...THAT THERE'S NO SUCH THING...
...AS A MEMORY THAT'S OKAY TO FORGET.

"EVEN IF THEY'RE MEMORIES THAT I'D RATHER FORGET, IF I KEEP THEM AND KEEP TRYING WITHOUT RUNNING AWAY...IF I KEEP TRYING, THEN SOMEDAY... SOMEDAY I'LL BE STRONG ENOUGH THAT THOSE MEMORIES CAN'T DEFEAT ME. I BELIEVE THAT. I WANT TO BELIEVE THAT."

"IT BECOMES SPRING! NO MATTER HOW COLD IT IS NOW, SPRING WILL COME AGAIN! WITHOUT FAIL. IT'S STRANGE, ISN'T IT?"

(Volume 2) Hatori asks Tohru the same question Kana once asked him...and Tohru gives him the exact same answer.

NO MATTER HOW COLD IT IS NOW...
IT'S STRANGE, ISN'T IT? BUT IT'S TRUE.
...SPRING WILL COME AGAIN!
WITHOUT FAIL.

•READERS' COMMENTS•

"When Tohru echoed those words to Hatori-san, it seemed to me that his frozen heart began to thaw again." (P.N. Ichigo Daifuku)

"SO EVEN IF YOU STUMBLE AND MAKE MISTAKES, THAT'S NOT USELESS. THINK OF IT LIKE FERTILIZER. SURE, IT FEELS LIKE CRAP NOW, BUT IT WILL HELP YOU GROW.

(Volume 7) Kyoko's advice to Arisa, who wanted to become a better person. It was wisdom she was able to share after experiencing the same pain herself.

SO EVEN IF YOU STUMBLE AND MAKE MISTAKES...
...THAT'S NOT USELESS.
THAT'S...
THINK OF IT LIKE FERTILIZER. SURE IT FEELS LIKE CRAP...
...BUT IT WILL HELP YOU GROW!

•READERS' COMMENTS•

"I was deeply moved and impressed. And I cried, because when I was being bullied, there wasn't anyone to say something like that to me. I'll never forget how those words touched me." (P.N. Yoshie)

"THERE WAS SOMETHING I WANTED. SOMETHING I ENVISIONED. LOVING PARENTS, A HAPPY HOME, EVERYONE SMILING AT ME. A ME THAT NO ONE WOULD EVER WANT TO LEAVE. A WARM PLACE, A WARM PERSON. IT EXISTS. I KNOW IT DOES."

A WARM PERSON.

(Volume 4) After Akito revived Yuki's painful memories, his heart was eased by Tohru-kun simply having fun with him.

•READERS' COMMENTS•

"There was a time in my life when I always distanced myself from people, because I didn't know how to deal with them. When I read this scene, I was reminded that I too have a place where I belong, and that there are warm people in my life." (P.N. Kanayo)

"...I'M GLAD. I'M GLAD. WAS I ABLE TO HELP A LITTLE? IF SO, I'M HAPPY. I'M HAPPY. I'M VERY HAPPY."

•READERS' COMMENTS•

"I believed all along that Yuki-kun had been the boy with the hat, so I was happy--but it kind of means that he was the one who brought Tohru-kun and Kyo-kun together. As a Yuki fan, I had mixed feelings." (P.N. Yuuki)

I'M...
WAS I ABLE...
TO HELP...
EVEN JUST A LITTLE
...
WAS IT
THAT MAKES ME SO HAPPY.
I'M SO HAPPY.
I'M SO, SO HAPPY!

(Volume 15) The chapter that revealed the identity of the boy in the hat. When Yuki saved Tohru, he also saved himself.

"......IT MIGHT BE THAT THE REASON PEOPLE ARE JEALOUS OF OTHERS IS THAT THEY CAN SEE THE UMEBOSHI ON THEIR BACKS."

•READERS' COMMENTS•

"She can just say such wonderful things without hesitation! I thought that Tohru-kun was amazing, with her knack for saying what people want to hear when they most need it." (P.N. Yoshihiro Tsuda)

THERE IS AN UMEBOSHI ON YOUR BACK.
MAYBE...
...THE REASON PEOPLE GET JEALOUS OF EACH OTHER...
...IS BECAUSE THEY CAN SEE SO CLEARLY THE UMEBOSHI ON OTHER PEOPLE'S BACKS.
I CAN SEE THEM TOO.

(Volume 2) Every line from "If you think of someone's good qualities as an umeboshi~" to "There's an amazing umeboshi on your back, Kyo" received votes!

"I WANT TO BE WITH YOU...!"

(Volume 9) Saki shares her true feelings with Tohru and Arisa.

•READERS' COMMENTS•

"I was so glad to see Hana-chan's suffering end that I cried." (P.N. Atsuko Yamaguchi)

"IT WOULD BE OKAY TO COMPLAIN, BE SELFISH, SAY WHAT YOU WANT ONCE IN A WHILE. IT'S OKAY TO LET YOURSELF BE SAD."

(Volume 1) Kyo comforts Tohru when she cries that she wants to go back to Shigure's house.

•READERS' COMMENTS•

"Those words are just full of his kindness to Tohru.♥" (P.N. Shizuku)

"DON'T LEAVE ME..."

(Volume 16) She finally met someone irreplaceable, only to lose him. Kyoko's sadness is so real it hurts.

•READERS' COMMENTS•

"Kyoko-san's lines as she cried were so sad they broke my heart. I couldn't stop crying." (P.N. Suika)

"WHAT'S MOST IMPORTANT IS THAT WE TRY TO RISE ABOVE OUR WEAKNESS."

(Volume 5) When Kisa was teased at school, she lost the ability to speak.

•READERS' COMMENTS•

"It really encouraged me. It made me think that I could stand up and face anything without running away." (P.N. Mameko)

"AND IF WE GIVE IN TO OUR EMOTIONS AND END UP STRIKING THEM, LET'S MAKE SURE TO APOLOGIZE. AND HOLD THEM AGAIN. TOGETHER. LET'S RAISE THEM LIKE THAT."

•READERS' COMMENTS•

"I'm sure I'd be happy if someone said that to me. Those were the lines that touched me the most. Seeing Katsuya-papa and Kyoko-san renewed my belief that married couples are lucky, and that it's wonderful to be with people." (P.N. Mayumi Isaki)

YOU'VE ALREADY PROVEN THAT YOU UNDERSTAND.
THIS BABY WILL BE A HUMAN BEING.
I'M SURE YOU'LL BE FINE.
AS FELLOW HUMAN BEINGS...
...WE JUST HAVE TO REMEMBER.
WE KNOW WHAT WE LIKE DONE TO US.
AND WE KNOW WHAT TEARS US APART.
WE'LL HOLD THIS CHILD OFTEN.
WE'LL TOUCH IT, LISTEN TO IT.
IF IT DOES SOMETHING WRONG...
WE'LL BE VERY CLEAR.
...WE'LL EXPLAIN WHY IT'S WRONG.

(Volume 16) There was reader support for everything Katsuya said to reason with Kyoko when she was afraid of raising a child.

(Volume 5) Tohru spoke for Kisa when she had been teased at school and was embarrassed about it.

WHEN SHE TOLD ME, "THERE'S NOTHING TO BE ASHAMED OF"...
...I WAS SO RELIEVED...
...THAT I STARTED CRYING AGAIN.
KISA-SAN...
...MIGHT BE FEELING THE SAME WAY.

"SO WHEN MOM TOLD ME, 'IT'S OKAY,' I WAS SO RELIEVED. WHEN SHE TOLD ME, 'THERE'S NOTHING TO BE ASHAMED OF,' I WAS SO RELIEVED, THAT I STARTED CRYING AGAIN."

•READERS' COMMENTS•

"When I was being teased, I felt just like Kisa--so reading those words hurt. But I also think what Tohru-kun said saved me back then." (P.N. Eri)

"...IT MIGHT BE A GOOD IDEA TO START WASHING THE LAUNDRY RIGHT AT YOUR FEET."

(Volume 8) When Tohru makes herself uneasy by thinking too hard about her future goals, Shigure advises starting with the things right in front of her.

IT MIGHT BE A GOOD IDEA...
...TO START WASHING THE LAUNDRY RIGHT AT YOUR FEET.

•READERS' COMMENTS•

"When I was worrying about my career path, this advice helped clear my mind. I realized, 'Oh, that's right,' and it made me happier." (P.N. Tera Suama)

"BECAUSE IF YOU STAY TRUE TO YOURSELF AND LIVE YOUR LIFE BOLDLY, SOMEDAY, YOU MIGHT BE ABLE TO MEET SOMEONE WHO WILL WANT TO EAT TAKOYAKI WITH YOU MORE THAN WITH ANYONE ELSE..."

(Volume 9) When Ritchan anguishes over whether his lack of redeeming qualities means he has no right to live, Tohru tells him what she believes.

BECAUSE IF YOU STAY TRUE TO YOURSELF AND LIVE YOUR LIFE BOLDLY, SOMEDAY...
...YOU MIGHT BE ABLE TO MEET SOMEONE...
...WHO WILL WANT TO EAT TAKOYAKI WITH YOU MORE THAN WITH ANYONE ELSE.

•READERS' COMMENTS•

"I often question my own worth and reason for living, so reading those words really saved me." (P.N. Hekiru)

You chose: Favorite outfits

もみじ
でしゅ
羽がついててかれんでかわいい♪♡
33話の最後のページのコスチューム♥

(P.N. Kurage★)

第53話より もみっちの うさみみフード
めちゃ×2 カワイイ…♡
紅葉は何を着てもかわいいです…
フルーツバスケット⑨ P.153～

(P.N. Hiroko Kawano)

The undisputed winner!

MOMIJI'S WARDROBE!

(Volume 4) The adorable costume Momiji wears at the end of volume 4. He was like a ray of sunshine in a sad story.

TOMORROW, WE SET OUT WITH A BOOM!!
GET READY FOR SOME VA-VA-VOOM!!

(Volume 9) The western clothes (with a bunny-ear hood!) that Momiji wears at the summer home. This outfit was actually designed by Banri Hidaka-sensei and adapted for the manga by Takaya-sensei.

5巻 第30話 熱を出した透の代わりにバイトをするため、掃除の服を着てたトコ、めちゃ可愛♡
服がダボダボなところもまたカワイイ♡

(P.N. 3392)

(Volume 5) When Tohru is sick, he goes to work for her! Maybe it's because of the short notice that the jacket swims on him. But the nametag was a clever touch.

The uniforms were popular, too!

SCHOOL UNIFORMS

FRUITS BASKET
KYO
都立海原高校の学制服(冬)
TOHRU

(P.N. Hiyoko)

...AND I JUST WANT TO SMILE.
IT'S THAT KIND OF KINDNESS.

KAIBARA PUBLIC HIGH SCHOOL UNIFORMS

This is the girls' winter uniform for Kaibara High. The school isn't too strict about rules, so students can choose their own shoes or book bags.

KISA'S MIDDLE SCHOOL UNIFORM

This is the summer uniform for the private girls' middle school that Sohma girls attend. Kagura and Isuzu used to be students there.

ISUZU'S HIGH SCHOOL UNIFORM

This is the summer uniform for the private girls' high school that Isuzu attends. It's similar to the middle school uniform, but there are small differences.

CONTEST

We've reproduced some of your favorite outfits that appear in the series, and some original ones designed by readers!

So cute!

ORIGINAL DESIGNS

依鈴
オリジナル

This is an original design for Isuzu. It's sexy in a way that's very Isuzu, with just a bit of cuteness. It's a wonderful look.

[P.N. Reina Matsubara]

Outfits for Momiji and Hatsuharu. The rabbit tattoo on Momiji's arm and the ox tattoo by Haru's navel add an interesting touch.

Hatsuharu & Momiji

[P.N. Rukia]

ふるーつばすけっと
透くん♥

A slightly more hardcore Tohru than we're used to. If Kisa wore matching clothes, the two of them would be even cuter.

[P.N. Yayoi]

It's a cat overload! And the ears on the cat hat even move!

[P.N. Shizuku]

KYO-KUN IS A FAVORITE!

[Volume 1] This is a favorite outfit that's appeared many times in the series. Kyo wore it when Tohru had a fever, and when he went to fetch her.

THEN WE'RE GOING HOME NOW!
All right already!
!

Kyo
うまかねぇよ
そんなん
おまえの料理よか
全然
1巻から度々着ていたこの上着が大好きです。なので最近見れないのが残念です。高屋先生！
是非書いて下さい！
フルバ大好き

[P.N. Haru Okazaki]

CHIBI-KYON'S JUMPER

[Volume 15] This is a jacket Kyo wore a lot when he was young. He's liked this kind of clothing since he was little.

[P.N. Minaki]

DRESSES LIKE THAT ONE!

[Volume 6] This is the dress that Mine made Tohru wear to impress Yuki. It really was the Day of Yuki's Romantic Fantasy!

WHAT DO YOU THINK?
HA!
COME ON, YUKI! GIVE HER

[P.N. Yuki Mikami]

You chose: **Coolest Scenes**

"...NN? WHAT'S WRONG...?"

...NN?
WHAT'S WRONG...?

[Volume 13] This is another scene that received an incredible amount of support. The kindness in his eyes when he looks at Tohru is overwhelming.

•READERS' COMMENTS•

"Kyo had been cold to another girl just before this scene, so it really highlighted his kindness toward Tohru. So cool..!" [P.N. Kirara]

"I WON'T APOLOGIZE FOR KISSING YOU."

I WON'T APOLOGIZE...
...FOR KISSING YOU...

[Volume 11] Yuki says and does a lot of cool things, and this scene in particular won many readers' hearts.

•READERS' COMMENTS•

"Yuki's super cool. This line makes me feel like he's growing, and it suits him--he really is Prince Charming. If a normal guy said that, it would tick me off." [P.N. Sumie Sakamaki]

FOR TOHRU...

TEACH HER HOW TO BREATHE!
YOU WANT FUN? I'LL GIVE YOU FUN!
spin
WAAAAHH!

[Volume 10] Kyo hates water, but he jumps into the ocean for Tohru. And to make her happy, he even played with her floatation ring.

•READERS' COMMENTS•

"In the ocean, it was so clear how badly Kyo-kun wanted to take care of Tohru. It was wonderful! And it was fun when he played with the floatation ring (laugh)." [P.N. Hii-chan]

"I WOULD PROTECT KYO SINGLE-HANDEDLY IF I HAD TO."

YOU, WHO CANNOT HAVE THE HEART OF A PARENT...
...WOULD NEVER UNDERSTAND.
THAT IS MY HUMBLE OPINION.

[Volume 9] Kazuma directs those words at Kyo's real father. You can feel his resolution and love for Kyo. Now that's cool!

•READERS' COMMENTS•

"It's those lines more than the whole scene--they had so much impact coming from Kazuma, who's usually so kind." [P.N. Hatsuki]

CONTEST

After "Most Touching Lines", we received the most postcards for the coolest scene!

"...I'M SURE IT WOULD BE VERY PRETTY."

...IT WOULD BE VERY PRETTY.

(Volume 2) Is this what Kakeru was talking about when he called Yuki a "natural princess old man"? It's just too cool.

•READERS' COMMENTS•

"Well, I think this is probably the coolest scene in all of *Fruits Basket* (laugh). It should be illegal to be that cool while crossdressing." (P.N. Hajime)

"MAKE IT COME TRUE WITH YOUR OWN POWER."

IN THAT CASE–PRINCE CHARMING, SUPPORT THEM IN THEIR BUSINESS.
I THOUGHT YOU WERE GRANTING THE WISH.
PRINCE CHARMING...
...I WON'T ASK WHAT YOU WISH FOR.
I ONLY HOPE IT COMES TRUE BY YOUR OWN TWO HANDS.

(Volume 15) Yuki's advice in the "Sorta Cinderella" play. It's a line from the play, but he says it so persuasively!

•READERS' COMMENTS•

"It's great that it sounds like he's saying it so seriously, even though it's part of a play." (P.N. Mai Sugisaki)

"THE KNIGHT WHO PROTECTS TOHRU."

THEY DON'T PUT UP ANY RESISTANCE YOU KNOW!
IT'S ANNOYING WHEN GIRLS GET ALL ASSERTIVE, DON'T YOU THINK?
SHE DOES LOOK LIKE SHE'LL BUY ANYTHING.
MAYBE I SHOULD GO TALK TO H–
?!
!

•READERS' COMMENTS•

"It's so cute that Kyo-kun gets so possessive of Tohru-kun, even though he doesn't know why he's reacting that way." (P.N. Terasato)

(Volume 4) There were a lot of readers who said, "I'm so jealous of Tohru-kun, having Kyo-kun protect her like that!"

"CHOOSE ME, KYOKO."

CHOOSE ME.
KYOKO.

(Volume 16) Katsuya's composure is so charming! Who could refuse that kind of proposal?

•READERS' COMMENTS•

"Katsuya Honda! I love him so much it's a crime.♥" (P.N. Sumiko Ito)

"I thought, 'Ooohh, I want someone to say that to me!" (P.N. Suika)

"I'M ME."

DON'T TALK DOWN TO ME!!
WHO THE HELL DO YOU THINK YOU ARE?!
Ah?!
I'M ME.

(Volume 11) This exchange received votes for both "cool scene" and "funny scene". We decided to go with "cool"!

•READERS' COMMENTS•

"He's so cool. Only Yuki could pull that off." (P.N. Floral)

ザ

You chose: Most Hilarious Scenes

"TOHRU HONDA WILL HUMBLY SMASH THE WATERMELON!"

ONG ONG ONG
...CO-
CONGRATULA... TIONS...
ARE YOU CRYING BECAUSE YOU COULDN'T BREAK IT, OR BECAUSE YOUR HAND HURTS?
drip drip
drip drip
You really are a moron...
shudder shudder
drip drip
I- I'LL...
...DO MY BEST TO CELEBRATE... TOO...
GYAH
I'M BEGGING YOU, KISA! STOP!!

[Volume 10] We feel bad for Tohru when she tears up, but it's still funny. Yuki and Kyo's panic as they scramble to stop her is pretty entertaining, too.

Air-heads unite!

•READERS' COMMENTS•

"It was great when Tohru tried to smash the watermelon with her bare hands, and it was funny that Kisa wanted to do it too!" [P.N. Yuna Takashi]

"IF IT COMES DOWN TO 'ATTACK' OR 'ACCEPT,' I CHOOSE 'ACCEPT'!!!"

No. 1 idiot!

IF IT'S COMES DOWN TO "ATTACK" OR "ACCEPT"...
...I CHOOSE TO "ACCEPT"!!
YOU IDIOT!!!
HE REALLY WAS AN IDIOT!!
SUCH AN IDIOT!!
NO NEED TO WORRY, HATORI! I MAY APPEAR FRAGILE, BUT I'M IN CONTROL!
......

[Volume 4] The whole Kandora-sama story was incredible, but your postcards said this scene had the most impact!

•READERS' COMMENTS•

"Insanely funny! That was the best scene!! Where did that crazy idea come from??! I almost died laughing." [P.N. Blue Cherry]

"YES?"

LISTEN TO THIS, GURE-SAN!!
YUKI--YES, THAT YUKI--
--CAME TO ME WITH TEARS IN HIS EYES SAYING THAT BY ALL MEANS HE WOULD LIKE TO COME VISIT ME AT MY SHOP!!
YES?

[Volume 6] Ayame doesn't stop at telling Hatori about his conversation with Yuki--he even reports it to Shigure, who's taking a bath. It's an annoying habit.

•READERS' COMMENTS•

"I laughed at the way he burst in on Gure-san's bath, and the normal way Gure-san responded." [P.N. Kotone Ugetsu]

"I CAN SEE THAT."

[Volume 3] Tohru's earnest "I missed!" and Kyo's deadpan response play off each other beautifully.

I MISSED!!
I CAN SEE THAT.

•READERS' COMMENTS•

"I laugh myself silly every time. They have a great airhead/straight man dynamic--I can't get enough of it." [P.N. Miki Takeuchi]

CONTEST

Lots of responses said there are too many hilarious scenes to choose just one! We've selected some scenes that many people thought were funn

BLACK!! CINDERELLA IS WEARING BLACK!!

HERE WE ARE.
THE BALL.
WATCHING FOR AN OPPORTUNITY, CINDERELLA ARRIVED.
Wow!
THAT WOMAN IS SO BEAUTIFUL!
BLACK!
CINDERELLA'S WEARING BLACK!

Of course she's in pure black!

[Volume 15] Hana-chan asked Mine to make her a pure black dress. The beautifully-made dress gets a major response from the audience (laugh).

•READERS' COMMENTS•

"Hana-chan's black-clad Cinderella was very unexpected, compared to the Cinderella I'd imagined. I really just kept laughing and laughing." [P.N. Rie Funenokawa]

"PLEASE HURRY TO KIMI~♥"

Yun-Yuuun♥

Yun-Yuuuun!♡
MY BELOVED PRESIDENT YUN-YUN-SAAAAN! ♡
THE MEEEETING IS ABOUT TO STAAART, SO PLEASE HURRY TO KIMI, 'KAAAY?
OH NO! MY MISTAKE! I MEANT, "HURRY TO THE COUNCIL ROOM!" KIMI MADE A BOO-BOO! SORRY, YUN-YUN! ♡
BUT KIMI WILL BE WAITING FOR YOU. SO PLEASE HURRY HERE! ♡

[Volume 14] A school PA announcement that sounds like taunting from the "other woman" (laugh). A lot of votes came in for Kakeru's line after this, too.

•READERS' COMMENTS•

"It's funny that she does things that annoy people so much. That announcement made me burst out laughing★." [P.N. Yuki]

"WAIT A SECOND, GRANDPA!!"

DEEP DOWN...
...THEY'RE JUST EVIL PEOPLE.
WAIT A SECOND, GRANDPA!
YOU DON'T MEAN THAT!
WHAT? WHAT DID I SAY?

[Volume 1] "Deep down, they're just evil people," Grandpa declares--as expected from Katsuya's father.

•READERS' COMMENTS•

"I love that her grandfather just smiles and says that without hesitation!" [P.N. Rie Watanabe]

"WHAT HAVE YOU DONE...?"

PUT IT ON FORTHWITH!!
WHAT HAVE YOU DONE?

[Volume 8] The hilarious embroidery that makes everyone but Shigure fall to the floor laughing. Although Shigure's reaction is questionable, too...

•READERS' COMMENTS•

"I laughed a lot. I wanted him to wear it (laugh)." [P.N. Yuu]

You chose: Most Moe-moe Scenes

YUKI AND MACHI'S MOE-MOE HEATED ARGUMENT♥

[Volume 16] The two of them argue about whether or not it's the maple leaf Yuki gave her, whether or not she was taking good care of it, and--most importantly!--whether or not she'll be giving it back. To anyone watching, it's obviously a lovers' quarrel. There were a lot of votes for this first real display of Machi's feelings.

HUNH.
I KINDA WANNA ASK, BUT I ALSO KINDA DON'T.
Do I risk it?
shake shake
grab
ASK.
TAKE THE RISK.

......!
I...
I'M NOT TAKING CARE OF IT!
HUH?

Do I dare?

•READERS' COMMENTS•

"Machi-chan is always so expressionless that I was surprised by how cute she was when she got embarrassed and blushed." [P.N. Yuri Daidoji]

I'M BACK, I'M BACK!

I'M BACK! I'M BACK! I'M BACK!
TOHRU!!
MOMIJI! WHY, YOU LITTLE--!

[Volume 11] There were a lot of people who loved the Momiji/ Tohru hugging scenes! (Momiji is cute no matter what he does.)

•READERS' COMMENTS•

"It was adorable how much Momiji-kun wanted to see Tohru-kun (plus, his rabbit form...!). Kisa-chan was cute, too.♥" [P.N. Yuka Ezure]

KISA-SAN = BIIIIG HUGS! ♥

Hearts fill the air ♥

MOM...
...AND ALL OF YOU...
...YOU'RE ALL HERE... FOR ME.
THAT'S WHY I CAN DO MY BEST...
I love you!!
きゅう♥
SO MANY HEARTS...

[Volume 7] We received votes for Kisa and Tohru's various hugging scenes, and we chose this one to represent them.

•READERS' COMMENTS•

"Gure-san's 'So many hearts' line is cute, too." [P.N. Kanro-chan]

CONTEST

You sent a whole variety of choices for the most adorable scenes, and the scenes that made your hearts flutter.

......! CU--! ♥

Uh, er, um, it's really, really, true!!
That's not the reason!!
......!
CU--!
Moron...

Entering teasing mode

[Volume 12] Two things about this scene brought in votes: Tohru going red, and Kyo impulsively thinking, "She's cute."

•READERS' COMMENTS•

"It's too cute when Kyo-kun asks Tohru-kun if it's a date, and she blushes and frantically denies it. And it's even cuter when he sees her panicking and starts blushing too (laugh) ♥" [P.N. Satsuki]

OH MY......♥

OH MY...
CUT IT OUT!!
HARU...
IF YOU DON'T STOP NOW, I'LL DISOWN YOU FOREVER...
RELAX! I WAS JUST MAKING A POINT. DON'T BE MAD. ♡

[Volume 4] Yuki wearing the girls' school uniform also received nominations for the best costume. (Even though he said not to imagine it...)

•READERS' COMMENTS•

"He's even cuter than any of the girls! He's seriously super-ultra-cute♥ I'd like to see him like that again!" [P.N. Fugu]

YUKI AND MACHI'S MOE-MOE HEATED ARGUMENT♥

...ALL RIGHT.
LOOK ME IN THE EYE AND SAY IT.
YAH!
YAH!
YAAAH!
NOT QUITE.
......!

Just like grade school ...

[Volume 15] Ahh, youth: the two of them squabbling over the script for the play. Now that's a "moe" scene.

•READERS' COMMENTS•

"Ohhh, Tohru-kun is adorable. Her face gets so red, and Kyo-kun teasing her is just great." [P.N. Ayametsuki]

MEEEEEP

SH-SHE-SHE'LL GET MAD!
...SAYS I SHOULDN'T TALK TO STRANGERS.
MY MOM...
DRAG
DRAG
DRAG
SHE WON'T GET MAD! I'M LIKE YOU! I'M IN THE ZODIAC! I'M THE BOAR!

[Volume 12] Apparently Kagura was incredibly strong even as a child! Chibi-Kyon being dragged along the ground is far too cute.

•READERS' COMMENTS•

"Kyo-kun's tiny 'meeep!' is so cute--I love it. ♥ And him being dragged is unbearable (laugh)." [P.N. Kumi]

You chose: Best Couple & Combo Rankings

#1 THE OBVIOUS CHOICE!

Tohru & Kyo 495 votes

WELCOME BACK...
WELCOME BACK, KYO-KUN!

......
AH HA HA HA!
......!
DON'T--
--LAUGH--
--LIKE--
--THAT!
Y-YES!
AH HA HA!

HIS EYES SAY, "I LOVE YOU ♥"!

To no one's surprise, these two won first place by a landslide. Akito's probing forces Kyo to admit his own feelings to himself, and Tohru's heart pounds when she thinks about him. What does their future hold...?

YEAH.
IT'S GOOD TO BE BACK.
I LOVE YOU.

•READERS' COMMENTS•

"It's not a one-sided, forced love; they really do care for each other. That's why it's so great that he doesn't act on his feelings!" (P.N. Miyabi)

"I want to talk to Tohru and Kyo and tell them, 'It's true love!' (laugh)." (P.N. Mairi Hosozawa)

#6 Tohru & Arisa & Saki

79 votes

...AND I HAVE...
...THE TWO BEST FRIENDS IN THE WORLD...
...HANA-CHAN AND UO-CHAN...

•READERS' COMMENTS•

"They've had a unique relationship ever since Furuba began. It's an amazing, strong friendship. Right now, Hana-chan is my favorite after Tohru-kun." (P.N. N)

#4 Hatsuharu & Isuzu

81 votes

•READERS' COMMENTS•

"They feel so strongly about each other, and yet things just don't work out for them...I reeeeeeally like Hatsuharu, so I definitely want him to be happy." (P.N. Kanaha Nagai)

#4 Tohru & Yuki

81 votes

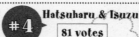

•READERS' COMMENTS•

"There's a gentle vibe between them that I like. It's heartwarming--they give the impression that they've been married for years (laugh)." (P.N. Tokiya Rien)

CONTEST

We've tallied all your postcard votes for the best couple so we can present them by their rankings. (Couples and combos are combined.)

Others

COUPLES & COMBOS OUTSIDE THE TOP TEN

- #11: Hiro & Kisa
- #12: Yuki & Ayame
- #13: Kyo & Saki
- #14: Kyo & Kazuma
- #15: Saki & Megumi
- #16: Tohru & Isuzu
- #16: Kyo & Kagura
- #18: Tohru & Kisa
- #19: Kyo & Arisa
- #19: Tohru & Kyo & Yuki

 # 20 and below

Many unique combinations were nominated but didn't make it past 20th place, like Ayame & Kakeru, President Takei & Motoko Minagawa, and Kyo & Momiji.

#2 THE NATURAL CLOWN & STRAIGHT MAN

Yuki & Kakeru

108 votes

•READERS' COMMENTS

"It's like Kakeru is dragging the real Yuki out ♫" (P.N. Tsubasa)

You're a Princess. ♡
PAT
OWWWWW!
I'M SORRY—I'LL SHUT UP, PRINCESS!
THESE FEEL-INGS.

YES. I WAS GIVEN A HIGH-SOCIETY UPBRINGING.
strangle
I'm jealous!
THEN I'LL SEND YOU OUT SHOPPING AT NIGHT SOME DAY.
......

Their relationship is getting to the point where they can just freely speak their minds to each other. Their clown/straight man act is getting out of control...

#3 A PREMONITION OF ROMANCE♥

Yuki & Machi

107 votes

•READERS' COMMENTS

"It's wonderful how Yuki's traumatic past makes him want to understand the people around him. And Machi's cute, too, as she becomes more honest about her feelings." (P.N. Keishi Kawakami)

WHAT DOES THE WORLD LOOK LIKE THROUGH YOUR EYES?
YOU MAKE ME WONDER.

LONELY.
YES.
AND HE MAKES THINGS...
HE'S ALWAYS SURROUNDED BY PEOPLE.
AND HE'S KNOWN AS "PRINCE CHARMING."

Right now, their relationship is the one readers are most curious about, and it made it into the top three. Machi has started to recognize her romantic feelings for Yuki. What will he do?

#7 Tohru & Momiji

54 votes

I CAN'T WAIT TO GO TO THE ONSEN!!
YES!!

•READERS' COMMENTS•

"I like the bright, warm, fuzzy feeling when those two are together." (P.N. Hiraku Fukuoka)

#8 Shigure & Akito

50 votes

"I'LL BE HERE."

•READERS' COMMENTS•

"Akito is violent, but there's something damaged in her heart. I want Shigure to heal that 'something'." (P.N. ERIKO)

#9 Kyoko & Katsuya

45 votes

LET ME TAKE YOU SOMEWHERE YOU WANT TO GO.
HUH?

#9 Mabudachi Trio

45 votes

ALL right!!
YOU NEVER GET TIRED OF THAT, DO YOU?

Hana to Yume Character Rankings

HANA TO YUME 2004, ISSUE 22

#1 TWO-TIME CHAMPION!

Kyo Sohma | **7725 points**

Kyo made a strong showing, with two landslide victories in a row!

#2 THE HEROINE, OF COURSE!

Tohru Honda | **4680 points**

Tohru, who has started trying to break the curse for Kyo's sake. She has the look of a girl in love♥

#3 EVERYONE'S PRINCE CHARMING♥

Yuki Sohma | **3134 points**

Maybe he's actually happy that Tohru ranked higher than he did...?

#4 Hatori Sohma

1498 points

#5 Hatsuharu Sohma

1224 points

......
OR HAVE YOUR FEELINGS MADE YOU DIZZY?

#6 Momiji Sohma

1193 points

Hatori and Hatsuharu are as popular as ever, and Momiji is now in the top six! His kindness and inner strength are bringing his popularity up dramatically.

7TH-20TH PLACE

#7: Kakeru Manabe, 1025 points	#14: Kisa Sohma, 495 points
#8: Ayame Sohma, 928 points	#15: Machi Kuragi, 358 points
#9: Kureno Sohma, 798 points	#16: Hiro Sohma, 331 points
#10: Shigure Sohma, 741 points	#17: Kazuma Sohma, 254 points
#11: Isuzu Sohma, 715 points	#18: Akito Sohma, 252 points
#12: Saki Hanajima, 534 points	#19: Arisa Uotani, 223 points
#13: Ritsu Sohma, 527 points	#20: Kagura Sohma, 211 points

*The "Character Rankings" and "Best Couple & Combo" were calculated differently.

CONTEST

Re-presenting the Hana to Yume character rankings from 2004 and 2000.

HANA TO YUME 2000, ISSUE 8

EVERYONE'S EMOTIONAL SUPPORT

#2 Tohru Honda 11,922 points

Tohru, who heals everyone's heart, is universally loved.

FIRST PLACE BY A LANDSLIDE!

#1 Kyo Sohma 17,218 points

In the character rankings, he's already beaten Yuki!

IT'S JUST LIKE YUKI TO AVOID THE LIMELIGHT A LITTLE.

#3 Yuki Sohma 11,187 points

Yuki thinks people aren't drawn to him, but here he is!

#5 Shigure Sohma 5,614 points

#4 Hatori Sohma 6,885 points

#6 Hatsuharu Sohma 5,589 points

As of the 2000 vote, Shigure is in fifth place! Are there a lot of people who were charmed by his appearance, like Mitchan? (laugh)

7TH-20TH PLACE

#7: Ayame Sohma, 3684 points	#14: Megumi Hanajima, 301 points
#8: Momiji Sohma, 1654 points	#15: Kyoko Honda, 267 points
#9: Saki Hanajima, 1581 points	#16: Arisa Uotani, 182 points
#10: Kagura Sohma, 1184 points	#17: Mogeta, 123 points
#11: Kisa Sohma, 975 points	#18: Concubine-san, 89 points
#12: Kazuma Sohma, 613 points	#19: Tohru's grandfather, 67 points
#13: Akito Sohma, 525 points	#20: Mayuko Shiraki, 42 points

How much are you like Kyo? And how can you be lucky in love?

Furuba-themed Personality Test

We'll chart your answers to a series of questions to see how much you're like Yuki, Kyo, or Shigure! The results can reveal things like your ideal job.

Q1:
How do you spend your days off?

A: I PREFER GOING OUT; IF I'M GOING TO WATCH A MOVIE, I GO TO A THEATER. (→ Q2)

B: I PREFER STAYING IN; IF I'M GOING TO WATCH A MOVIE, I RENT A VIDEO. (→ Q3)

Q2:
How do you feel about competition?

A: I CAN'T STAND TO LOSE! (→ Q4)

B: AS LONG AS I HAVE FUN, IT'S OKAY! (→ Q5)

Q3:
People say it's easy to tell what you're thinking.

A: YES. (→ Q5)

B: NO. (→ Q6)

Q4:
When you were in elementary school, what did you do for fun?

A: I PLAYED WITH EVERYONE OUTSIDE. (→ Q7)

B: I WAS REALLY INTO PLAYING GAMES AT HOME. (→ Q5)

Q5:
At cultural festivals and athletic meets, you wind up getting into the spirit of things even if you started off thinking they were a pain.

A: YES, FESTIVALS ARE EXCITING! (→ Q7)

B: NO, THEY REALLY ARE A PAIN. (→ Q8)

Q6:
You get absorbed in things you like, but you can't be bothered doing boring things.

A: YES. (→ Q5)

B: NO. (→ Q9)

Q7:
You've had an unrequited love for over a year.

A: YES. (→ 100% like Kyo)

B: NO. (→ Q8)

Q8:
When something ticks you off, you take it out on other people.

A: YES. (→ 100% like Kyo)

B: NO. (→ 70% like Kyo)

Q9:
You don't mince words.

A: YES. (→ 70% like Kyo)

B: NO. (→ 30% like Kyo)

100% like Kyo
If you're 100% like Kyo, you're the reliable older-sister type. But your weakness is that you suddenly get tongue-tied around the person you like...

HOW TO BE LUCKY IN LOVE:
Have confidence in yourself and be assertive!

70% like Kyo
If you're 70% like Kyo, you're cheerful and well-liked. But although you make friends easily, it might be hard for you to take a friendship to the next level.

HOW TO BE LUCKY IN LOVE:
Casually express your love every day!

30% like Kyo
If you're 30% like Kyo, you may be too reserved to stand out much. The first step is to make sure the person you like knows who you are!

HOW TO BE LUCKY IN LOVE:
Find out what you have in common to increase your opportunities to talk to your crush!

M E N T A L ● G A M E

How much are you like Yuki?

And what diet strategy is best for you?

Q1:
You take leadership roles in class and club activities:

A: OFTEN.

B: RARELY.

Q2:
When faced with things that just need to be done, like homework, do you finish them quickly and systematically?

A: I FINISH THEM.

B: I PLANNED TO, BUT...

Q3:
What would you plant in a garden?

A: STRAW-BERRIES.

B: CACTI.

Q4:
How concerned are you about how people see you?

A: VERY CONCERNED.

B: IT DOESN'T DO ANY GOOD TO WORRY ABOUT IT, SO I'M NOT CONCERNED.

Q5:
How are you at cleaning and tidying up?

A: NOT GOOD. I THINK ABOUT ORGANIZING THINGS, BUT CAN'T GET MOTIVATED.

B: AVERAGE, I GUESS. OR EVEN GOOD AT IT.

Q6:
Do you have trouble waking up in the morning, or wind up going back to sleep?

A: I HAVE A HARD TIME.

B: I LIKE GETTING UP EARLY.

Q7:
What do you do with your favorite food?

A: I SAVE IT FOR LAST.

B: I EAT IT FIRST.

Q8:
Do you think it's important to work hard and improve yourself?

A: I DO THINK SO. I'LL WORK HARD!

B: IF I'M BAD AT SOME-THING, I DON'T HAVE TO DO IT.

Q9:
Do you wish people who are teased would stand up for themselves instead of relying on outside help?

A: I DON'T.

B: I DO. DO YOUR BEST!

100% like Yuki

If you're 100% like Yuki, you're a serious, kind person. You may be a bit sloppy, but you're trying to improve your habits. But you tend to let your stress levels build, so try to relax sometimes!

YOUR MOST EFFECTIVE DIET STRATEGY:
A diet with a regular exercise regimen.

70% like Yuki

If you're 70% like Yuki, you're a moderate combination of serious and laid-back. But just a little more effort could make you accomplish things you thought were impossible!

YOUR MOST EFFECTIVE DIET STRATEGY:
A diet involving supplements and spa treatments.

30% like Yuki

If you're 30% like Yuki, you have the skill to handle all sorts of things. You should follow Ayame's example and play up your individuality--but don't go overboard! (laugh)

YOUR MOST EFFECTIVE DIET STRATEGY:
A low-carb diet while counting calories.

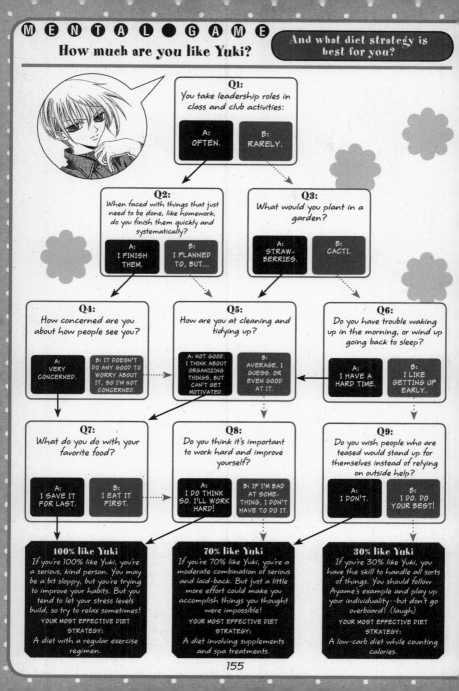

How much are you like Shigure?

And what's your ideal career?

Q1: Which is more important?

- A: MONEY.
- B: LOVE.

Q2: Living a normal lifestyle...

- A: IS HARD FOR ME.
- B: IS EASY FOR ME.

Q3: What do you do when your friends fight?

- A: I CALM EVERYONE DOWN WITH A JOKE.
- B: I PERSUADE THEM TO TALK IT OUT CALMLY.

Q4: If they're funny, are pranks that upset people okay?

- A: YES.
- B: NO, THEY'RE NOT OKAY.

Q5: How often do you forget where you put your cell phone?

- A: OFTEN.
- B: RARELY.

Q6: It it worth a little extra effort to make people laugh?

- A: YES.
- B: NO.

Q7: So, about the person you love...

- A: I TORMENT THEM.
- B: I DO ALL I CAN FOR THEM.

Q8: Do you have a dream that's so important that nothing will keep you from making it come true?

- A: I DO.
- B: I DON'T THINK I'D GO THAT FAR...

Q9: What do you do if you feel obliged to give someone Valentine's chocolate?

- A: I GIVE CHOCOLATE WITH WASABI IN IT AS A JOKE.
- B: I GIVE HIGH-QUALITY CHOCOLATE, I GUESS.

100% like Shigure

If you're 100% like Shigure, you express yourself freely without worrying about other people's opinions--or common sense. That sounds very nice, but is it really good to be that much like Shigure...? (laugh)

IDEAL CAREERS:
Author, artist, game designer, etc.

70% like Shigure

If you're 70% like Shigure, you've found moderation and balance in your life. Keep it up, and your dreams should come true!

IDEAL CAREERS:
Shop clerk, beautician, researcher, etc.

30% like Shigure

If you're 30% like Shigure, you're a serious, honest person. But remember to let loose and get rid of your stress sometimes!

IDEAL CAREERS:
Civil servant, doctor, accountant, etc.

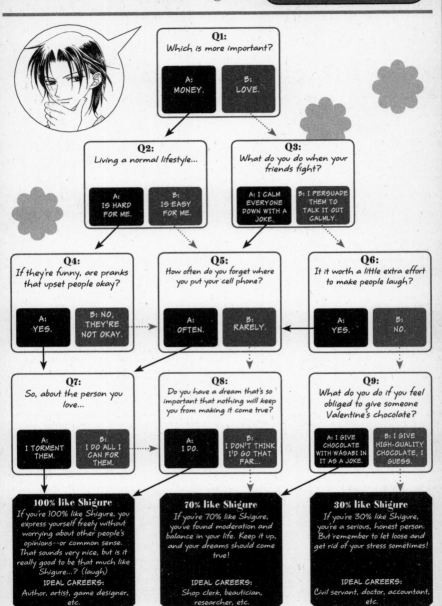

Q U I Z

Furuba-themed

Multiple-choice Quiz for the Total Fanatic

Furuba-themed Quizzes

YOU'RE ONE OF THEM.
ONE OF THOSE PEOPLE WHO STUDIES ALL THE TIME BUT ENDS UP BLOWING TESTS BECAUSE HE STUDIED ALL THE WRONG THINGS.
Heh heh!
YOU DIDN'T DO THAT AGAIN, DID YOU?
I'M GOING TO STRANGLE YOU BOTH!

CHOOSE A, B, OR C TO ANSWER EACH QUESTION.

Q1: WHAT IS THE BEST DESCRIPTION OF *FRUITS BASKET*?
a: A lighthearted romantic comedy about the exciting school life of the Zodiac members--a story for the whole family!
b: A heartwarming school romance with a hint of fantasy--something for everyone!
c: An intense story about the end of the world, with comedic school drama and a bit of mystery thrown in.

Q2: IN CHAPTER 1, WHAT DOES TOHRU THINK IS HER REDEEMING QUALITY?
a: She never gets depressed, no matter what happens.
b: She can become friends with anyone.
c: She is good at housework.

Q3: WHAT FOODS DID YUKI LIKE WHEN HE WAS LITTLE?
a: Crabs and peaches.
b: Shrimp and strawberries.
c: Salmon roe and grapes.

Q4: KYO HATES LEEKS, ONIONS, AND MISO. WHAT ABOUT MISO SOUP?
a: He still hates it, unless it's made into a Japanese-style soup.
b: He can handle it if it's watered down.
c: He doesn't mind miso soup.

Q5: SHIGURE WROTE A BOOK OF SCARY STORIES. IT INCLUDES THE STORY ABOUT THE COCKROACH ON A HOT DAY, AND WHICH OF THESE OTHER STORIES?
a: A story about grated cheese.
b: A story about cola.
c: A story about daifuku (rice cake stuffed with bean curd).

Q6: WHAT DOES AYAME HAVE ATTACHED TO HIS CELL PHONE STRAP?
a: A rat charm.
b: A snake charm.
c: A seahorse charm.

Q7: WHAT MADE ARISA CRY WHEN SHE WAS CASHIERING AT THE CONVENIENCE STORE?
a: An old man buying a convenience store lunch.
b: An old man who was worried because he didn't know how to warm up his lunch.
c: A child throwing away the candy that came with a toy.

Q8: WHY DOES SAKI PAINT HER FINGERNAILS BLACK?
a: To seal her waves.
b: As a sign that she is a witch.
c: As proof that she is a sinner.

Q9: YUN-YUN IS RED, KAKERU IS BLACK, AND KIMI IS PINK, SO WHAT COLOR IS NAOHITO?
a: Green.
b: Blue.
c: Yellow.

Q10: WHAT DID KURENO TRANSFORM INTO?
a: A rooster.
b: A sparrow.
c: A crow.

Q11: MAYUKO SHIRAKI'S FAMILY RUNS A USED BOOKSTORE. WHAT DOES MOTOKO MINAGAWA'S FAMILY RUN?
a: A noodle shop.
b: A flower shop.
c: A vegetable shop.

Q12: WHEN UO-CHAN ASKS YUKI AND KYO WHAT COLOR LOOKS BEST ON TOHRU, WHAT ARE THEIR ANSWERS?
a: Light blue (Yuki) and pink (Kyo)
b: White (Yuki) and red (Kyo).
c: Blue (Yuki) and orange (Kyo).

Q13: IN THE MADE-UP STORY ABOUT THE FINE, UPSTANDING YOUNG MAN WHO IS EASILY MOVED AND LIKES ANIMALS AND COOKING, WHAT DOES HE DO ON SUNDAYS?
a: Vote in elections.
b: Look for another job.
c: Volunteer.

Q14: WHAT IS THE NAME OF THE SUPERMARKET THAT KYO AND YUKI WERE FIGHTING IN FRONT OF IN CHAPTER 13?
a: Super "Dodoitsu".
b: Super "Koi-Koi".
c: Super "Yotteke".

Q15: WHAT WAS RITCHAN'S IDOL, AYA-NIISAN, EATING WITH SUCH CONFIDENCE IN CHAPTER 45?
a: Katsudon.
b: Gyoza.
c: Soba.

Q16: WHAT IS THE TITLE OF THE BOOK KAZUMA WAS READING WHILE HE COOKED IN CHAPTER 52?
a: "In the Moonlight".
b: "Heartthrob".
c: "Maliciousness".

Q17: WHICH OF THESE IS A LINE FROM THE POEM THAT CAME TO MOTOKO MINAGAWA'S MIND IN CHAPTER 66?
a: His hair that shines silver in the sun, his white skin, his resonating voice, his eyelashes that cast shadows on his cheeks when he closes his eyes.
b: Because your smiling face is better than any gift! Like a bird, it spreads its white wings, soaring to great heights in the blue sky that is my heart.
c: Since then, I knew our destinies were intertwined, like roses winding their way up a black gate! A sweet pain in my heart!

Q18: WHAT WAS WRITTEN ON THE PERMIT THAT THE SCHOOL PRINCIPAL GAVE AYAME AND MINE SO THEY COULD ENTER THE SCHOOL IN CHAPTER 87?
a: Permitted.
b: It's all good.
c: Do what you want.

Q19: WHAT DOES THE PROVERB "YOU CAN'T SEE THE FOREST FOR THE TREES" MEAN?
a: Seeing trees means you're in a forest.
b: If a tree falls on your head, it covers your eyes.
c: "Sometimes it's easier to understand a situation if you look at it from a distance."

ANSWERS ON PAGE 170!

Furuba-themed Fill-in-the-speech-bubble Quiz

From the selections below, choose the lines that go in the empty speech bubbles from each panel.

Q1

GOOD MORNING!

Q3

OH... HEARING THAT...
...I FEEL SO BAD...
YES... SORROWFUL, ISN'T IT ...?
喧嘩上等
*Primed for a fight!

CHOOSE THE LINES THAT GO IN THE BUBBLES!

Q2

My God, man, you're dense !!
THE FACT THAT YOU STILL DON'T UNDERSTAND AFTER I'VE MADE IT SO CRYSTAL CLEAR IS PROOF THAT YOU'RE AN IDIOT OF THE HIGHEST ORDER!
Wh-
WHAT'S THE MATTER?!

Q4

Such rudeness!!
EEHH ?!!
HOW DO YOU COME TO THAT CONCLUSION...?!
TRY IT AND I'LL CRUSH YOU WITH ALL MY MIGHT!!

Q5

tremble
NO! I'LL GO IN. I'LL GO IN. I'LL CONQUER MY FEARS.
N-NO...!!
IT'S OKAY IF YOU AVOID IT.

SELECTIONS

a: "A man like you has no right to have summer!! Pack your bags and leave this place at once!!"
b: "I have no choice but to sleep while embracing Tohru-kun!!"
c: "N-n-n-no, I'm all right. B-b-b-b-bring it on."
d: "I don't know if it's surprising or expected that Yuki is actually an over-sleeper. By the way, I am the type who sleeps when he wants to sleep and wakes when he wants to wake!!"
e: "If I ever see that jerk again, I'll rip his head off! I'll kick his ass into the sky before he can even get a word in, then I'll punch right through him with all my strength...!"
f: "What the hell are you talking about!!"
g: "Mon frère magnifique!!"
h: "Well, yes! But my mother always told me that we need to face our fears because if we stay afraid, then those fears will rule our lives, so I mustn't keep avoiding it!"
i: "You need to calm down! What was it Kinpachi-sensei said? Oh! You might not know. It's from a school drama about razzle-dazzle youth being lifted from ignorance like fish from a dried up stream."
j: "You're as dense as an ogre! Dense as lead! If a tack is sharp, you're the thing farthest from it!!"
k: "If you must know, my hair has to be long because it is said that the first king, the honorable Rurubara-sama, received a message when he reached the age of four."
l: "Up, up, little brother! It is certainly time for a cheerful song to sweep you sonorously into a wonderful new day!!"
m: "If you're going to be so difficult, then I am left with no alternative!!"

QUIZ

Furuba-themed Comedic Dialogue Quiz

We've made a quiz out of some of Furuba's more memorable comedic moments. We think the answers will pop right into your head!

Q1

USING THE PICTURES AS HINTS, COMPLETE THE CONVERSATIONS BY FILLING IN THE MISSING DIALOGUE.

(1)

...
TH-THAT MEANS I'M YOUR SENPAI*, DOESN'T IT?!
patter patter patter patter

(2)

DON'T ACT LIKE YOU'RE SO SMART!!
WHO GIVES A DAMN IF SOME BEAR SHOWS UP IN A HORROR MOVIE?!!

(3)

PLEASE, YOU HAVE TO STOP FIGHTING!!

(4)

I SHALL EXERCISE MY SKILL SO THAT MY BELOVED LITTLE BROTHER CAN SPARKLE MORE GLORIOUSLY THAN ANYONE ON STAGE!
AHEM!
AND HOW MANY TIMES WILL YOU BE CHANGING OUTFITS, YUKI?

Q2

COMPLETE THE CONVERSATIONS BY DRAWING LINES BETWEEN THE DIALOGUE IN THE TOP SECTION AND THE MATCHING REPLY BELOW.

A: "Yuki-kun is cold today, as usual..." (Shigure)
B: "Please drink as much as you like from this dish! I've hardly touched it...!" (Ritsu)
C: "In fact, perhaps it would be easier if we just discussed me instead." (Ayame)
D: "I've never heard such a wonderful story..." (department store clerk)
E: "It never does. Aaya-nii as an older brother doesn't fit, either" (Hatsuharu)
F: "Good luck, Chibi-suke. You're on your own in this one." (Kakeru)
G: "Please...take good care of Yuki." (Hatsuharu)
H: "The old man is always alone!!" (Momiji)
I: "Besides, Shishou-san has the wonderful Hana-chan..." (Tohru)
J: "Did you know!!? There's a devil who pretends to be human adrift at sea and gets on the boat!!" (Mitsuru)

a: "You're right...You're right. You don't have to remind me." (Yuki)
b: "He's subtly mixing references..." (Hiro)
c: "Let go of her. Your vulgar germs will rub off on her." (Yuki)
d: "What would be the point in that?" (Yuki)
e: "...can you please not pick fights like a drunk person?" (Yuki)
f: "Don't just decide. On those things. On your own. And don't say that." (Kyo)
g: "What are you talking about?" (Boss)
h: "I'd rather die." (Kyo)
i: "He's a moron!! This place is crawling with idiots!!" (Kyo)
j: "Yes...! I promise I will make your daughter happy...!!" (Kakeru)

ANSWERS ON PAGE 172!

Step 1

Find Your Chinese Astrology Color

Furuba-themed Juusanshi Fortune-Telling

First, use the chart below to find your Furuba Chinese Zodiac color (you need to know your Chinese zodiac sign).

Chinese Zodiac Sign	Color
Rat	Pink
Ox	Green
Tiger	Red
Rabbit	Pink
Dragon	Red
Snake	Black
Horse	Green
Ram	Blue
Monkey	Yellow
Bird	Yellow
Dog	Blue
Boar	Black

How the fortune-telling works:

Step 1 will tell you what your Furuba Chinese Zodiac color is, according to your Chinese Zodiac sign. Next, the chart in Step 2 will indicate your blood type number (you need to know your blood type, too!). Once you have both pieces of information, go to Step 3 to determine your Juusanshi Sign.

This fortune-telling game adds the Year of the Cat to the zodiac, since we're dealing with Furuba. It indicates your romance "type", and which character you're compatible with!

ONCE YOU'VE LOOKED UP YOUR COLOR AND NUMBER, GO TO STEP 3!

This has no relation to wave fortune-telling.

HEY, HANAJIMA--NORMALLY I HATE GIRLY STUFF LIKE FORTUNE TELLING...
...BUT I WOULDN'T MIND IF YOU PREDICTED WHETHER OR NOT I'LL BEAT YUKI.
...OKAY.

Step 2

Find Your Blood Type Number

Start with Q1 and follow the arrows as you answer the questions.
The number you end up with is your blood type number.

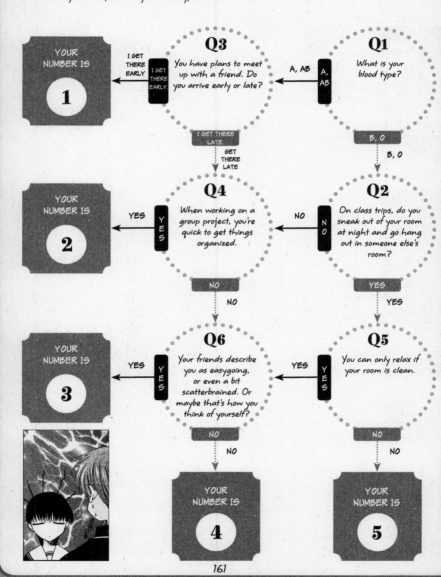

Q1
What is your blood type?
- A, AB → Q3
- B, O → Q2

Q2
On class trips, do you sneak out of your room at night and go hang out in someone else's room?
- YES → Q5
- NO → Q4

Q3
You have plans to meet up with a friend. Do you arrive early or late?
- I GET THERE EARLY. → YOUR NUMBER IS 1
- I GET THERE LATE. → Q4

Q4
When working on a group project, you're quick to get things organized.
- YES → YOUR NUMBER IS 2
- NO → Q6

Q5
You can only relax if your room is clean.
- YES → Q6
- NO → YOUR NUMBER IS 5

Q6
Your friends describe you as easygoing, or even a bit scatterbrained. Or maybe that's how you think of yourself?
- YES → YOUR NUMBER IS 3
- NO → YOUR NUMBER IS 4

YOUR NUMBER IS 1

YOUR NUMBER IS 2

YOUR NUMBER IS 3

YOUR NUMBER IS 4

YOUR NUMBER IS 5

Use your color and number to find your Juusanshi Sign!

Your Juusanshi Sign is based on the number and color you identified in Steps 1 and 2. The character you're most compatible with also indicates the sign of people with whom you're generally most compatible.

COLOR	NUMBER	JUUSANSHI SIGN	COLOR	NUMBER	JUUSANSHI SIGN
Red	1	Cat	Pink	1	Dragon
Red	2	Snake	Pink	2	Ox
Red	3	Monkey	Pink	3	Rat
Red	4	Ram	Pink	4	Rat
Red	5	Rabbit	Pink	5	Rabbit
Black	1	Cat	Green	1	Cat
Black	2	Snake	Green	2	Ox
Black	3	Monkey	Green	3	Tiger
Black	4	Ram	Green	4	Dragon
Black	5	Boar	Green	5	Boar
Yellow	1	Cat	Blue	1	Rat
Yellow	2	Horse	Blue	2	Horse
Yellow	3	Rat	Blue	3	Tiger
Yellow	4	Bird	Blue	4	Bird
Yellow	5	Dog	Blue	5	Dog

Juusanshi Descriptions

Your romance "type," and which character you're most compatible with.

An explanation of your approach to romance,
and which of the male Furuba characters is your best match.

Cat Type

You're a bit dense when it comes to romance--you may be completely oblivious to it when someone has feelings for you. However, once you fall in love, your heart will belong completely to that special person.

•YOUR MOST COMPATIBLE *FURUBA* CHARACTER•

Your most compatible character is Momiji. You rush headlong into situations, and sometimes it gets you hurt; Momiji's inner strength and cheerfulness will cushion life's blows.

Rat Type

When you're in love, you're very serious and a bit awkward. You put the other person's happiness first, so you watch out for them. You also have a hidden sloppy side, so you tend to look for a romantic partner who isn't a perfectionist.

•YOUR MOST COMPATIBLE *FURUBA* CHARACTER•

You tend to be reserved when it comes to love, so outgoing, forceful people like Ayame are a perfect balance for you. Taking things too seriously can wear you out, but matching Ayame's pace can open up whole new worlds!

Ox Type

You have a big heart, but you may not experience sudden flares of romance. On the other hand, your capacity to love just one person for a very long time is its own flavor of passion. You also have a tendency to change your interests and style to be more like the person you love.

•YOUR MOST COMPATIBLE *FURUBA* CHARACTER•

Your ability to see through other people's selfishness makes us think Kyo is a good match! His intense personality won't frighten you off, and you have the power to bring out the kindness hidden under his rough behavior.

Tiger Type

You probably express your love passively. Even if you like someone, you often won't tell them; instead, you'll wait for them to approach you. Be careful not to let opportunity pass you by!

•YOUR MOST COMPATIBLE *FURUBA* CHARACTER•

You are compatible with Hiro! He can seem bold or even self-important, but he's kind and prone to worrying. He's a perfect balance for someone like you, who wants to be protected.

Rabbit Type

You do everything you can for the person you love. You go out of your way to find gifts or to plan events to make them happy, and charm them with your smile.

•YOUR MOST COMPATIBLE *FURUBA* CHARACTER•

You are perfectly compatible with Kureno! His composure and maturity compensate for your exuberance and playfulness, and he can rein you in if you get a bit out of control.

Dragon Type

You have your own feelings under control, and don't force your opinions on others. You're so quiet that the people around you may be surprised when you have romantic feelings for someone, but that very restraint probably makes you popular.

•YOUR MOST COMPATIBLE *FURUBA* CHARACTER•

Yuki is an ideal match for you--your intellectual, peaceful aura appeals to Yuki's need for calm surroundings. The two of you would be a couple with a sympathetic, stable love.

Snake Type

You're the energetic sort, and other people trust you. Your love is naturally intense, and you express it frankly; you use every method you can think of to catch the attention of the person you love.

•YOUR MOST COMPATIBLE *FURUBA* CHARACTER•

Because you're so vibrant and overwhelming, we think Hatori is a natural match for you. His calm personality will help keep you from rushing into things, and being with him will probably help you settle down a little.

Horse Type

You come across as calm and composed, but you're capable of loving so intensely that you'll sacrifice anything for the person you love--and sometimes you may be badly hurt as a result.

•YOUR MOST COMPATIBLE *FURUBA* CHARACTER•

You love too strongly for your own good, so Hatsuharu is perfect for you: his heart is big enough to not be overwhelmed by your feelings. Simply being with him may be enough to give you some peace of mind.

Ram Type

No matter how much you love someone, you can't just be honest and admit it. But your attitude reveals your feelings, and the person you love-- and everyone else around you--will notice your emotions right away.

•YOUR MOST COMPATIBLE *FURUBA* CHARACTER•

Yuki is your perfect partner. He's very sensitive about other people, and will notice your feelings right away. It's safe for you to entrust him with your heart.

Monkey Type

Your personality is so hesitant that people might never suspect you can confess your feelings to someone you like--but when the crucial moment comes, you can surprise them with your boldness. You may well win them over!

•YOUR MOST COMPATIBLE *FURUBA* CHARACTER•

You're easygoing in some ways, and so is Shigure--which could make a solid match! They say that no one ever knows what Shigure is thinking, but being around him will help you grow as a person.

Bird Type

You don't rely on anyone else, and you love patiently. If you fall in love with someone whose heart belongs to someone else, you'll quietly back down. But if you try being selfish once in a while, you never know what could come of it!

•YOUR MOST COMPATIBLE *FURUBA* CHARACTER•

Because you tend to suppress your own feelings, we think Hatsuharu would be ideal for you. He tries so hard to understand other people's emotions that you can't help but be honest with him, which would help you relax.

Dog Type

Many people are attracted to your mature aura, but the truth is that you have a selfish streak. If you do date anyone, it doesn't last long. But if you really fall in love, that love could last your entire life.

•YOUR MOST COMPATIBLE *FURUBA* CHARACTER•

When it comes right down to it, you only really care about the person you love. Ritsu, who has trouble seeing past himself, is perfect for you. It's the kind of relationship that other people might not understand, but what matters is that it works for the two of you.

Boar Type

You're the type to rush headlong into things, and you love wholeheartedly. Your cheerful love doesn't weigh heavily on people or hold them back, which means you can have a good relationship with almost anyone.

•YOUR MOST COMPATIBLE *FURUBA* CHARACTER•

You're most compatible with Kyo! His personality is a bit rough, but you know yourself well enough that you won't be intimidated by it. You can deal with his intensity, and may even be able to help him think more like you do.

G A M E ● O F ● L I F E

This "Game of Life" is based on events in Furuba.
You can play it by yourself or with friends!

Furuba-themed Game of Life

HOW TO PLAY

(YOU'LL NEED)
- Pencil
- Die
- Something to use for pawns
- Calculator (optional, if you're not confident about math)

(RULES)
- You start with 50,000 yen.
- Roll the die and move your pawn forward the number of spaces shown on the die.
- Follow the instructions written on the space you land on.
- When you reach the "Finish", the player with the most money wins.
- The player who gets there last has to play a penalty game!

Start

Start here to play the Furuba Game of Life! (You start with 50,000 yen.)

I'M SO EXCITED!
LET'S GO!!
がしっ

1 Tonight you're having hamburger for dinner. (minus 500 yen)

2 Hana-chan uses waves to tell your fortune. (minus 7,000 yen)

WHY ARE YOU LOOKING AWAY?!!
YOU'RE... VERY SUPER-STITIOUS, AREN'T YOU?
......

3 Tonight you're having curry for dinner. (minus 500 yen)

4 You hit your head really hard at the haunted house! They charge you 10,000 yen to cover your medical bill. (minus 10,000 yen) + (lose one turn)

IT'S NO GOOD. AT THIS RATE...
...SHE'LL DIE!
EEK! WHAT'S THAT?!
IT'S...
THERE'S NO POINT IF THE SOUNDS ARE GOING TO SCARE YOU!!
...ALL

5 Uo-chan and Hana-chan buy you a swimsuit. (plus 5,000 yen)

TH-
THANK YOU SO MUCH.
I'LL... I'LL TAKE GOOD CARE OF IT!

6 Tonight you're having nira-tama for dinner. (minus 500 yen)

7 Tonight you're having shark fin for dinner. (minus 500 yen)

8 Mitchan writes a suicide note in front of your house. (minus 5,000 yen)

tremble
...BUT YOUR DAUGHTER MITSURU CAN NO LONGER BEAR THE HARASSMENT OF A CERTAIN AUTHOR...
MITCHAN —
...SAN?
tremble tremble

←

9

You are invited to stay at a Sohma hot springs inn. (plus 10,000 yen)

...ONSEN...
I COULDN'T GO TO SUCH AN EXTRAVAGANT PLACE AND FORGET ABOUT MOM.
I WONDER IF SHE'D FORGIVE ME...
UM, TOHRU-KUN, IT'S JUST AN ONSEN. HE'S NOT ASKING YOU TO GO TO PARIS OR ANYTHING.

10 Tonight you're having a gyoza combo for dinner. (minus 500 yen)

11

Ayame embroiders something idiotic on your clothes. (minus 7,000 yen)

THERE IS NO NEED TO HESITATE! I AM IN THE HIGHEST OF HIGH SPIRITS TODAY!
AS YOU WISH, I SHALL EMBROIDER "I LIVE FOR KAGURA" FOR YOU!
DON'T SEW ANYTHING! DON'T COME NEAR ME! DON'T TOUCH ME!!
I don't want it!

12 Tonight you're having hand-rolled sushi for dinner. (minus 500 yen)

13

You are given ribbons as a White Day gift. (plus 5,000 yen)

...PRINCESS?
DO YOU...
...LIKE IT...
EH?!

14 Tonight you're having soumen for dinner. (minus 500 yen)

22

You smash a watermelon with your bare hands! ...and hurt yourself. (minus 10,000 yen)

IN CELEBRATION OF HIRO-SAN'S BABY--
I TOLD YOU IT'S NOT MY BABY!!
--TOHRU HONDA WILL HUMBLY SMASH THE WATERMELON!!
TU--!
EH?!

23 You get hit by a skyrocket firework. (minus 15,000 yen)

Oh.
IT SAYS NOT TO HOLD IT IN YOUR HANDS OR POINT IT AT PEOPLE OR BUILDINGS.
HE'S POINTING IT AT ME!!

24

You get infected by Ritchan's panic, and lose some years off your life. (minus 20,000 yen)

NOOOOOOOOO!!!
I'M SORRY! I'M SORRY!
I'M SORRY!
JUST KIDDING!
NO, NO. SERIOUSLY, I WAS JOKING.

GAME OF LIFE

15 Snack time: aburi-mochi! (minus 500 yen)

16 Uh oh! Megumi Hanajima learns your real name!! (minus 10,000 yen) + (go back two spaces)

...AND "MOTOKO"...
...SAN?

17 Tonight you're having tororo soba for dinner. (minus 500 yen)

18 You come down with a cold! (minus 3,000 yen) + (lose one turn)

WELL... MORE OR LESS. THAT NIGHT, EVERYONE WAS SICK WITH COLDS.
WHAT DID THEY EXPECT, PLAYING OLD MAID OUTSIDE IN SUCH COLD WEATHER...?
Of course they'd catch colds!
I ONLY TAKE FAMILY AS PATIENTS, AND I STILL GET WORKED TO DEATH...

19 Snack time: pancakes! (minus 500 yen)

20 You are invited to the Sohma beach house. (plus 10,000 yen)

......!
STAG BEETLES! WE HAVE TO CATCH STAG BEETLES!
YES!!

21 Tonight you're having monja-yaki for dinner. (minus 500 yen)

The loser has to play this penalty game!

Roll the die to discover your penalty. See if you can manage it without bothering anyone.

- ♦If you roll 1 or 2 .... Imitate Kimi
- ♦If you roll 3 or 4 .... Imitate Aaya
- ♦If you roll 5 or 6 .... Imitate Ritchan

Finish

......
I AM HAPPY...

- * First player to arrive .... Plus 10,000 yen
- * Second player .... Plus 8,000 yen
- * Third player .... Plus 6,000 yen

※Players who don't mind being called ingrates can sell the "ribbons" and "swimsuit" they were given as gifts during the game for 5,000 yen.

Furuba-themed Quiz Answers

Here are the answers to each of the quizzes. If you couldn't answer more than half of the questions, maybe you should read the story again!

Multiple-choice Quiz for the Total Fanatic

Q1...b: A heartwarming school romance with a hint of fantasy--something for everyone!
Q2...a: She never gets depressed, no matter what happens.
Q3...a: Crabs and peaches.
Q4...c: He doesn't mind miso soup.
Q5...a: A story about grated cheese.
Q6...a: A rat charm.
Q7...a: An old man buying a convenience store lunch.
Q8...c: As proof that she is a sinner.
Q9...b: Blue.
Q10...b: A sparrow.
Q11...c: A vegetable shop.
Q12...c: Blue (Yuki) and orange (Kyo).
Q13...c: Volunteer.
Q14...c: Super "Yotteke".
Q15...c: Soba.
Q16...a: "In the Moonlight".
Q17...b: Because your smiling face is better than any gift! Like a bird, it spreads its white wings, soaring to great heights in the blue sky that is my heart.
Q18...b: It's all good.
Q19...c: "Sometimes it's easier to understand a situation if you look at it from a distance."

Fill-in-the-speech-bubble Quiz

Q1...(1) g: "Mon frère magnifique!!" **(2) l:** "Up, up, little brother! It is certainly time for a cheerful song to sweep you sonorously into a wonderful new day!!" **(3) d:** "I don't know if it's surprising or expected that Yuki is actually an over-sleeper. By the way, I am the type who sleeps when he wants to sleep and wakes when he wants to wake!!"

Q2...(4) j: "You're as dense as an ogre! Dense as lead! If a tack is sharp, you're the thing farthest from it!!" **(5) a:** "A man like you has no right to have summer!! Pack your bags and leave this place at once!!" **(6) f:** "What the hell are you talking about?!"

Q3...(7) e: "If I ever see that jerk again, I'll rip his head off! I'll kick his ass into the sky before he can even get a word in, then I'll punch right through him with all my strength...!"

Q4...(8) m: "If you're going to be so difficult, then I am left with no alternative!!" **(9) b:** "I have no choice but to sleep while embracing Tohru-kun!!"

Q5...(10) h: "Well, yes! But my mother always told me that we need to face our fears, because if we stay afraid, then those fears will rule our lives, so I mustn't keep avoiding it!!"

Comedic Dialogue Quiz

Q1
(1) ..."Senpai, you really suck at this."
(2) ..."You really are an idiot."
(3) ..."You stop swinging that thing around!!"
(4) ..."It's not a wedding ceremony!"

Q2
A:"Yuki-kun is cold today, as usual..." and **c:**" Let go of her. Your vulgar germs will rub off on her." [Shigure → Yuki]
B: "Please drink as much as you like from this dish! I've hardly touched it...!" and **h:** "I'd rather die." [Ritsu → Kyo]
C:" In fact, perhaps it would be easier if we just discussed me instead." and **d:**"What would be the point in that?" [Ayame → Yuki]
D:" I've never heard such a wonderful story..." and **i:** "He's a moron!! This place is crawling with idiots!!" [department store clerk → Kyo]
E:" It never does. Aya-nii as an older brother doesn't fit, either." and **a:**" You're right...You're right. You don't have to remind me." [Hatsuharu → Yuki]
F:" Good luck, Chibi-suke. You're on your own in this one." and **e:** "...can you please not pick fights like a drunk person?" [Kakeru → Yuki]
G:"Please...take good care of Yuki." and **j:** "Yes...! I promise I will make your daughter happy...!!" [Hatsuharu → Kakeru]
H:"The old man is always alone!!" and **b:** "He's subtly mixing references..." [Momiji → Hiro]
I: "Besides, Shishou-san has the wonderful Hana-chan..." and **f:** "Don't just decide. On those things. On your own. And don't say that." [Tohru → Kyo]
J: "Did you know?!! There's a devil who pretends to be human adrift at sea and gets on the boat!!" and **g:** "What are you talking about?" [Mitsuru → Boss]

Chapter 5: God

INTERVIEW 2
COMIC

This final section includes the second half of the written interview with Takaya-sensei, and special bonus comics! In the interview, we asked Takaya-sensei more questions about Furuba, and a bit about her private life!

About the Sohma Family

Natsuki Takaya WRITTEN INTERVIEW Part 2

We asked Takaya-sensei to tell us more about the Furuba characters and about herself. Questions marked with a star were received from readers.

★Q1: HOW DID YOU COME UP WITH THE NAMES OF THE CHARACTERS WHO AREN'T POSSESSED BY THE ZODIAC? (P.N. GACHAPIN, OTHERS)

There isn't really a story to those names. It's actually unusual for me to choose characters' names the way I did for the Zodiac. Usually, I get a sense of what a character's name should be like after I establish their personality and looks. One thing I do, although it's not really an "origin" for names, is give masculine names to female characters to balance them out. That's what I did with Tohru. What else...Kakeru was supposed to have a different surname, but the night after I drew my rough draft of his first appearance, when I was trying to sleep, he shouted "The true pot flies!" in my head (laugh). So I changed his name to "Manabe".

Q2: WHAT KIND OF RESPONSIBILITIES DOES AKITO HAVE AS HEAD OF THE FAMILY?

It'd be stretching it to say Akki does any work (laugh). She leaves it all up to other people, like Kureno. I think the only thing she puts effort into is existing.

★Q3: DID AKITO GO TO SCHOOL? WAS IT THE SAME SCHOOL AS THE OTHER MEMBERS OF THE ZODIAC? (P.N. CHIGUSA, OTHERS)

She didn't exactly attend school. She always stayed home. She did high school by correspondence, and I think she was enrolled at better (more expensive, anyway) elementary and middle schools than the other Zodiac members. It's just like our Akito-sama to stay home from even that kind of school (laugh). Incidentally, I pretend family registers and whatnot don't exist in the Furuba world.

Q4: THE WOMAN WHO LOOKS AFTER AKITO IS VERY HIGH-HANDED WITH THE ZODIAC MEMBERS, BUT WHAT ARE HER ACTUAL DUTIES? AND WHAT IS HER NAME?

She is someone who has been with the Sohmas for a long time, and has been sucked into their distorted world. She is in charge of the maids, and is mainly responsible for taking care of Akito, as she once took care of Akira-san. She doesn't have a name (again?).

Q5: YOU'VE SAID THAT THE PEOPLE WHO RAISE THE JUUNISHI ARE GIVEN A LOT OF MONEY TO TAKE CARE OF THEM, BUT JUST HOW MUCH MONEY ARE WE TALKING ABOUT? AND WHAT OTHER SPECIAL PRIVILEGES DO THEY HAVE?

No way, this is really good!
Yeah, it's good.
I'm surprised.
It's delicious, isn't it?
Enjoying Pri-Yuki's Candy
Appeared in Volume 13
So carefree...

Haru was thinking of confessing his love to Rin when his height surpassed hers. He's caught up by strange things.
?
Just a little more...
Appeared in Volume 14
Rin is two years older than Haru.

Celebrating volume 13!!
Sadly, we're not going to be able to make an appearance in this volume.
We're off to fight evil things right now!
Mogeee!
Today is also today.
Appeared in Volume 13
Mogeta & Ari

I LOVE YOU! EVEN IF YOU GO BALD, OR LIKE UNDERAGE GIRLS, I CAN HANDLE IT!
I'm crazy with love!
YES, YES, I LOVE YOU, TOO.
BUT THAT HURTS.
hug
hug
hug
squeeze
hug
Long live the stupid couple.

Appeared in Volume 16
Long live the bakappuru

AWESOME! VOLUME 15'S OUT! NOW I GET TO HEAR MORE OF YUN-YUN'S STORY! LET THE SOMBER TALE BEGIN!
Woo!
PLEASE DON'T CALL MY LIFE SOMBER.
Sorry for the delay.

Appeared in Volume 15
Sorry to make you wait....

I don't have a specific amount in mind, but they're given enough money that it generates strong feelings; they're also given the kind of privileges that make them start to think they're better than other people. But the trade-off, I think, is that the Sohmas find (or create) a weakness that inescapably binds them to the family.

Q6: DID THE SOHMA FAMILY CHOOSE THE HIGH SCHOOL THAT SHIGURE, AYAME, AND HATORI WENT TO?

That's right. They also chose the girls' high school that Kagura, Kisa, and Isuzu attend(ed).

Q7: WHEN ISUZU AND KISA WERE HOSPITALIZED, WERE THEY IN A SOHMA-OWNED HOSPITAL?

Yes, they were.

★Q8: I UNDERSTAND THAT HATORI-SAN'S HYPNOSIS IS VERY STRONG, BUT IS IT POSSIBLE TO REVERSE IT? I WANT MOMIJI-CHAN TO BE HAPPY, BUT I DON'T THINK THAT CAN HAPPEN UNLESS HATORI-SAN'S HYPNOSIS IS UNDONE (AND UNLESS HIS MOTHER ACKNOWLEDGES HIM AS HER SON)...(P.N. SAKI KITAMAKI)

Oh, wow...I'm sorry, I've never really thought about it. Can he undo it...? But I think that even if he could, Momiji wouldn't ever ask him to. I think Momiji empathizes too much with the pain Hatori goes through, being the only one who can do (or undo) it. But Momiji's happiness could come from somewhere else--like Momo. It's a work in progress.

About the Furuba Characters

★Q9: IS THERE ANY KIND OF FOOD TOHRU DOESN'T LIKE, OR CAN'T MAKE? IF SO, WHAT KIND? (P.N. SAE ★ARATSU)

As long as she has a recipe, I think she can make just about anything. She's probably not up to cooking everything as well as a trained chef, though. Incidentally, they often eat Japanese food at Shigure's house.

Q10: ARE UO-CHAN AND HANA-CHAN GOOD COOKS? WHAT DO THEY MAKE WELL?

Hana-chan can't cook. She won't even try (laugh). Uo-chan is good at it, but I haven't really thought about what she's best at making...

Q11: YUKI'S MOTHER ALWAYS SEEMS SO BUSY, BUT WHAT IS SHE ACTUALLY DOING?

Going shopping, to salons, to the theatre, to parties...Those kinds of things keep her very busy.

★Q12: WHAT KIND OF PERSON IS KYO'S FATHER? (P.N. FRANK)

He's a difficult man. He's very anxious, and tries to make himself feel better by taking it out on other people, but it just makes things worse.

Q13: HOW MANY PEN NAMES DOES SHIGURE REALLY HAVE? IS MITCHAN HIS EDITOR FOR THE ROMANCES HE WRITES AS "NOA KIRITANI", OR THE STORY ABOUT THE COCKROACH? HAVE HE AND MITCHAN EVER HAD A SERIOUS MEETING?

I think he has about three or four. Mitchan edits the books he publishes under his own name.

Q14: HOW GOOD IS KAGURA AT KARATE? DOES SHE BEAT EVERYONE AT THE DOJO?

I wouldn't say she beats everyone (laugh), although I think of her as stronger than normal girls. The reason she seems to outclass Kyo so badly is that he won't actually fight back against a girl. Shishou's teachings live on, at least in him.

Q15: I GET THE IMPRESSION MOMIJI LIVES BY HIMSELF (NOT COUNTING SERVANTS), BUT HOW BIG IS HIS HOUSE? DOES HE EAT HIS MEALS ALONE?

In terms of the rooms he actually lives in, I guess there's the one you see in Volume 13, and one more (a room for his clothes?). That seems to be enough for him. As far as meals go, he usually eats alone, but sometimes he visits the other Zodiac members' houses. And Hatori-san worries about him and invites him over a lot.

Q16: WHEN HATORI TURNS INTO A SEAHORSE, IS IT ACTUALLY BEST TO PUT HIM IN FRESH WATER, WARM WATER, OR SEAWATER?

Hmm, I wonder. Hatori is naturally human, but when he transforms, he's a seahorse, so I...I don't know. We should ask Hatori-san. (laugh)

Q17: WE DON'T REALLY SEE MUCH OF HATSUHARU'S PARENTS. WHAT ARE THEY LIKE?

I feel like they're decent people. But if you're asking whether they're responsible parents...maybe not so much. At this point, though, Haru has stopped being bothered that they used to laugh at him and tease him.

Q18: ROUGHLY HOW MUCH DOES A CUSTOM-MADE COSTUME FROM AYAME'S SHOP COST? AND HOW LONG DOES IT TAKE THEM TO FINISH IT ONCE IT'S ORDERED?

It all depends on the individual costume--materials, labor, etc. Among enthusiasts, those outfits have an excellent reputation for quality.

Q19: WHERE DID AYAME AND MINE MEET?

At Ayame's shop. I'd like to draw the story, so I've had it on the back burner for a long time, but it looks like the series is going to end without it being included (laugh).

Q20: DOES KISA ENJOY SCHOOL NOW?

I'd be lying if I said she was having a lot of fun. But Kisa's learned not to look in just one place to have fun, or to determine her own self-worth, so she'll be okay. She's still trying hard.

Q21: DOES HIRO QUIBBLE LIKE THAT (OR DID HE) WITH HIS TEACHERS AND FRIENDS AT SCHOOL?

He doesn't hate studying.

Appeared in Volume 14
He won't show up much.

Appeared in Volume 15
Prince in a hat.

Appeared in Volume 10
A one-piece or a bikini...

Appeared in Volume 11
This is Kagura.

Appeared in Volume 8
Tease Mitchan in moderation.

Not exactly, no. He used to be ruthless about snapping at high-and-mighty people who tried bossing others around, but now he's grown up enough that he's started being able to let things slide.

Q22: HOW IS RITSU AND MITCHAN'S RELATIONSHIP GOING?

I think if you read the special bonus comic, it will be obvious (laugh).

Q23: HOW WAS IT DECIDED THAT KAGURA'S FAMILY WOULD TAKE ISUZU IN?

The people around them thought it would be a good environment for Isuzu, since she and Kagura are both female Juunishi, and are almost the same age. But it backfired.

Q24: WHEN KURENO USED TO TRANSFORM, WHAT KIND OF BIRD DID HE TURN INTO?

A sparrow. I initially thought he'd be a rooster, but then that didn't seem to mesh with his character, so I changed my mind.

Q25: WHAT KIND OF PART-TIME WORK DOES KAKERU DO?

I guess he usually works at a convenience store, but he probably does temporary jobs, too. Right now, he's stopped taking as much extra work, though. If I can fit it in, I'll draw the reason for that into the story. (Or so I say, but the reason isn't really that important.)

Q26: WHY DOES KIMI DO SO MANY THINGS TO OFFEND THOSE GIRLS?

Because she's Kimi-sama (laugh). I think she doesn't care if girls don't like her, as long as guys do.

★Q27: WHO NOMINATED HANA-CHAN TO PLAY CINDERELLA IN "SORTA CINDERELLA", WHEN THE CLASS WAS CHOOSING THE CAST? AND WHAT WAS THEIR MOTIVATION? (P.N. YUMERIA)

It was almost all the boys in the class--Hana-chan is secretly very popular! Their reasoning was, "She's mysterious, so it'll be interesting; I wanna see what kind of Cinderella she'll play!"

★Q28: WHAT HAPPENED TO YUKI-KUN'S COSTUME FROM "SORTA CINDERELLA" AFTER THE SHOW? DID THE PRI-YUKI MEMBERS DIVIDE IT UP LIKE LAST TIME? (P.N. SAE, OTHERS)

Ayame and Mine put in a lot of work on the costumes, so the cast took them home as mementos. But I think Kyo would have refused to keep his, so one of his admirers probably gave it a good home.

Q29: WHAT IS "MOGETA" ABOUT, REALLY?

There's an evil emperor who targets a country, and that country's princess hires Ari and Mogeta to defeat him. Every episode is an absurd story where they have an absurd battle with the emperor's absurd minions. I'm a bit mystified about why something like that would be so popular--so I wonder about my own sanity, since I'm the one who came up with it. But there's no way they've ever had a serious discussion about it. Mitchan is more like his servant, or maybe his plaything.

Q30: ARE THERE THINGS ABOUT ANY OF THE CHARACTERS THAT MAKE YOU THINK, "DARN IT! I SHOULDN'T HAVE DESIGNED THEM THIS WAY!" WHILE YOU DRAW THEM?

Haru and Rin's outfits. Ayame and Mine's clothes. Long hair, blond hair, black hair (especially Ren-san. When I'm inking Ren-san, I call it "Ren Hell"), etc., etc., etc...Those are all hard to work on. I think my assistants have trouble with the tone of Kyo's hair (laugh).

★Q31: IF YOU COULD BE A FRUITS BASKET CHARACTER, WHO WOULD YOU WANT TO BE, TAKAYA-SENSEI? (P.N. HAMBURGER, OTHERS)

Since I created them myself, I don't think I "want to be" any of them. There's a bit of me in each of them. And I think that without idealizing someone you can't be like--no matter how much you want to be like them--you can't recognize who you really want to be. So even if you become just like the person you wanted to be like, you'll never really "be them" as long as you're still "you" in your mind. You're still always yourself...Was that too complicated? (sweatdrop)

★Q32: WHICH OF THE FRUITS BASKET CHARACTERS WOULD YOU WANT AS A BOYFRIEND, A HUSBAND, A BEST FRIEND, OR A SIBLING? (P.N. HIZUKI, OTHERS)

As I said before, I don't really think that way about characters I created myself. I think they're all very close to me--like my reflection, or a "what if" part of me. So I don't want to get too close to them; I need some distance. It's not that I'd push them away, of course--it's just that I'm always thinking about my characters, and they're incredibly important to me. So I worry about them a lot, but I don't want to make them the center of my life and lose track of things that are more important. It's a personal rule of mine when I'm drawing a series. I'm sorry, maybe that explanation doesn't really help...(sweatdrop)

About Takaya-sensei Herself

Q33: WHAT IS YOUR MONTHLY SCHEDULE LIKE?

I don't have a consistent schedule. I arrange my life around each month's deadlines.

Q34: WHAT ABOUT YOUR DAILY SCHEDULE? ARE YOU A DAY PERSON OR A NIGHT PERSON?

Sometimes I'm a day person, and sometimes I'm a night person. I fluctuate too much to settle down as one or the other. If I don't answer the phone, it usually means I'm asleep.

Q35: ROUGHLY HOW MUCH OF YOUR LIFE IS TAKEN UP BY MANGA, TAKAYA-SENSEI?(P.N. HIROMI MIO)

Appeared in Volume 8
Ritchan, having a wonderful dream

Appeared in Volume 11
A flower with a flower

Appeared in Volume 12
A mystery...

INTERVIEW

I too... feel like it's summer...
In the story, it's the height of summer...

Appeared in Volume 11
We get hot just looking at you.

Appeared in Volume 12
Inking her in is too hard...

I feel like I spend about 80-90% of my time thinking of nothing but manga, no matter what I'm doing. Sometimes it exhausts me, and I feel like I need a break from it--but then I immediately start missing it and wanting to get back to drawing. So in the end, I think it suits me best to sit at my desk, quietly thinking about and drawing manga.

Q36: WHAT MUSIC DO YOU LISTEN TO WHILE YOU WORK?
Various kinds of Japanese music and game soundtracks. I'm always listening to something while I work; if I don't, I can't seem to get myself into working mode.

Q37: HOW DO YOU USUALLY DRESS? WHAT KIND OF WESTERN CLOTHES DO YOU WEAR A LOT? (PLEASE USE FRUITS BASKET CHARACTERS AS EXAMPLES.)
When I'm working--I mean, when I'm at home, I wear sweats; kind of sports casual, I guess. When I go out, I usually wear some kind of pants. I like the Agnès brand. To give a character as an example... Hmm. Maybe Mayuchan-sensei?

Q38: WHAT ARE THE MOST FUN OR EXCITING THINGS ABOUT DRAWING MANGA?
When I come up with a story and shape it, and someone reads it and thinks it was good. When my voice reaches people. There is nothing better than that.

★Q39: ARE THERE ANY ART SUPPLIES YOU'RE PICKY ABOUT? (P.N. YUKAKO)
I try hard not to get too fussy. I'm the type who's prone to over-thinking that kind of thing too much to get any work done. But I still wind up being picky: I find myself needing to use kuretake for inking, and AIR-IN erasers...

★Q40: OF ALL THE COLOR ILLUSTRATIONS YOU'VE DRAWN SO FAR, WHICH ONE DO YOU LIKE BEST? (P.N. ORANGE)
It's hard to choose! I'd like to know which one the readers like best. Hmm...Maybe the Haru and Rin picture I drew recently?

Q41: WHAT IS YOUR FAVORITE OUT OF ALL THE INSERTS, SPECIAL OFFERS, PRIZES, AND MERCHANDISE HANA TO YUME HAS RELEASED SO FAR?
The Zodiac / Cat / Onigiri ornaments.

★Q42: DO YOU EVER HAVE A CHANCE TO TAKE A WHOLE DAY OFF, TAKAYA-SENSEI? IF SO, HOW DO YOU SPEND IT? (TOSHIHARU TAKETSUGI, OTHERS)
There aren't any official "days off", because there's always work to do. I make them by announcing (to myself), "Today I won't work! I won't do anything! I said I won't, and I won't!" As for what I do then, I play video games. I ♥ games! There are also times when I spend the whole day staring blankly at the TV. When that happens, it's a dead giveaway that I'm very tired.

★Q43: WHEN YOU GET OVERWHELMED BY WORK, WHAT ARE THE THINGS THAT GIVE YOU THE ENERGY TO PUSH FORWARD? (SUMIKO NISHIDA)

The moment I finish a manuscript. That makes me feel incredibly liberated. And dollhouses and miniatures refresh my mind--gazing at a dollhouse gives me the feeling that I'm traveling to another world.

Q44: WILL YOU SHARE YOUR FAVORITE PHRASE OR MOTTO?

I have a few, but they're secret--especially my motto. I want to keep it vibrant in my heart, where no one else can see it, so I can aspire to it on my own. It's like when I'm discouraged--I want the person who slaps sense into me to be me, with my own strength. (Sometimes I slap myself too hard and fall over, though.)

Q45: WHAT IS THE SOURCE OF YOUR STRENGTH, TAKAYA-SENSEI?

I think in the end, it might really be drawing manga.

Q46: AND WHAT IS YOUR WEAKNESS?

I have a lot of weaknesses. But I can't tell them to you, because they're my weaknesses (laugh). And there are a lot of things that scare me. I'm amazed I've made it this far, given all that.

Q47: WHAT ARE YOUR FAVORITE AND LEAST FAVORITE FOODS?

I like abalone. I like cotton candy. I like curry, too. And I like soba and udon, and crepes. I guess the answer is that I like a lot of things (laugh). But I hate peppers; maybe I'm being childish, but I just can't do it. Oh, but I've recently made a little progress with yuzu.

Q48: IS THERE SOMEWHERE YOU'D LIKE TO GO?

Somewhere that's just a grassy field, as far as the eye can see. I think I'd feel both incredibly fulfilled and incredibly empty. Oh, and Kyoto--I've been there tons of times, but I love it.

Q49: WHAT DO YOU WANT MOST RIGHT NOW?

Time. I'm afraid of my left hand relapsing, so I can't push myself--but I often think, "I wish I could draw a lot more."

Q50: WHAT IS YOUR FAVORITE SEASON?

Autumn. I can relax then, because I feel as if the things that woke up in the summer are quieting down and going back to sleep.

Q51: WHAT IS YOUR FAVORITE ANIMAL? HAVE YOU EVER HAD A PET?

Dogs! Puppies! Doggies! I've never had one of my own, but I really, really want to welcome one into my family someday...!

★Q52: WHAT ZODIAC YEAR DO YOU WISH YOU'D BEEN BORN IN, TAKAYA-SENSEI? (P.N. N)

Hmm...Maybe the Bird? The Bird can fly. I'd like to try flying.

Appeared in Volume 10
Not near. Not far. Someday.

Appeared in Volume 11
Summer memories

Q53: WHAT KINDS OF TRADITIONS DID YOUR HIGH SCHOOL HAVE?

Wow, you're really asking me to go back in time...(laugh). I'm sure it was a completely typical, normal high school. It didn't have traditions like Kaibara High's. (Maybe I should have put more thought into naming the school. Kaibara...I don't know....)

★Q54: WHAT WERE YOU REALLY INTO WHEN YOU WERE IN HIGH SCHOOL? (P.N. AYANO HAYAMI)

Drawing manga. Music, and listening to songs. I guess I haven't changed much (laugh). I wasn't in a club; the school didn't have a manga club or anything.

Q55: WHEN YOU WERE IN HIGH SCHOOL, WHAT DID YOU DREAM OF BECOMING?

I desperately wanted to be a manga artist. I thought my life would be over if I couldn't become one.

Appeared in Volume 9
His identity will become clear in chapter 49.

Cat Kyon Chibi

Appeared in Volume 12
Why he was drawing fried eggs...

Q56: WHAT WAS THE FIRST VIDEO GAME YOU EVER PLAYED?

Romancing Saga for the Super Nintendo. The very first time you do anything is always new and exciting, and makes a deep impression. In my case, I don't really remember the game itself, but I clearly remember thinking, "That was interesting! It was really fun!"

Q57: WHAT WAS THE FIRST MANGA YOU EVER READ?

Doraemon, maybe? And after that, I think it was my older sister's Nakayoshi magazines.

Q58: WHAT ARE SOME BOOKS, MUSIC, OR MOVIES THAT HAVE INFLUENCED YOU?

Momo and The Neverending Story are the first books that come to mind. In terms of music, I'd have to say Mackie. And as for a movie, there's Castle in the Sky. Those are the things that have left the deepest, longest-lasting impressions on me. The truth is, I sometimes feel as if it's presumptuous of me to draw manga, when the world already has incredible things like those in it. But I still draw (laugh).

Q59: DO YOU HAVE ANY PLANS TO DRAW EXTRA STORIES ABOUT THE CHARACTERS AFTER *FRUITS BASKET* HAS ENDED?

I don't. I've known all along that I wouldn't be able to draw every story I thought of, and they just keep coming. I can't say for sure that I won't want to come back to them a few years after the manga ends; I mean, lately I've started thinking I'd like to draw a continuation of Tsubasa o Motsu Mono. But I suspect that if I actually started drawing it, I'd think, "On second thought, I wanna draw something new" (laugh).

Q60: THIS MAY BE A BIT PREMATURE, BUT WHAT KIND OF STORY WOULD YOU LIKE TO DRAW NEXT?

I've considered various genres: a school drama, a fantasy, or some sort of home drama. I have a lot of fun thinking about things like that (laugh). I think next time I'd like to try a story with only a few characters, but that might be impossible....

Q61: DO YOU HAVE A CLOSING THOUGHT FOR YOUR FANS?

As always, thank you so much. Thank you for everything. Whenever I'm asked to give you all a message, I never know what I should say or how I should say it (laugh), but what I most want to express is how grateful I am. All of your support reaches me, so thank you for that. I really want to thank everyone who reads my work, and everyone who's helped me. Furuba still has a long way to go before it gets to its final chapter (laugh), but I hope you'll keep watching over the characters as they go through their mountains and valleys. I'll do my best!

Special Bonus Section

Sohma Family Journal

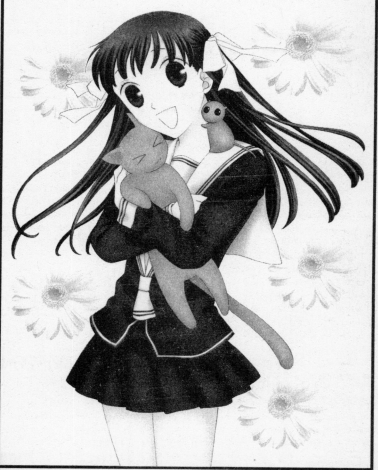

Something that makes even Shigure-san so uncomfortable that he wants to flee.

SHIGURE-SAN WRAPPED MY END-OF-THE-YEAR GIFT IN SUCH LOVELY PAPER.

OH, AND IT WOULD BE A SHAME TO THROW THIS STRING AWAY. THERE MUST BE SOMETHING I CAN USE IT FOR...

:

It does work!

I CAN USE IT JUST LIKE A HAIR RIBBON!

I'LL BE SURE TO WEAR IT TO SCHOOL TOMORROW.

I'LL BUY YOU RIBBONS!

I'LL BUY YOU RIBBONS! JUST PLEASE STOP DOING THAT...!!

EH?!

Blood will tell.
WHEN AAYA AND MINE ARE GOING OUT...
...HE ALWAYS PUTS HER SHOES ON FOR HER.
I GET FLUSTERED EVERY TIME!
信用第一
HE'S ALWAYS DOING THAT, YOU KNOW? ALWAYS!
I get embarrassed just watching!!
Ayame's regular customers.
MINE IS MINE, BUT THE BOSS IS THE BOSS! HOW DENSE CAN THEY BE?!
OTOUTO-KUN, SINCE YOU STOPPED BY TO VISIT, YOU SHOULD BE CAREFUL GOING IN THERE!
HA HA...
ARE THEY RIGHT? IS IT THAT STRANGE?
IT SEEMS LIKE SOMETHING I'D DO, TOO...
WHATEVER IS THE MATTER? YOUR DUMBFOUNDED VISAGE BETRAYS YOUR BEWILDERMENT OVER THE VERY NOTION THAT WE MIGHT LACK PERFECT UNDERSTANDING!!
My brother!!

Take that! (Or not.)

OH, KYO-KUN...? WHAT ARE YOUR FATHER'S HOBBIES?
WHAT KINDS OF THINGS DOES HE LIKE...?
ISN'T THIS DAMN WOMAN EVER GONNA GIVE UP?
I'LL DO ANYTHING TO GET IN HER WAY! I'LL LIE IF I HAVE TO!
YOU'RE OUTTA LUCK, HANA-JIMA...
OUT OF LUCK ...?
SHISHOU REALLY CAN'T STAND GIRLS WHO WEAR ALL BLACK!
TAKE THAT!!
OH, REALLY ...?
HEE HEE ...
WHO DO YOU THINK I'M TALKING ABOUT???
I MEAN YOU!!
WHAT'S WITH THAT SMUG LOOK?!!

Is it okay for me to draw such happy people
(given how they are in the actual story)?
IN CHAPTER 74...
HE WOULDN'T EVEN NOTICE IF HE STEPPED IN DOG CRAP...
THAT'S WHAT ARISA SAID ABOUT KURENO-SAN...
BUT HOW WOULD SHE FEEL IF SHE REALLY SAW IT HAPPEN?
Aaaah!
KURENO-SAN, YOU STEPPED IN CRAP!
Eh ...?
YOU'RE RIGHT. I DIDN'T EVEN NOTICE.
Ha ha!
I NEED TO PAY MORE ATTENTION.
......
I LOVE YOU, YOU DORK!!
ずぎゅーん
ACTUALLY, IT LOOKS LIKE SHE'S TOTALLY FINE WITH IT.

W c = c c
GURE-SAN, DID YOU HEAR? WHY TORI-SAN--OUR TORI-SAN!--COULD NOT PERFORM ON THE DRAMA CD???
IN THE END, HE WOULD NOT GRACE US WITH THE HONOR OF HIS VOICE! THE END OF THE WORLD IS AT HAND!
WASN'T IT BECAUSE WE COULDN'T MAKE YOU STOP TALKING, AAYA?
AND SO I HAVE CONSIDERED THE MATTER!!
IF HE WILL NOT SPEAK ON HIS OWN, WE HAVE NO CHOICE BUT TO MAKE HIM SPEAK, BY FORCE IF NEED BE!
TO THIS END, WE WILL MAKE HIM READ STORIES ALOUD!!
MOMOTARO
How-ever!!
TORI-SAN SPEAKS SO RARELY THAT READING SUCH A LONG STORY MIGHT RENDER HIS BEAUTIFUL VOICE HOARSE-- IT WOULD BE A GRAVE TRAGEDY FOR THE SOHMA ESTATE!
THEREFORE, I, AYAME, WILL JOYFULLY TAKE TORI-SAN'S PLACE, THAT MY OWN VOICE MAY BE RENDERED HOARSE!
THE LINE, "ONCE UPON A TIME, THERE WAS AN OLD MAN WHO LIVED WITH HIS WIFE," WILL LEAVE YOU STRICKEN WITH AWE!!
READ QUIETLY.
ROGER THAT, TORI-SAN!!
Why a folk-tale?

All you need is love.
RITCHAN AND MITCHAN.
TODAY, THEY'RE ON ANOTHER FRIENDLY DATE.
THE WIND IS A LITTLE COLD TODAY, ISN'T IT?
Gasp!
SPRING IS STILL CHILLY, ISN'T IT? YOU CAN WEAR THIS SHAWL IF YOU LIKE, MITSURU-SAN...
I UNTHINKINGLY WORE FURISODE AGAIN...!!
THANK GOODNESS...
LUCKILY, MITSURU-SAN IS NOT A WOMAN WHO IS BOTHERED BY SMALL FAILINGS...!
I WONDER WHY HE ALWAYS WEARS FURISODE...?
I KEEP MEANING TO FIND OUT IF HE'S A MAN--I THINK HE IS, BUT MAYBE...OH, IT COULDN'T BE...!
AH...!
LOOK! THERE ARE SAKURA OVER THERE!
YOU'RE RIGHT...! LET'S GO GET A BETTER LOOK!
THEY SEEM HAPPY.

You wouldn't think it to look at them, but they're all at the top of their class.
SEEMS LIKE YOU AND MACHI ARE GETTING ALONG LATELY, YUN-YUN, BUT YOUR FENCE-SITTING'S GETTING OLD.
The math doesn't add up...
I'M NOT SITTING ON THE FENCE.
UH HUH. AS HER OLDER BROTHER, I CAN'T LET IT SLIDE.
FIRST NII-SAN, NOW HIM. WHY DO THEY ONLY WANT TO ACT LIKE BROTHERS WHEN IT DOESN'T MATTER?
There are times that matter, right?
IS IT MACHI YOU LIKE?
A REAL MAN IS UPFRONT ABOUT HIS INTENTIONS!
IT'S KIMI, RIGHT?
Right, Yun-Yun?
YOU?!
OR ME???
NOBODY CARES! GET TO WORK!!!

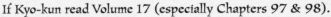

If Kyo-kun read Volume 17 (especially Chapters 97 & 98).
WHAT WOULD HE SAY WAS THE MOST MEMORABLE PART OF FURUBA 17?
MAYBE IT WAS ALL THAT STUFF ABOUT AKITO-SAN...
Cow udders!
Flat chest!
OR THE MESSY PARENT/CHILD WAR WITH REN-SAN, THAT BELONGS ON A SOAP OPERA.
IT COULD HAVE BEEN HATORI-SAN, WHO SEEMED LIKE HE'D BE CRUSHED WITH WORRY WHEN HE GOT CAUGHT BETWEEN THEM.
No, don't worry about me...
OR WE COULD FORGET ALL THAT--MAYBE IT WAS SHIGURE-SAN, WHO LIVES ONLY FOR HIMSELF.
I'm telling you, that's not true. I think about things around me.
You've got it all wrong.
IT COULD BE ANY OF THOSE...
WHAT THE HECK...?
HE'S JUST EXPLAINING THE SITUATION TO HER, BUT HE'S ALL OVER HER EVERY CHANCE HE GETS! KURENO! TOUCHING TOHRU!!!
He's got that "I'm such a gentleman" look, but he just tells her and runs away!
Ah!
KYO-KUN! IS THERE ANYTHING SPECIAL YOU'D LIKE FOR DINNER!?
FRIED CHICKEN ...!
ふるば
ふるば 17
SOHMA FAMILY JOURNAL: THE END

Works by Natsuki Takaya

Year	Publication	Title	# of pages	Notes
'91	Hana to Yume extra issue, Winter	Sickly Boy wa Hi ni Yowai (The sickly boy is weak in the sun)	17	Runner up in the 178th HMC (Hana to Yume Manga-ka Course)
'91	Hana to Yume Planet special edition, issue 9/1	Long Range!	40	Runner up for 18th BC (Big Challenge) Award
'92	Hana to Yume Planet special edition, issue 9/1	Born Free	32	Debut work
'92	Hana to Yume Planet special edition, issue 11/1	Knockin' on the Wall	32	HC Tsubasa o Motsu Mono 1
'93	Hana to Yume Planet special edition, issue 1/5	Ding Dong	32	HC Boku ga Utau to Kimi ga Warau Kara (Because when I sing, you smile)
'93	Hana to Yume extra issue, November	Voice of Mine	45	HC Boku ga Utau to Kimi ga Warau Kara
'94	Hana to Yume extra issue, February	Double Flower	40	HC Boku ga Utau to Kimi ga Warau Kara
'94 〜 '97	Hana to Yume Planet special edition, issue 4/15 〜 Hana to Yume Step special edition, issue 9/30	Gen'ei Musou	896	HC Gen'ei Musou 1-5
'95	Hana to Yume, issue 6	Midori no Saidan (Green Altar)	46	————
'95 〜 '98	Hana to Yume, issue 22 〜 Hana to Yume, issue 11	Tsubasa o Motsu Mono	1122	HC Tsubasa o Motsu Mono 1-6
'96	Hana to Yume, issue 5	Gen'ei Musou Gaiden	41	HC Gen'ei Musou 4
'96	Bonus comic	Kikyuu (Aspiration)	4	HC Gen'ei Musou 1
'97	Bonus comic	Gen'ei Musou Epilogue	4	HC Gen'ei Musou 5
'98	Hana to Yume Step special edition, issue 1/15	Ankoku Hime (Dark Princess)	32	HC Boku ga Utau to Kimi ga Warau Kara
'98	Hana to Yume, issue 14	Boku ga Warau to Kimi ga Warau Kara	44	HC Boku ga Utau to Kimi ga Warau Kara
'98	Hana to Yume, issue 19 ~	Fruits Basket	Ongoing	HC Fruits Basket 1 ~

TOKYOPOP.COM

WHERE MANGA LIVES!

JOIN the
TOKYOPOP community:
www.TOKYOPOP.com

LIVE THE MANGA LIFESTYLE!

EXCLUSIVE PREVIEWS...
CREATE...
UPLOAD...
DOWNLOAD...
BLOG...
CHAT...
VOTE...
LIVE!!!!

WWW.TOKYOPOP.COM HAS:

- News
- Columns
- Special Features
- and more...

A kiss sweeter than poison

SHINSHOKU KiSS

From the creator of tactics!

An exciting new story filled with beautiful girls and boys, black magic and enchanted spirits by the co-creator of tactics! Aspiring teen doll maker Kotoko Kashiwagi always dreamed of meeting her idol, the famous doll maker "Fool." But when the two meet, Kotoko finds herself not just under Fool's spell, but cursed to be his servant--or else!

DRAMA

OT OLDER TEEN AGE 16+

© 2004 KAZUKO HIGASHIYAMA.

Trinity Blood™
DVD BOX SET
Available November 13th
WATCH
TRINITY BLOOD ON
[adult swim]™
© 2005 Trinity Blood Partners. Licensed by FUNimation® Productions, Ltd. All Rights Reserved.
ADULT SWIM and logo are trademarks of and © Cartoon Network.
A Time Warner Company. All Rights Reserved.
GONZO
FUNIMATION ENTERTAINMENT
A NAVARRE CORPORATION COMPANY

KING OF THORN

YUJI IWAHARA

ACTION

OT
OLDER TEEN
AGE 16+

**WARNING:
Virus outbreak!**

Kasumi and her sister, Shizuku, are infected with the fatal Medusa virus. There is no cure, but Kasumi is selected to go into a cryogenic freezer until a cure is found. But when Kasumi awakens, she must struggle to survive in a treacherous world if she hopes to discover what happened to her sister.

From Yuji Iwahara, the creator of the popular *Chikyu Misaki* and *Koudelka*.

© YUJI IWAHARA

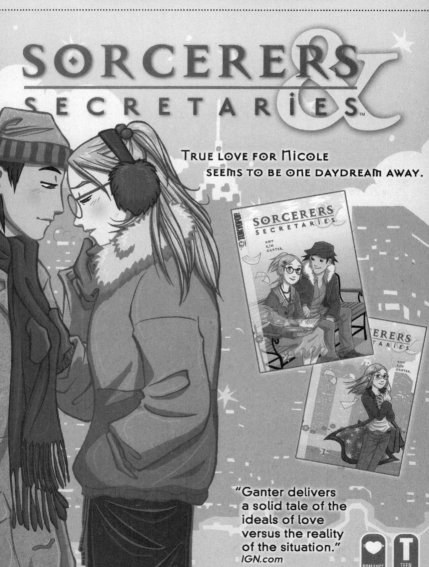

SAKURA TAISEN
TOKYOPOP
1

ACTION

T TEEN AGE 13+

SAKURA TAISEN

BY OHJI HIROI, IKKU MASA AND KOSUKE FUJISHIMA

I really, really like this series. I'm a sucker for steampunk-type stories, and 1920s Japanese fashion, and throw in demon invaders, robot battles and references to Japanese popular theater? Sold! There's lots of fun tidbits for the clever reader to pick up in this series (all the characters have flower names, for one, and the fact that all the Floral Assault divisions are named after branches of the Takarazuka Review, Japan's sensational all-female theater troupe!), but the consistently stylish and clean art will appeal even to the most casual fan.

~Lillian Diaz-Przybyl, Editor

BATTLE ROYALE 1
TOKYOPOP

ACTION

M MATURE AGES 18+

BATTLE ROYALE

BY KOUSHUN TAKAMI AND MASAYUKI TAGUCHI

As far as cautionary tales go, you couldn't get any timelier than *Battle Royale*. Telling the bleak story of a class of middle school students who are forced to fight each other to the death on national television, Koushun Takami and Masayuki Taguchi have created a dark satire that's sickening, yet undeniably exciting as well. And if we have that reaction reading it, it becomes alarmingly clear how the students could so easily be swayed into doing it.

~Tim Beedle, Editor

TOKYOPOP
Angel Cup
JAE-HO YOUN

ACTION
T
TEEN AGE 13+

ANGEL CUP

BY JAE-HO YOUN

Who's the newest bouncing broad that bends it like Beckam better than Braz—er, you get the idea? So-jin of the hit Korean manhwa, *Angel Cup!* She and her misfit team of athletic Amazons tear up the soccer field, whether it's to face up against the boys' team, or wear their ribbons with pride against a rival high school. While the feminist in me cheers for So-jin and the gang, the more perverted side of me drools buckets over the sexy bust-shots and scandalous camera angles... But from any and every angle, *Angel Cup* will be sure to tantalize the soccer fan in you... or perv. Whichever!

~Katherine Schilling, Jr. Editor

THE GOOD WITCH OF THE WEST
TOKYOPOP

FANTASY
T
TEEN AGE 13+

GOOD WITCH OF THE WEST

BY NORIKO OGIWARA AND HARUHIKO MOMOKAWA

For any dreamers who ever wanted more out of a fairytale, indulge yourself with *Good Witch*. Although there's lots of familiar territory fairytale-wise—peasant girl learns she's a princess—you'll be surprised as Firiel Dee's enemies turn out to be as diverse as religious fanaticism, evil finishing school student councils and dinosaurs. This touching, sophisticated tale will pull at your heartstrings while astounding you with breathtaking art. *Good Witch* has big shoes to fill, and it takes off running.

~Hope Donovan, Jr. Editor

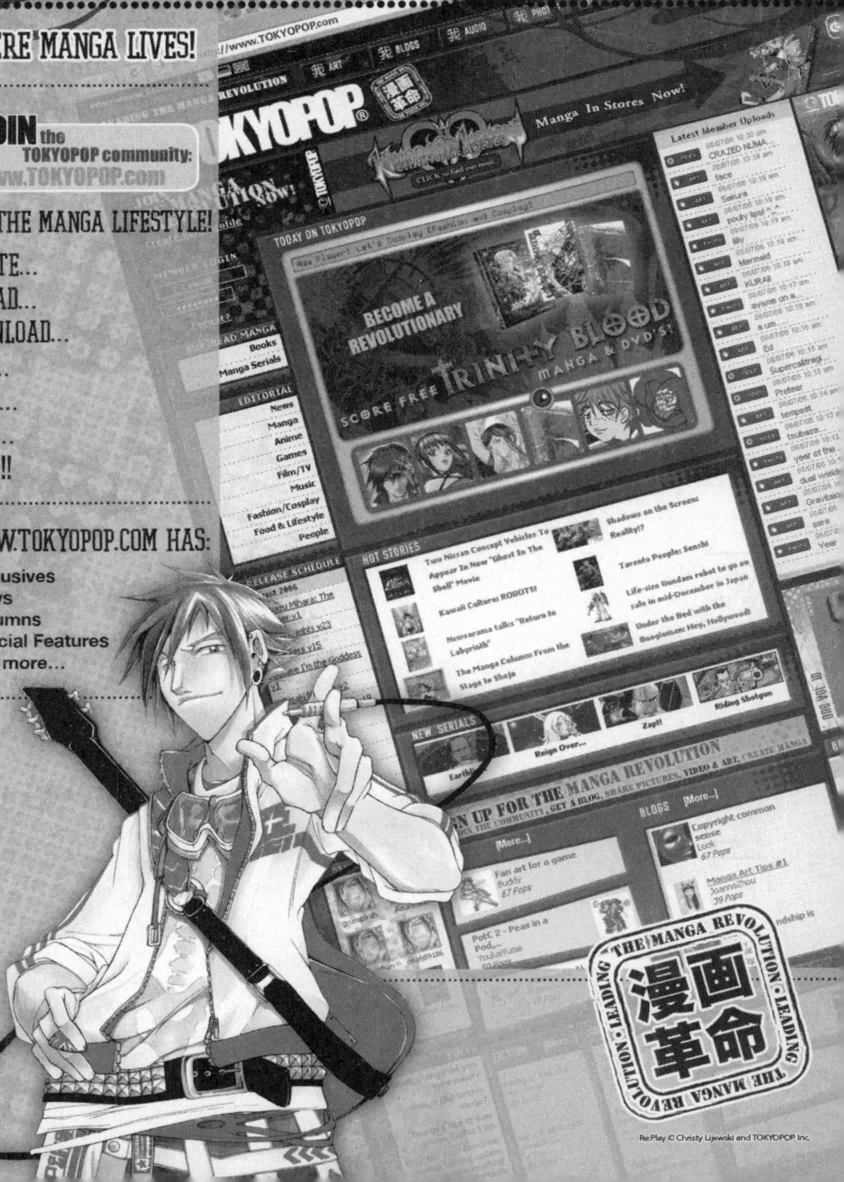

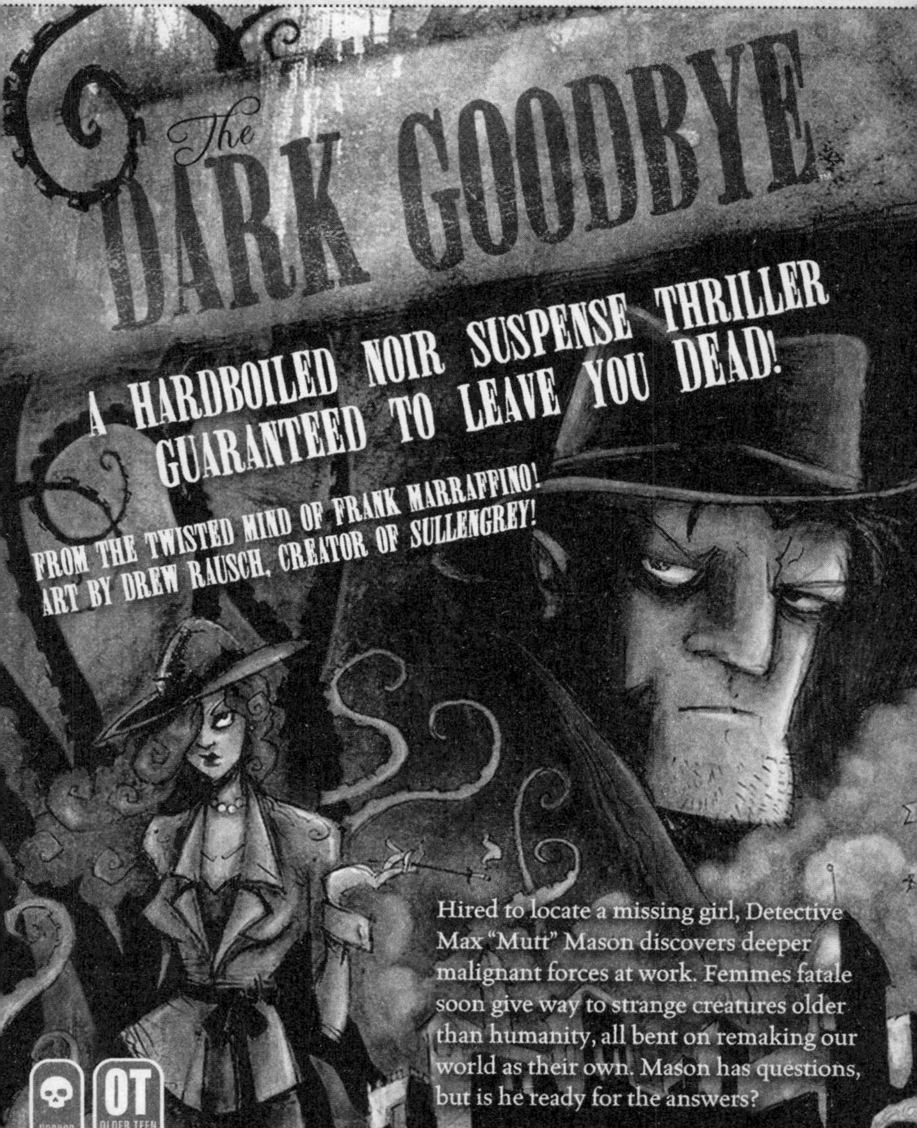

Lunatics run rampant and madness thrives in...
KING CITY™
BY BRANDON GRAHAM
After being gone for years, Joe returns to King City, a city where everyone has a secret, with spy gangs, monsters and aliens lurking behind every door. But this time, Joe has The Cat with him. The Cat is the ultimate weapon, and Joe will need it to survive the war brewing over the resurrection of a long-dead alien demon king.
From Brandon Graham, the off-the-wall creator of October Yen, Universe So Big and Escalator.
SCI-FI
OT OLDER TEEN AGE 16+
© Brandon Graham and TOKYOPOP Inc.
COMIC SHOP LOCATOR SERVICE
COMICS
888-COMIC-BOOK
csls.diamondcomics.com
This title is exclusively available at Diamond Retailers for the first three (3) months.

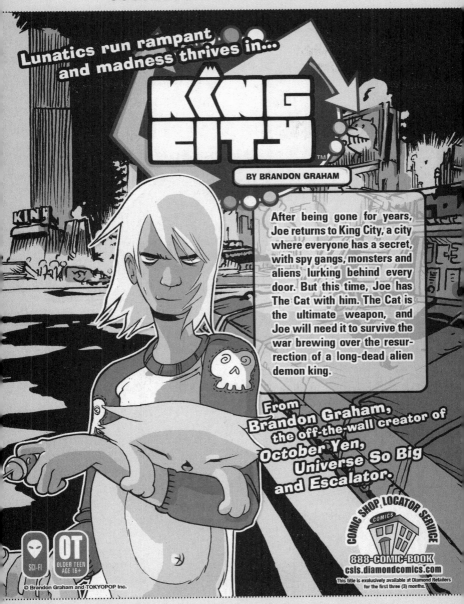

STOP!

This is the back of the book.
You wouldn't want to spoil a great ending

This book is printed "manga-style," in the authentic Japanese right-to-le format. Since none of the artwork has been flipped or altered, readers get to experience the story just as the creator intended. You've been asking for it, so TOKYOPOP® delivered: authentic, hot-off-the-press, and far more fun!

DIRECTIONS

If this is your first time reading manga-style, here's a quick guide to help you understand how it works.

It's easy... just start in the top right panel and follow the numbers. Have fun, and look fo more 100% authentic manga from TOKYOPOP®!

1
2
3
4
5
6
7
8
9
10

THE MANGA REVOLUTION · LEADING
漫画革命